DATE DUE

THE UNSEEN
WALL STREET
OF 1969–1975

THE UNSEEN WALL STREET OF 1969–1975

And Its Significance for Today

ALEC BENN

QUORUM BOOKS
Westport, Connecticut • London

Library of Congress Cataloging-in-Publication Data

Benn, Alec, 1918–
    The unseen Wall Street of 1969–1975 : and its significance for today / Alec Benn.
      p. cm.
    Includes bibliographical references and index.
    ISBN 1–56720–333–7 (alk. paper)
    1. New York Stock Exchange—History—20th century. 2. Wall Street—History—20th
century. 3. Stock exchanges—United States—History—20th century. I. Title: Unseen
Wall Street of nineteen sixty nine–nineteen seventy five. II. Title.
HG4572.B46 2000
332.64'273—dc21   99–462243

British Library Cataloguing in Publication Data is available.

Library of Congress Catalog Card Number: 99–462243
ISBN: 1–56720–333–7

First published in 2000

Quorum Books, 88 Post Road West, Westport, CT 06881
An imprint of Greenwood Publishing Group, Inc.
www.quorumbooks.com

Printed in the United States of America

The paper used in this book complies with the
Permanent Paper Standard issued by the National
Information Standards Organization (Z39.48–1984).

10 9 8 7 6 5 4 3 2

Copyright Acknowledgment

Every reasonable effort has been made to trace the owners of copyright materials in this
book, but in some instances this has proven impossible. The author and publisher will be
glad to receive information leading to more complete acknowledgments in subsequent
printings of the book, and in the meantime extend their apologies for any omissions.

To Robert M. Bishop
whose efforts to preserve The New York Stock Exchange
have never been fully appreciated

As protection against financial illusion or insanity memory is far better than law.

—John Kenneth Galbraith,
author of *The Great Crash*

Those who do not remember the past are condemned to repeat it.

—George Santayana, philosopher

Contents

Preface

Men of vision and daring radically changed Wall Street in the seven years 1969–1975 into the Wall Street often taken for granted today. During some of those years, other men, led by one who was unusually wily and stubborn, prevented The New York Stock Exchange from collapsing, with the possible loss of many millions of dollars by millions of investors and immeasurable damage to the economy. Furthermore, these were years during which economic conditions forced Wall Streeters to lead the nation in reducing discrimination based on class, religion, and race.

Yet the names of some of these men are little known. Furthermore, much of how they actually achieved what they did—as well as how very, very close The New York Stock Exchange came to collapsing—has been hidden until now.

What really occurred during those years is sometimes more fascinating than business-tale fiction, besides providing insights into human character and ways of the world.

The concealments have contributed to misunderstandings of how changes beneficial to society actually are accomplished. Contrary to most previous descriptions of the many reforms of 1969–1975, the opposition to nearly every reform that would benefit investors was formidable. Even proposed measures that would benefit members of The New York Stock Exchange were also sometimes vigorously opposed by many members of the Exchange as well—sometimes by a majority. (This is true even today.)

This book may be of practical value. Men and women who wish to reform—or to resist the reform—of any kind of organization or institution may benefit by knowing how reforms of The New York Stock

Exchange actually were accomplished. More specifically, knowing how financial crises of the past really arose and the measures that were taken to correct them can be helpful in deciding what should be done in similar crises today and in the future. Furthermore, investors may benefit from an intimate look at Wall Street—specifically by what is revealed about insider trading.

I was peripherally involved in some of the critical events on Wall Street during 1969–1975. Some of the principal clients of the advertising agency I headed were investment firms whose financial difficulties most endangered the existence of The New York Stock Exchange.

Yet there was much I didn't know. In fact, no single individual knew all that went on.

To get as near to the truth as possible, I interviewed more than thirty people at length. Some men had actually proposed the radical changes that took place. Others were intimately involved or were close observers. Most had been partners in member firms of The New York Stock Exchange or officers of The New York Stock Exchange. Some have been long-time friends, some were friends of friends, a few strangers till I approached them.

A few would not allow their names to be used as sources. I did not ask them why they wished to remain anonymous. I guessed in some instances the interviewees did not wish to damage friendships they had with others who were involved. Others may have feared being sued.

In two instances, interviews were arranged with men whom I did not personally know, but at the last minute were cancelled. One man refused on the advice of his lawyer. The other, dying of cancer, refused at the last minute—right after I had set up my tape recorder—even though his irritated wife, who had gone to considerable trouble to arrange the interview and was present, said, "What are you worried about? By the time this book is published, we'll all be dead!"

Many interviewees felt free to say today much they could not say years ago. Some had been in the investment business and might have lost clients or offended their bosses; now that they were retired they could talk freely. Others would have lost friends if they had talked in the seventies, but by the nineties, those friends were dead. More than a dozen ·men mentioned in this book died prior to 2000.

The most important of those interviewed was Jim Lynch. He occupied several near-top positions, sometimes that of general counsel, at the firm whose bankruptcy would have caused the collapse of The New York Stock Exchange. He too can say much now that he could not reveal before. And his presence at many of the interviews as a questioner and commentator was invaluable.

Members of the research department of The New York Stock Exchange were as cooperative as they could be, but the 1990s top management of The New York Stock Exchange restrained them in one specific way. A previous management had been wise enough to compile extensive oral histories telling the true extent of the dangers that beset investors and The New York Stock Exchange in the sixties and seventies. In these oral histories, participants who struggled for and against the reforms reveal many startling details about what really happened. But the 1990s management tried to keep those oral histories secret.

I learned of the existence of these oral histories while browsing in the research department of The New York Stock Exchange. I saw a loose-leaf binder on the bookshelves. I took it down, looked through it, and discovered it listed oral histories taken of men who were officers of the Exchange during the period I was studying (as well as from other men whose experiences might be pertinent).

I asked the Research Director if I could look at the histories. He said he would need to check. Some days later he told me I could not have the histories. I protested to the secretary of the Exchange. He adamantly refused to release the oral histories.

When I told Jim Lynch of this, Jim telephoned the president of the Exchange, Richard Grasso, whom he had known for many years, and asked him to release the oral histories. Mr. Grasso refused.

When I next visited the research department of The New York Stock Exchange, the binder listing the oral histories was no longer on the shelves available to visitors.

I later learned that one chairman of the Exchange, Bernard J. Lasker, had asked that the original oral history he gave be sent to him so that it would no longer be in the files of The New York Stock Exchange—and thus not in danger of becoming publicly available.

However, two men who were officers of the Exchange in the sixties and seventies, Lee Arning and Robert Bishop, lent me their personal copies of their oral histories, containing what each of them had told the oral histories researcher (five volumes).

The information in them differs in many respects from that in press releases, booklets, and books distributed by The New York Stock Exchange—and from books and articles based on those sources.

Alec Benn
May 2000

Acknowledgments

More than sixty people helped me write this book. Each helped make it what it is. I am especially grateful to the men and women who spent time and thought talking to me about their experiences and what they personally observed. Most were interviewed in their offices, a few in their homes, a few at mine, and a few over the telephone. Usually one interview was enough, but Jim Lynch was interviewed several times. He also reviewed the several previous drafts of the manuscript.

Of those who helped in other ways, two stand out. The editorial guidance of Eric Valentine, publisher of Quorum Books, was invaluable in shaping this book. We often argued heatedly about important matters as well as a few that made little difference, such as the correct use of a preposition. But he was usually right, and I am grateful for his intense scrutiny of what I wrote while at the same time providing valuable guidance in the overall organization of the book. What is more, the winner always made an intense effort to soothe the loser's ego.

The other editor was my wife, Caroline M. Benn. She read and criticized the many drafts of this book. Her advice was invaluable not only because of her editorial judgment but also because she lived through this period on Wall Street (and later) as a general assistant at Benn & MacDonough, Inc., a vice president of Hornblower & Weeks–Hemphill Noyes, a vice president of Loeb Rhoades, Hornblower, and as communications director of The Bond Market Association, retiring at the end of 1998 as a senior vice president.

PERSONS INTERVIEWED (In order of their appearance in this book)

Norman F. Swanton
.   In 1966, an accountant with Hayden, Stone & Co.; in the 1990s, a successful consultant, venture capitalist, and entrepreneur.

Dan W. Lufkin
In 1969, a partner in Donaldson, Lufkin & Jenrette and a governor of The New York Stock Exchange; in the 1990s, a successful venture capitalist.

Lee D. Arning
In 1969, a senior vice president of The New York Stock Exchange in charge of operations, with overall responsibility for the liquidity and solvency of member firms; in the mid-1980s, retired vice chairman and chief investment officer of USLIFE CORP.

R. John Cunningham
In 1969, executive vice president and chief operating officer of The New York Stock Exchange; in the 1990s, a financial consultant.

Robert M. Bishop
In 1966, a vice president of The New York Stock Exchange with responsibility for the liquidity and solvency of member firms; in the 1990s, a consultant to Lloyds of London and several foreign stock exchanges.

Jim Lynch
In 1970, an officer and voting stockholder of Glore Forgan Staats, Inc.; in 1999, chairman of National Discount Brokers Group, Inc.

Edward I. O'Brien
In 1969, executive vice president of Bache & Co.; from 1974 to 1992, president of the Securities Industry Association; in the 1990s, a corporate director, consultant, and private investor.

Theodore H. Focht
In 1970, Special Counsel, House Interstate and Foreign Commerce Committee (the House committee that introduced a bill that eventually established the Securities Investors Protection Corporation); in the 1990s, retired.

Harry W. Colmery
In 1968, executive president of Glore Forgan Staats, Inc.; in the 1990s, vice president of Capital Guardian Trust Company following retirement as senior vice president, Crocker National Bank.

Richard J. McDonald
> In 1970, a partner in Francis I. duPont; in the 1990s retired from being a vice president of Merrill Lynch & Co.

Kenneth G. Langone
> In the late 1950s, looking for a job on Wall Street; in the 1990s, a venture capitalist who founded Home Depot and other companies and a director of several corporations.

Gilbert Bach
> In 1970, a partner in Hirsch & Co.; in the 1990s, a managing director of Lehman Brothers, then retired.

Thomas C. Hofstetter
> In 1973, a vice president of Walston & Co.; in the 1990s, vice president, investments, Salomon Smith Barney.

R. Tippen Cullen
> In 1973, assistant sales manager and a director of Walston & Co.; in 1995, retired from Unicorp Financial Group.

Harvey J. L'Hommedieu
> In 1973, a first vice president of Walston & Co., in the 1990s, retired vice president of Paine Webber.

Douglas L. Blair
> In 1970, a market maker in over-the-counter stocks at Walston & Co.

George W. Thomson
> In 1973, chief financial officer and a director of Walston & Co.; in 1995, retired from the real estate business.

Willard H. Smith, Jr.
> In 1969, a vice president and syndicate manager of Glore Forgan Staats, Inc.; in the 1996, retired managing director of Merrill Lynch & Co.

Mrs. Willard H. Smith, Jr. (Barbara)

Paul H. Fitzgerald
> In 1973, a vice president of The New York Stock Exchange; in the 1990s, President, Josephthal & Co. Inc.

Walter E. Auch
> In 1973, president of duPont Walston, Inc.; in the 1990s, retired chairman of the Chicago Board Options Exchange.

John C. Whitehead
> In 1947, a trainee at Goldman, Sachs & Co.; in 1976, co-chairman

of Goldman, Sachs & Co.; in 1999, chairman, AEA Investors, Inc. and chairman, Federal Reserve Bank of New York.

PERSONS INTERVIEWED WHOSE NAMES DO NOT APPEAR IN THE TEXT

Mrs. Allan Blair
> In 1973, the wife of Allan Blair; in 1995, a widow.

Sterling Dimmitt
> In 1970, personnel manager of Glore Forgan Staats, Inc.; in the 1990s, a personnel consultant.

Robert J. Gersky
> In 1969, a vice president and Eastern Regional Sales Manager, Glore Forgan Staats, Inc.; in the 1990s, a managing director of Banc of America Securities.

Maurice Meyer, Jr.
> In 1970, a partner in Hirsch & Co.; in the 1990s, chairman, Texas Pacific Land Trust.

George B. Munroe
> In 1970, a NYSE governor and president of Phelps Dodge Corporation; in the 1990s, retired.

Michael Reid-Schwartz
> In 1969, vice president, Schroeder Naess & Thomas; in the 1990s, retired.

Frederick D. Schroeder (son of Frederick H. Schroeder)
> In 1973, a lawyer with Hughes, Hubbard; in the 1990s, retired.

OTHERS WHO WERE HELPFUL INCLUDE:

Steve Wheeler, archivist at The New York Stock Exchange and his assistant, John R. Kret

William H. Donaldson, former DLJ CEO and former NYSE chairman

Henry Hecht of Merrill Lynch & Co.

Mrs. Henry P. Wheeler, daughter of J. Russell Forgan

John G. Stewart, former editor at the *New York Times*

Irving Strauss, public relations executive

Joseph G. Krassy, attorney

Paul C. O'Shea, in 1973, public relations and advertising manager at Walston & Co., Inc.; in the 1990s, senior vice president and communications director for MBIA, Inc.

William H. McElnea, Jr., former chairman, Caesar's World, Inc.

Gerald Baumgarten, ADL researcher

John Heine, Deputy Director, Office of Public Affairs, U.S. Securities and Exchange Commission

Barry Burris, accounting executive

Pam I. Faber, vice president of the Securities Industry Association

Susan Linton, Merrill Lynch public relations executive

James R. Beams, risk analysis executive

David B. Morris, portfolio manager, Security Capital Trading

Arlene Driscoll, public relations, Automatic Data Processing, Inc.

Jacqueline (Mrs. Jim) Lynch

Alexander W. Benn, writer

Richard Renwick Benn, insurance company executive

Librarians at the Millburn Public Library (especially Barbara Simmonds and Leighton Williams Wright), the Newark Public Library, the Library of Congress, the Library of Commerce, the New York Public Library, the Brooklyn Public Library, the Palm Desert Library, the University Club Library (especially Jane Reed), the Dana Library of Rutgers University, and the library at Donaldson, Lufkin & Jenrette, Inc.

Some of the People of Historical Importance Who Appear in this Book

William J. Casey
>Director of Central Intelligence 1981–1987; that is, during the Iran-Contra scandal. Previously: manager of Ronald Reagan's presidential campaign in 1970; Chairman, Securities and Exchange Commission, 1971–73.

Frank R. Lautenberg
>U.S. Senator from New Jersey, 1983–2000.

Arthur Levitt, Jr.
>Chairman of the Securities and Exchange Commission, 1993–.

William McChesney Martin, Jr.
>Chairman of the Federal Reserve, 1951–1970; that is, during the presidencies of Truman, Eisenhower, Kennedy, Johnson, and Nixon.

John Mitchell
>Attorney-General of the United States during the presidency of Richard Nixon. In the Watergate scandal, he was convicted of conspiracy, obstruction of justice, and perjury.

Edmund S. Muskie
>U.S. Senator, 1958–1980; candidate for the presidency of the United States, 1972; Secretary of State, 1980.

Richard M. Nixon
>President of the United States, 1968–1973.

Lawrence F. O'Brien

> In 1972, when he was Chairman of the Democratic Party, his offices in the Watergate Hotel were broken into.

H. Ross Perot

> As candidate for President of the United States in 1992 he received far more votes than any other third-party candidate since Theodore Roosevelt. Also a presidential candidate in 1996.

Donald T. Regan

> President of Merrill Lynch, Pierce, Fenner & Smith Inc., 1968–1970; chairman and CEO, 1971–1980; Secretary of the Treasury, 1981–1985; Chief of Staff to President Reagan, 1985–1987.

Felix Rohaytn

> Managing director, Lazard Freres, 1960–1998; leader in saving New York City from bankruptcy in 1972; Ambassador to France, 1998–.

Arlen Specter

> In 1971, Federal District Attorney in Philadelphia; from 1981 on, U.S. Senator from Pennsylvania.

Stanley Sporkin

> SEC official, 1961–1981; CIA general counsel, 1981–1985; federal judge, 1985–2000. Among other newsworthy actions, barred the U.S. Navy from discharging a gay sailor in 1998.

Maurice H. Stans

> Chief fund raiser for President Nixon; Secretary of Commerce, 1969–1973. Indicted but not convicted in the Watergate scandal.

Frank G. Zarb

> Energy czar during the administration of President Ford; chairman of the National Association of Securities Dealers, 1997–.

1

How Members of The New York Stock Exchange Gained the Right to Sell Shares in Their Firms to the General Public Despite the Opposition of a Majority of the Members

In 1969, most of the 1,366 members of The New York Stock Exchange were partners in a firm. Some operated as individuals. And some were officers in a corporation, but only people working for a member firm could own common stock in that firm.

If an official of The New York Stock Exchange were asked, "Why are member firms forbidden to sell stock in their firms to the general public?" the official usually replied, "To prevent criminals from obtaining control of a member firm."

This was nonsense. The rules that prevented people with bad reputations from controlling a partnership or a partnership-like corporation could have just as effectively been applied to officers of publicly owned firms. More likely, I believe, the purpose of the rule was to maintain the control of many firms, not by the most competent, but by the most wealthy and their personal friends.[1]

Each super-rich family in the United States tended to have its own brokerage firm—one which family members used to buy and sell securities as well as to underwrite securities of companies in which the family had an important interest. The firm was usually controlled by a member of the family. The Henry Fords had McDonnell & Co.; the managing partner was Henry Ford II's brother-in-law. The patriachs of the R. J. Reynolds tobacco people put a man who had married into their family in charge of the brokerage firm they founded. The Harrimans (big in railroads) owned much of Harriman, Ripley & Co. The Peabodys (big in coal) had Kidder, Peabody & Co. The Bradys had Dillon, Read. The Astors had close ties to Kuhn, Loeb & Co. The family that owned Marshal

Field in Chicago founded Glore Forgan & Co. The Morgans, Whitneys, Pews, and Phipps had Morgan Stanley.

The largest of the rich family–dominated brokerage firms was Francis I. duPont & Co. In 1969, it was the third-largest firm in number of customers and offices—325,000 customers served by over 100 offices around the world. Even so, it was a partnership. By reason of his wealth, the controlling partner was Edmond duPont, a scion of the family that founded and controlled the giant chemical firm, E. I. duPont & Co.

Edmond duPont seldom concerned himself with the nitty-gritty of managing the firm. He didn't study the firm's balance sheet and other reports but usually had their contents explained to him.[2] He maintained his principal residence in Delaware even though the firm's headquarters were in downtown New York. And he took long vacations.

He put a school chum in day-to-day charge of the firm.[3] When the chum's drinking during the working day seriously damaged his ability to direct the firm, Edmond delayed firing him—and when Edmond did, he replaced him with a charming young man with no experience or skill in managing a large enterprise.[4] The result was disastrous, as will be described in a later chapter.

Norman F. Swanton, who will also figure prominently in later chapters, learned about the power of wealth early in his career.

In 1966, when 25-year-old Norm was employed in the record-keeping department of Hayden, Stone & Co., he discovered facts that led him to believe one of the partners was a thief.[5] Hayden, Stone at the time was one of the country's largest firms with 77 offices across the United States and around the world.

The partner's expense accounts were so padded that "unreasonable" would be an understatement, Norm felt. The partner was also depositing much bigger sums—millions of dollars—in mysterious accounts in Switzerland and Nassau. Norm thought he could prove that two hundred thousand dollars of the foreign deposits circled around and ended up the partner's pocket. Norm couldn't trace the rest. He guessed that some had been embezzled and some consisted of kickbacks or bribes designed to get more business.

Norm Swanton reported what he had discovered to a member of Hayden, Stone's top management—who was shocked. He suggested Norm collect more evidence.

Swanton did so.

When the offending partner was confronted, he offered to resign from the firm, taking his capital with him.

This was horrifying. If the offending partner withdrew his capital, the firm would be forced to dissolve.

The accused partner said he would stay only if Norm were fired.

Norm was fired and the partner—and his capital—stayed.[6]

So anyone who tried in the sixties to change the status quo—especially anyone who advocated a change that would diminish the power of the wealthy—faced a formidable foe: the richest families in the United States and their friends.

Yet that is what William H. Donaldson, Dan W. Lufkin, and Richard H. Jenrette did in 1969.

Bill, Dan, and Richard were true pioneers. Ten years earlier, when Bill and Dan were not yet 30 and Richard just 30, they had founded Donaldson, Lufkin & Jenrette. They succeeded in making the new firm highly profitable and themselves multimillionaires on paper by applying a tried and true entrepreneurial principle: See a need and fill it.

They took one of Charles E. Merrill's principles to a higher level. Charlie Merrill had transformed Merrill Lynch, Pierce, Fenner & Beane (the then-largest investment firm) from near bankruptcy to great profitability partly by pioneering and promoting securities research as an aid for investors.[7] Naturally Merrill Lynch's reports concentrated on the best known companies with large numbers of stockholders.

Bill, Dan, and Richard saw that pension funds and other institutional investors also wanted analyses of smaller, lesser-known companies with capital gains potential. They also sensed that institutional investors wanted more detailed research than individual investors could digest.

Before Bill, Dan, and Richard founded DLJ—and other firms followed their lead—there actually were many small companies with growth potential that few investors knew about.

Today a well-established theory of investing—the Efficient Market Theory—says that one stock is as good a buy as another because all there is to know about each stock is widely known. Consequently investors bid stocks up and down so their prices take into consideration all the known risks and rewards.

But before DLJ was founded in 1959, the Efficient Market Theory didn't apply to many stocks—or didn't seem to apply—because of the dearth of widespread, intensive securities research.

Some of the people who managed the portfolios of pension funds, banks, insurance companies, and mutual funds wanted detailed information to help them improve the performance of their portfolios. Others wanted the information to protect themselves—that is, to show their bosses or clients that when a stock they bought went down, they had exhaustively investigated it first; they couldn't be blamed.

Donaldson, Lufkin, & Jenrette profited handsomely[8] by offering pension funds and other institutions the kind of securities research they wanted.

The three partners and the security analysts they employed investigated corporations and the securities they issued more thoroughly than ever before and provided the results of their investigations to pension funds, mutual funds, banks, and other institutional investors as incentives to buy and sell securities through DLJ. The firm did not try, as Merrill Lynch did, to appeal to all investors. For an individual to be a DLJ customer, he or she had to have an account worth $5 million or more.

The three partners of DLJ profited handsomely for two reasons: (1) The orders that institutions placed were huge—*thousands* of shares at a time rather than the *hundreds* of shares placed by individuals; and (2) NYSE commissions were fixed at a high percentage of the number of shares bought or sold and the dollar amount of the investment. Any member of The New York Stock Exchange who charged less than the established commission would be expelled from the Exchange.

Even so, the three partners found after a while that lack of capital prevented their expanding in other ways where they saw profit potential. With more capital, they could, for example, buy large blocks of stock from institutional investors for their own account. This "block positioning" was a growing activity engaged in by investment firms with large amounts of capital. It benefited the institution that wished to sell a block which it could not otherwise sell at a decent price. (The larger the number of shares that an investor wished to sell, the less liquid the market.) The brokerage firm that bought the stock usually profited by selling the shares piecemeal over a period of time or by finding another institution that wanted to buy the block.

What was the best way for the trio to obtain the millions of dollars they needed? Borrowing money did not seem sensible, considering the risky use to which they intended to put much of their new capital. And taking in wealthy partners would weaken their freedom to manage the firm as they wished.

The logical solution was to sell common stock in Donaldson, Lufkin & Jenrette to the general public.

Besides enabling the trio to obtain permanent capital without losing control, selling stock to the general public would benefit each of them personally. Establishing a public market for DLJ stock would make it easy for them eventually to sell some of the shares they owned, converting paper profits into cash without giving up control of the firm.

Unfortunately, there was that NYSE rule forbidding the sale of common stock in a member firm to the general public. Sure, repealing the rule was long overdue. Other firms could benefit just as DLJ would by selling stock in their firms to the general public. And it was absurd that firms were so dependent upon the capital supplied by wealthy partners that the survival of the firm could be imperilled by the partner withdrawing all or part of his capital.

Yet a majority of the members of The New York Stock Exchange could not be persuaded to make the change, Bill, Dan, and Richard decided after much thought and discussion.

It was not a new idea. A committee of the board of governors had been debating *for five years* how member firms could obtain more capital.[9] "Twiddling their thumbs," the trio often said to each other.[10]

The committee's inaction reflected the attitude of the Exchange's members. Most members didn't want change. They liked things as they were. Allowing member firms to sell shares in their firms to the general public would benefit large, diversified firms like Merrill Lynch, Paine Webber, Francis I. duPont & Co., and Bache & Co. (to be renamed Prudential Securities in the 1990s). Big firms would be able to expand further into niches occupied by small firms. Small firms would find it more difficult to compete. And among the voting members of The New York Stock Exchange—and among the governors of the Exchange—small firms outnumbered large firms.

Persuasion wouldn't work, the trio decided. They had to use force.[11]

Without informing anyone at the Exchange, Bill, Dan, Richard, and their lawyers prepared a preliminary prospectus that would be used when DLJ offered its shares to the public. The night before they were to file the prospectus with the Securities and Exchange Commission— which was also the night before a meeting of the board of governors of The New York Stock Exchange—Dan took the first overt step in this enterprise. Dan, who would attend his first meeting as a governor on the morrow, told Bernard J. Lasker, a close friend who would be installed as chairman of The New York Stock Exchange that same day, of his firm's intention. This was the only warning DLJ gave to anyone.[12]

"Bunny" Lasker loved the Exchange—loved it as it was. Fifty-nine years old in 1969, he had been working for, with, or as a floor broker for 32 years. He had never gone to college but started out as a runner at 17 for a modest-sized Jewish brokerage firm. (More about the division of investment firms into Christian and Jewish firms in a later chapter.) Bunny became a member of the Exchange himself 22 years later. His firm, Lasker, Stone & Stern, executed orders on the floor of the Stock Exchange—often sizable, very profitable institutional orders—for other brokers who dealt directly with customers.

Lasker's nickname was a joke, like that of "Little John" for Robin Hood's giant lieutenant. "Bunny was larger than life, aside from the fact that he was about six foot three or four," recalls Edward I. O'Brien, executive vice president of Bache & Co. at the time. "Bunny thought big. Acted big. There was a certain awe of Bunny."[13]

Dan, standing next to Bunny, seemed short even though he was of average height, even younger than 39 because of the twenty-year difference in their ages, and even handsomer than he really was because of the way Lufkin's blue eyes and perky nose contrasted with Bunny's rugged, big-featured face with large eyes staring through black-rimmed glasses.

A swear word jumped out of the astonished Bunny's mouth when Dan told him what DLJ planned. He asked whether Dan was sure he wanted to do it.[14]

Dan went through the three partners' logic in detail, explaining that public ownership would not only benefit DLJ but many other firms as well—that, in fact, it was inevitable.

Bunny said that he wasn't going to argue with Dan—that it was a decision that Dan and his partners had obviously thought through. But he asked Dan, in a kindly way, whether Dan and his partners were fully aware of the possible consequences.

The three DLJ partners were. Two-thirds of DLJ's income came from New York Stock Exchange commissions. And each would suffer equally as they were equal partners.

Dan told Bunny they had long pondered, together and each alone, the risk they would be taking.

Bunny replied, after a polite preliminary, that as chairman, he would respond in the best interest of The New York Stock Exchange. Pointedly, he did not say he would support Dan.[15]

The next day, shortly before noon, the governors, unaware of the bombshell about to explode in their midst, assumed their seats in the governors' room. It was fundamentally an amphitheater with the new chairman, Bunny Lasker, presiding from the elevated stage.

A few minutes later, the president of the Exchange rushed in, brandishing a piece of paper torn from the Dow Jones Newswire, colloquially called the "broad tape." He glared at Dan and handed Bunny the piece of paper.

Bunny read from the broad tape to the assembled governors that at 12:01 that day the member firm Donaldson, Lufkin & Jenrette had filed a public offering for 800,000 shares at a maximum price of $30 a share.

Bunny then looked at Dan and asked in a controlled, almost sarcastic tone, whether the Exchange's newest governor, Mr. Lufkin, would like to give the governors further information about this rather startling development.[16]

Dan walked down to the base of the amphitheater, below the dais, clasping a bundle of freshly printed preliminary prospectuses under his arm. He looked up at 30 older, mostly angry, faces and explained forcefully and concisely what the trio planned and why what they planned would benefit many members of the Exchange. When he finished, nobody voiced support. Nobody.

"Some people on the Street thought it was the worst thing in the world," recalls Edward O'Brien.

Coincidentally, the NYSE governors held a ceremonial dinner that very evening. At the dinner, departing governors were given a token of appreciation—an engraved money clip with the NYSE seal—and incoming governors were usually made to feel welcome.

"Nobody'd talk to me," Dan recalls. "I was standing by myself. I had my drink, ate hors d'oeuvres by myself. The outgoing chairman, Gus Levy, bless his soul, one of my favorite people, came up to me."[17]

Gustave L. Levy was a wiry six feet tall, always tanned and vigorously healthy. He walked so fast others sometimes had to jog to keep up with him.

As chairman he had run meetings of the board of governors expertly, starting on time, finishing on time, allowing full pertinent discussion, but cutting off anyone who strayed from what was germane.

Even if he had never been a chairman of the Exchange, he would have been a powerful figure in the industry as senior partner of Goldman, Sachs & Co.

Many other people felt as warmly toward Gus as Dan did. "I don't know anybody who knew him that didn't like him," a former officer of the Exchange recalls.[18] Gus was unassuming. He answered his own phone. He was often being helpful to others regardless of their position. He was able to dominate and make others like his dominating.

Gus told Dan he didn't agree for one second with what Dan had done. And he didn't agree with the way Dan had done it. And he certainly didn't agree that public capital of the kind the trio proposed was needed for members of The New York Stock Exchange. But Gus did say that he admired the trio's guts. And that he was very, very impressed by that.

Gus was the only governor or ex-governor to talk to Dan the whole night.

Typically, Gus was being kind while at the same time voicing his opposition—which from his point of view was justified. Goldman, Sachs partners had no interest in incorporating their firm and thus paying corporate taxes on top of their personal income taxes. Nor did they want to share their profits with passive outsiders.

What is more, allowing many member firms to sell shares in their firms to the general public would strengthen Goldman, Sachs' competitors while conferring no benefit on Goldman, Sachs. The firm had plenty of capital and had very tough rules about partners withdrawing their capital.

Some other members of the financial community felt as admiring of the guts of the three young upstarts as Gus was. Many Bache partners were "aghast at the courage of DLJ. It was an extraordinarily iconoclastic and courageous act. They really went against the system. And some people admired that," Ed O'Brien recalls.

Also: When two DLJ floor brokers entered a lunch club popular with floor brokers the next day, several brokers rose to their feet and cheered and cheered.[19]

In the following weeks, some heads of firms voiced their support of the young trio's initiative, but something stronger than logic or public spirit, however, pushed many governors toward allowing DLJ (and therefore all member firms) to sell shares in their firms to the public.

Increasingly institutional investors were not being seduced by the entertaining, gifts, and devious devices of New York Stock Exchange firms seeking their orders. Instead of paying the high, fixed commissions NYSE members charged, many institutional investors were buying and selling blocks of stock through regional exchanges or over-the-counter. Weeden & Co., conspicuously, had grown from a small over-the-counter firm to a sizable one by specializing in this so-called "third market."

If DLJ were forced to resign from the Exchange and traded through regional exchanges and in the third market, these markets would be immensely strengthened and other institution-oriented firms would follow DLJ's lead. The New York Stock Exchange might be destroyed. At best, it would become a remnant of its former self.

So the governors of the Exchange gave in to DLJ's request, reluctantly voting to allow member firms to sell stock in their firms to the general public as of March 1970.

The 1969 *Fact Book* of The New York Stock Exchange chronicled this momentous, dramatic event only with the following paragraph:

"In the search for additional capital to finance the manifold needs of securities firms, the tradition of partner-supplied capital was augmented by the authorization of outside financing through public ownership of member firms."[20]

No hint that the reform was forced upon the Exchange by a single firm. No hint that a member had first proceeded to raise capital publicly and that the governors had simply bowed to a *fait accompli*. No hint that nearly all the members opposed the reform. And no hint that no governor had stood up and supported the proposer. Most readers of the *Fact Book* are likely to conclude that the governors had intelligently, amicably and foresightedly initiated the reform.

The media, however, did appreciate the importance of the trio's accomplishment at the time. The Associated Press ranked the event with the landing of a man on the moon, the Jets' surprise winning of the Super Bowl, and a near-revolutionary change in the government of France. Bill Donaldson, as senior partner of DLJ, was named one of the top seven newsmakers of 1969. The other six were Neal Armstrong, Joe Namath, Charles deGaulle, Norman Mailer, Bishop James A. Pike, and George Meany.[21]

The next year Merrill Lynch followed DLJ's lead and went public. The following year Merrill Lynch would go even further, listing its own stock on The New York Stock Exchange.

Other large firms slowly but steadily followed DLJ's lead. Fifteen additional firms went public during the next four years, including Bache (now Prudential Securities), Paine Webber, Dean Witter, and others whose names have vanished because of mergers. But not until 1999 did the last of the big firms—Goldman Sachs—sell some of its shares to the general public.

Over the long term, the benefits of public ownership have proved to be momentous. Firms are much better managed; personal wealth has little influence over management and policies. More and better services are offered investors—individual and institutional—as well as to corporations seeking capital and advice. And the permanency of so many firms' capital removes a key danger to the very survival of The New York Stock Exchange, as will be described in later chapters.

In the years that followed their *coup d'etat*, Bill, Dan, and Richard, like many successful revolutionaries, moved into the forefront of the establishment. In 1991, Bill Donaldson was elected chairman of The New York Stock Exchange.

2

How the Central Certificate System Was Introduced and Other Early Bumbling with Computers

The man most heavily and continuously involved in the application of computers to the processing of orders for stocks was Lee D. Arning. Even though, by his own admission, "My talent in computers was limited to kicking in the side of it when it doesn't work."[1]

But Lee had other talents. For computerization to function fully, people in the securities business or connected to it in one way or another had to be persuaded to adjust their thinking and ways of doing business. They had to be sold—and Lee had a salesman's personality. His height (six feet, seven inches), premature gray hair, good looks, and self-assurance commanded respect. His quick-witted diplomacy inspired liking in difficult situations.

Before joining the Exchange, he had spent eight years selling Dun & Bradstreet's credit services. At the same time, he had gone to Rutgers at night and received a degree in business administration. When he joined the Exchange in 1955, his principal task was persuading corporations with appropriate qualifications to list their common stocks on The New York Stock Exchange.

But Lee and his superiors also labored to make the transfering of the ownership of stocks more efficient. A big obstacle was the stock certificate. For centuries, investors who bought shares of stock in corporations had received handsomely engraved certificates as evidence of ownership. Filling in the names, transferring the certificates from one brokerage firm to another, and mailing them to customers was time consuming. The certificates of stocks transferred from customers at one brokerage firm to customers at another were trundled through the streets of downtown

New York on handcarts or in smaller amounts by gray-haired men carrying big wallets.

So as to eliminate the need for stock certificates, officials of The New York Stock Exchange had proposed back in the 1950s that a central certificate depository be established. Stock certificates would be kept in the depository while the proof of their ownership would be recorded in the books of member firms. This would make it easy to transfer stock ownership from one investor to another.

But: Many investors liked possessing stock certificates as proof of ownership. Many states required, by law, that stock certificates be issued. Bankers opposed the idea. Predating the anxieties about privacy of the 1990s, bankers didn't want an intermediary possessing the knowledge of ownership of stocks in portfolios of securities they managed. Similarly, insurance companies said they wouldn't insure loans based on stocks as collateral unless certificates proved ownership. And not all brokerage firms were enthusiastic.

Some objections to the proposed central certificate system were ludicrous. Some investment professionals thought it a "Nazi" idea.[2] Which was true. A central depository system had been functioning in Germany for decades. When the Germans successfully invaded France in World War II, they imposed the same efficient system on the Paris bourse. (Something few Frenchmen will admit today.)

An opposite political bugaboo caused some socialist-fearing investors to protest. They feared that lodging stock certificates in one convenient place would make it all too easy for the Federal government to seize ownership of corporations. (Remember, this was the fifties and sixties, when country after country was becoming socialist, when many influential Americans believed the ultimate triumph of socialism was inevitable, and protests over the U.S. war against Communist North Vietnam were mounting.)

In the late sixties, however, it became apparent to Lee and his superiors at The New York Stock Exchange that eliminating or at least reducing the use of the stock certificate had gone from being desirable to being necessary. The volume of trading had zoomed from only 2 million shares traded on an average day in 1950 to 7½ million in 1966.[3]

Post–World War II prosperity had expanded the ability of millions of people to own stocks. And the application of modern market methods to the investment business had turned many savers into investors. Merrill Lynch, the largest member firm of The New York Stock Exchange, led the way in funneling the increased incomes into common stocks. In the forties, Merrill Lynch adopted policies and began placing advertisements that soothed the fears of loss still lingering from the 1929 crash. The ads urged people to "Investigate, then invest."

Weekly ads, placed not just in the *Wall Street Journal* and the *New York Times*, but also in newspapers all across the country, told potential investors about policies Merrill Lynch had instituted to protect them. For example, account executives (Merrill Lynch's new name for stockbrokers) were paid salaries instead of commissions. Account executives would thus not be tempted to churn customers' accounts, the ads implied.

Investors flocked to Merrill Lynch.

Noting Merrill Lynch's success, Paine Webber, Bache & Co., Francis I. DuPont & Co., and many other firms placed persuasive advertising aimed at attracting individual investors.

In 1954, The New York Stock Exchange itself began an advertising campaign urging people to "own your share of American business."

Mutual funds stepped up their advertising. Dreyfus & Co. pioneered TV advertising; its emblematic lion roared out of the subway onto Wall Street.

An atmosphere was created in the 1960s of financial opportunities available for the taking. The number of people owning stocks soared. In the early forties, marketing people at Merrill Lynch guessed about a million people owned stocks. In 1952, the first year a survey was taken of stock ownership, 6½ million adults owned shares. By 1970, that number multiplied nearly five times—to 31 million. Only one in 16 adults owned stocks in 1952; one in four would in 1970.[4]

The stock market behaved in a very attractive way in the sixties, giving validity to the enticing advertising.

By 1966, stock prices were *five times* what they had been in 1949.

Corporate profits after taxes partly justified this rise in stock prices. Corporate profits tripled in the 17 years 1949–1966. (Some of these gains resulted from inflation, however. The consumer price index increased 36 percent from 1949 to 1966.)

But something besides more money in the hands of individuals, higher corporate profits, and inflation pushed stock prices up.

As wages rose in the 1950s and 1960s to levels that provided a comfortable living for most unionized workers, unions increasingly emphasized retirement in their bargaining. Corporations complied by setting up and increasing the benefits from private pension plans. By 1966, more than 26 million workers (half of all those employed in private, non-farm enterprises) were covered.[5] Pension plans accumulated billions of dollars which they had to invest.

Theoretically, managers of the pension plans could have invested the billions in bonds, but studies made at the time showed that common stocks provided a better return over the long term. The better a pension plan performed, the less money the corporation needed to contribute.

Stockholdings by corporate pension plans zoomed from half a billion dollars in 1949 to nearly $52 billion in 1970.

Insurance companies responded similarly. They invested more of their reserves in common stocks and sold insurance products whose return would benefit from a rise in stock prices. The value of stocks held by insurance companies increased from less than $3 billion in 1949 to more than $22 billion in 1970.[6]

The accelerating demand for stocks by individuals and institutions caused the volume of trading on The New York Stock Exchange to increase at a rate nobody in the investment business had anticipated.

Wall Street just couldn't handle the volume, even though by this time—the late sixties—The New York Stock Exchange and most member firms that dealt with the public were using computers.

The efficient processing of orders got a big boost when a new president of The New York Stock Exchange took office in 1967. The chairmanship of The New York Stock Exchange was then a part-time job. It was held by Gus Levy; much of his time was absorbed by his responsibilities as a partner of Goldman, Sachs & Co. The president of the Exchange was a full-time employee whose powers were traditionally, and according to the NYSE's bylaws, limited to administration.

The new president was Robert F. Haack, formerly president of the National Association of Securities Dealers. Before that he had been administrative vice president of a modest-sized but well-regarded Midwestern brokerage firm.

Bob Haack had not been the NYSE search committee's first choice. Two others had been approached and had turned[7] the job down—which was lucky. Bob was the right man at the right time. He was an outstanding administrator which was what the Exchange needed.

Bob had an MBA from Harvard, and his management methods could have been used as a textbook case history. He established objectives and thought out how those objectives could be achieved. He diplomatically manipulated his equals and superiors, and efficiently delegated responsibilities to subordinantes. His subordinates found, for example, that they could write letters for his signature that he didn't need to change. This contrasted with their experience with the previous president who continually rewrote their drafts. They also discovered they could talk frankly to him. He said he didn't want any Pollyannas working for him.[8]

However, some his subordinates were not happy to learn that he was an early riser—and demanded that those who worked for him be early risers as well. Meetings were often scheduled for 7:00 A.M.

Before assuming the presidency of The New York Stock Exchange, Bob assessed the abilities of the staff of The New York Stock Exchange. He discovered the staff had little knowledge of computers and how to apply computers to the securities business. So he recruited as executive vice president a man with 10 years of experience with computers, R. John Cunningham, 41. As a senior vice president of the Midwest Stock Exchange, John had set up a computer system that speeded up what is technically known as "clearing." At the end of the day, each member of an Exchange needs to know how it stands net with every other member. The process is "clearing." In developing the system, John had used Bob's old firm, Baird & Co., as a guinea pig, so Bob had more than a resume-reading knowledge of John's capabilities.

While Bob was disappointed with some of the staff of The New York Stock Exchange, he was enthusiastic about Lee Arning. He saw that Lee's people skills would make him a good team-mate[9] for John Cunningham, who, try as he might, often could not hide the scorn he felt for fools who opposed him. He had been a first sergeant in World War II and sometimes told how he admired another sergeant who cleaned several malingerers out of a hospital by taking away their crutches.[10] The new president jumped 44-year-old Lee up from assistant director of the Department of Member Firms to vice president in charge of operations.

The need for a central certificate system became even more imperative during Bob Haack's first years as president. In April 1968, the volume on an average day reached nearly 15 million—more than double 1966's overwhelming volume!

Many member firms of the New York Stock Exchange failed to perform their most important function: They failed to promptly deliver a tremendous number of shares of common stock to investors who had bought them. By April 1968, the first month "fails" were reported, the value of shares not delivered within four days totaled $2.7 billion! And even those not delivered within 30 days amounted to nearly half a million dollars![11]

Meanwhile John Cunningham worked feverishly to increase the efficiency of The New York Stock Exchange. He bought IBM 360 computers and hired programmers and systems analysts—more than a hundred additional people all told. Many functions of the Exchange were automated. The lobbying of state legislatures continued until all but Oklahoma had repealed their laws regarding stock certificates. And a central certificate system was set up.

John experimented with dry run after dry run until he was confident that a central certificate system would work. In February 1969, he told Bob Haack the Central Certificate System was ready. It was intended to deliver half a billion dollars worth of securities each day electronically. This, however, was only a third of all trades because the system had to be made voluntary. Many brokerage firms did not assent, but kept to their old ways.[12]

Bob approved the new system. A press conference was held, and the Central Certificate System was publicized with fanfare.

It failed.

It took too long. It took 26 hours to process a day's work. Settlements were backed up.

"CCS was held out as the great solution to our problems but recently it has been adding to them," an operations official at a large brokerage firm sarcastically stated.[13]

Bob Haack ordered the system shut down.

The vice president directly responsible under John Cunningham and Lee Arning for electronic data processing resigned.

John and the remaining data processing people worked furiously over the next several days finding and rectifying the glitches that slowed up the system. They got the Central Certificate System working more or less smoothly by the end of April.

Fails declined during the next few months, but not as a consequence of the Central Certificate System. Fails had already begun to decline before the Central Certificate System began to function properly. From a peak of over $4 billion in December 1968, fails had declined to $3.3 billion in January 1969, to below $3 billion in February, and to about $2½ billion in March.

Fails declined because the volume of trading declined. Fails continued to decline, to $1.4 billion in August as the volume of trading fell, but started climbing again in September when the volume of trading increased, reaching $1.8 billion in December.[14]

The Central Certificate System was only a necessary first step toward an efficient system for processing orders.

The faulty operations of many member firms impeded the proper functioning of the Central Certificate System. When any firm—especially such a large firm as Francis I. duPont—failed to get the correct information to the Central Certificate System on time, other firms suffered even though they processed orders efficiently. And the order processing in many firms was chaotic.[15]

The reasons were not just technical. The fundamental problem was cultural. The partners in member firms had traditionally paid little attention to the processing of orders. It had seldom been necessary in the many decades since the Exchange was founded in 1792.[16]

The partners of investment firms were like deck officers on a cruise ship. They concentrated on keeping the customers happy. Below-decks' problems were not their concern, but the responsibility of a rough-mannered crew.

The terminology used described the cultural gap. The men who processed the orders worked in "the back office." And, unlike today, most were poorly educated. Few had college degrees. Many had not graduated from high school.

The way most of them spoke indicated their working class backgrounds and that they were brought up in Brooklyn. (The differences in the way Americans speak have diminished in Pygmalion fashion since the fifties and sixties, perhaps because of the advent of television.)

And the people in the back office were poorly paid.[17]

In contrast, men in the front office—investment bankers, stockbrokers, office managers, lawyers—most had college degrees, often from Ivy League colleges, and most were extremely well-paid. Some were independently rich or were part of rich families. Some spoke with broad a's even though they weren't from Boston. And they seldom if ever set foot in the back office.

The top officers underrated the back office people partly because the problems had been smoothly handled in the past.[18] It's a mistake often made by executives in any business: An employee who makes his assignments look easy through intelligent organization may be underrated; and an employee who works hard and long because his methods are inefficient may be over-rated. His superiors can see the extra effort.

Incidents at Glore Forgan Staats, Inc., an investment banking and brokerage firm highly regarded in the sixties, illustrate the attitude that top managements of many investment firms had toward their back offices. Glore Forgan Staats' stature rivaled that of Morgan Stanley, and its chief executive officer, Maurice H. Stans, was a national figure.

Maury Stans had not inherited wealth. In fact, he had been born poor. And he was not incompetent. Quite the contrary. As a young man he had become a certified public accountant by taking courses at night, and then helped make the firm he worked for, Alexander Grant, the ninth largest accounting firm in the United States in 1953.

He became active in Alexander Grant's political efforts, and President Eisenhower appointed him, successively, controller of the Post Office Department, Deputy Postmaster General, and Director of the Budget. (As a souvenir of that experience, he would later usually wear cufflinks with the White House crest.)

When Kennedy became President in 1961, Maury Stans joined Wm. R. Staats, Inc., a West Coast investment firm, as president. When the firm merged with Glore Forgan & Co., he became president of the merged company.

So Maury was a notch better than the average CEO of a member firm of The New York Stock Exchange.

Yet look at his mistakes and his attitude toward order processing.

When Wm. R. Staats merged with Glore Forgan & Co. in 1965, the back offices of the two firms continued to operate separately because their systems were incompatible. In 1966, however, without checking on the capacity of the New York office, Maury ordered all orders were to be processed by the New York office. He failed to first investigate whether the New York office could handle the increased activity.

It couldn't.

The number of fails mounted. The administrative vice president tried to hire experienced back office people but with little success. The back offices of other brokerage firms were overloaded by the increase in volume as well. Few experienced, capable back office people were looking for work. The administrative vice president was forced to hire inexperienced people, some of whom could barely add—which resulted in more mistakes.[19]

In addition, Glore Forgan Staats' computers did not operate as anticipated. They were made by RCA, a glamorous company at the time. But no one—not even "experts" from RCA—really knew how to operate them. The software had been patched so many times, no one knew its intricacies.

The separation of front office people from back office people was so traditional, the administrative vice president never communicated his problems to Maury, and Maury never bothered to discover what was fundamentally wrong. Like an ignored cancer, the number of fails for which Glore Forgan Staats was responsible grew and grew—eventually to many millions of dollars.[20]

While Maury did not dig into the back office problems himself, he recognized that improvement was necessary. He asked Jim Lynch to help the administrative vice president recruit capable people for the back office. Jim, a lawyer, was Compliance Officer, but Maury felt that Jim, because he had previously been with the Association of Stock Exchange Firms (now the Securities Industry Association), "would know everybody on the Street."

Jim found Norm Swanton when Norm was fired from Hayden, Stone, and he was promptly hired.

"It didn't take me long," Norm recalls, "to figure out that everything was out of balance—nothing could be reconciled. On the plus side, the firm could do its business. Management could know, loosely, how profitable the company was, but basically the firm was without controls or record keeping of any kind."[21]

When Norm reported this back to Jim and Maury, the administrative vice president was summoned to Maury's office and promptly fired.

But anybody who knew anything about processing orders was so much in demand that Maury re-hired the offending administrative vice president the next day as a consultant.[22]

Norm, put in charge of operations, soon discovered that much more needed to be done than just reorganize the record keeping. Key members of the staff needed to be replaced. They had bad habits, were slovenly, and resented their new, dictatorial boss. They were accustomed to working at an easy pace. And they were considerably older than Norman. Most were twenty or even thirty years older.[23]

(This age gap was typical of Wall Street in the sixties. For more than 15 years—from the Crash of 1929 to after the end of World War II in 1945—few young people had gone to work on Wall Street.)

Behind the confident manner he assumed before his subordinates, Norm wasn't sure what he should do. This was the first time he had ever had responsibilities of such magnitude. He had been an enlisted man in the Air Force and his supervisory responsibilities at Hayden, Stone had been modest. Now he directly supervised two hundred men and women.

Emotionally overwhelmed by the size of the task before him, the usually self-reliant Norm decided he needed advice from top management. He tried to see Maury but discovered Maury was in Africa on a safari.

When Maury returned, his secretary fended off Norm's continual requests for an interview. Eventually, Norm cornered Maury in a hallway outside Maury's office.

"I have a crisis!" Norm pleaded. "I must see you."

Maury said he didn't have time for the next few days and then that he could only see Norm at 6:30 P.M.

On the appointed evening, Norm, loaded down with papers, walked into Maury's office.

"I had all my analyses; they could cover four walls," Norm recalls, "showing how we could do what needed to be done."

But Maury didn't give Norm a chance to speak.

An excited Maury said that he knew Norm had something important to say but that he had something important too. He told Norm to sit down and watch.

Norm sat down in a chair, facing a screen. Behind him, Maury operated a slide projector.

For nearly half an hour, Maury proceed to show Norm slides of animals he had shot on his African trip. Norm contained himself and politely commented despite his anxious need to tell Maury of the awful details of Glore Forgan's back office and get Maury's advice.

Suddenly Maury turned off the projector and swore.

Norm turned to see Maury looking at his wrist watch.

Maury said he didn't realize how late it was and that he had to be at a cocktail party. He was the speaker!

As he rushed out the door, Maury said he'd see Norm some other time.

Norm looked after him with amazement, gathered up his papers, and decided he would just have to proceed as best he could on his own.[24]

The chief executives of most other firms paid even less attention than Maury to the processing orders. And many other firms did not have a Norm Swanton in charge of their back offices.

"I promptly went to work—working night and day," Norm recalls. "I brought in specialists—a new team. I have always been a hard worker, but I never worked harder in my life. I worked seven days a week. I stayed nights at the nearby Downtown Athletic Club. I worked may staff hard as well—double shifts. I was a slave driver! I had two men die on me—literally. Die at their desks!

"After about nine months, I sat down and looked at where we stood. And I had to admit, for the first time in my life, I had failed! The firm was in worse condition than when I took over. The numbers were worse!"[25]

Norm was like a lone sailor in a dinghy nearly swamped by a fierce storm. It's raining so hard, no matter how fast he bails, the level of water in the boat rises.

Many other investment firms had the same problem, and the number of fails mounted.

In desperation, the governors of the Exchange voted to close the Exchange early—at 2:00 P.M.—beginning January 2, 1968. The early closing, they felt, would reduce the number of shares traded and give back offices more time to process the orders.

Fails declined, so a few weeks later the governors optimistically ordered that the regular closing time, 3:30 P.M., be resumed on March 1, 1968.

A mistake!

Fails climbed from nearly $2.67 billion in April to $3½ billion in May.[26] So the governors closed the Exchange every Wednesday in weeks without a holiday beginning June 12.[27]

Meanwhile Glore Forgan was contributing less to the fails problem than it had in previous years. Norm had figured out what he should do. Not being closely supervised can be an advantage to an executive with initiative. It can allow one, if one has the guts, to take chances one's superiors would not approve of—to try procedures that have never been tried before.[28]

Since the usual methods had failed, Norm desperately decided to start over. He replaced the old, much-repaired computer with a later RCA model, the RCA Spectra 70. And instead of trying to straighten out Glore Forgan's records, he set up an entirely new set of books early in 1968, as if he were originating the firm. He asked other firms to tell him what their records showed. If, for example, Paine Webber said, "You owe us 1000 shares of IBM," Norm in effect replied, "Prove it!" If Paine Webber could prove it, Norm sent them the shares. If Dean Witter said it owed Glore Forgan Staats 300 shares of General Motors, Norm accepted the shares. Slowly by this method, which seems so simple in hindsight but which was unheard of at the time, the number of Glore Forgan's fails slowly but consistently declined.[29]

No matter what Norm did, however, he couldn't reduce Glore Forgan's fails to zero because Glore Forgan couldn't escape the chaos in the back offices of other firms. Nearly every firm, at one time or another, denied it owed Glore Foran some securities or money.[30] Most did so, not maliciously, but because their own back offices were such a mess. But some firms denied they owed Glore Foran securities or money because they used a slick accounting trick never publicly revealed before. Merrill Lynch was one of those shrewd firms.[31]

Merrill was so big its books often showed fails that could offset each other. Merrill might, say, owe 200 shares of General Motors to one broker and be owed 200 shares of GM by another broker. The Merrill accountant would just cancel them both—as if one fulfilled the other. Two fails on Merrill's books were thus disposed of. But two fails were left on the books of other brokerage firms—one to buy 200 shares of GM, another to sell 200 shares of GM. Two irreconcilable fails!

The giant firms, even the the ones with well-run back offices, thus increased the number of fails at smaller firms. A small or medium-sized broker, such as Glore Forgan, suffered whether it had sound back office practices or not.

Thus, Glore Forgan's fails, because of the interdependence of broker-age firms, inescapably amounted to thousands of dollars in money and securities as 1968 ended. But not millions. Because of Norm's initiative and hard work, as well as the long hours put in by his staff, Glore Forgan's fails were small in number compared to those at most other firms—so comparatively small that when Glore Forgan's books were examined in late 1968, the auditors complimented the firm!

Before fails could become insignificant for New York Stock Exchange members as a whole, however, the efficient back offices of Glore Forgan, Merrill Lynch, Bache & Co., Paine Webber, Donaldson, Lufkin, & Jenrette, and a few other firms could not be exceptions. Top managements of more firms would need had to pay more attention to their back offices and pay the people who worked there better.

Merrill Lynch, for example, had the most efficient back office because Charles E. Merrill had recognized the importance of back office efficiency way back before World War II.

When Merrill Lynch, E. A. Pierce & Cassatt was formed in 1939, Charlie Merrill became chief executive officer with dictatorial powers. (One of the management problems of failing firms, because of the partnership arrangement, was getting a majority of partners to approve any forward-looking measure.)[32]

Charlie Merrill brought in executives from other industries with administrative skills. He and they revamped the firm's back office. In 1955, Merrill Lynch was the first firm to install computers.[33] And the CEOs who succeeded Charlie Merrill—Mike McCarthy and Jim Thompson—were efficiency minded back office types.[34]

Other obstacles besides improving back office efficiency needed to be overcome as well.

Interaction between the computers at all member firms with those at the Central Certification needed to be made possible. This was especially difficult because the firms used a variety of makes—RCA, Honeywell, UNIVAC, NCR, etc.

It was necessary that all but an insignificant percentage of orders be processed by the Central Certificate System. This meant getting the legislatures in a half dozen states, especially New York, to repeal laws that barred the use of CCS for shares owned by institutional investors.

It was also necessary for the Central Certificate System to be modified so it could process orders handled by a member firm for stocks not listed on The New York Stock Exchange. When a NYSE member firm bought an unlisted stock for one its customers, the dealer on the other side of the trade often was not located in New York City. Furthermore, clerks at banks that acted as transfer agents for over-the-counter stocks were often slow and inexperienced, and the banks involved were often located outside New York City, sometimes not even in the same city or town as the over-the-counter dealer; certificates, instead of being messengered in a few hours, suffered days of delay in the mail.[35]

It would be several years before the volume of fails would become insignificant—decades before The New York Stock Exchange could efficiently process hundreds of millions of shares.

The Exchange began reporting the volume of fails to the general public in 1968, yet the fundamental reason for the slow improvement in order processing escaped reporters and commentators. They didn't know how neglectful top managements of most firms were of the order processing system. Nor how neglectful many top officers (like Maury Stans) continued to be even as their ships were sinking.

Furthermore, no one at the time realized that much of the problem derived from class distinctions. The managing of the back offices, now that they were computerized, required at least college-caliber expertise and analysis. But few men with college educations who knew the investment business were interested in, shall we say, getting their hands dirty in the back office. Better to have lunch with a customer one had gone to Harvard with. Upper-class men (very few women) dealt with customers. Lower-class men and women processed the orders and were supervised by lower-class men who rose through the ranks.

Without the establishment of the Central Certificate System and the efficient, remarkably swift processing of orders by computers, it would be impossible for The New York Stock Exchange to process the hundreds of millions of shares traded everyday in the 1990s. Yet John Cunningham has never gotten the recognition he deserved for pushing the Central Certificate System onto members of The New York Stock Exchange, most of whom resisted and resented his efforts.

3

The Hair-Raising Way Brokerage Accounts Came to Be Insured

In the late sixties and early seventies, Robert M. Bishop was the most hated man on Wall Street.[1] It was not his appearance or manner that aroused antagonism. His voice was well modulated and controlled, his words well chosen and precise, never communicating anger or warmth. He wore gold-rimmed glasses, was not tall or muscular—verged on appearing frail—and was invariably polite. Seeing him for the first time in a neutral setting, say across the room at a friend's cocktail party, one might take him to be an English professor at a New England college—which would not be far wrong.

Back in the forties, Bob had been director of public relations at Trinity College, where his writing skills, directness, and lack of equivocation earned him the respect of the press—even though he did not fit the stereotype of a hearty, comradely public relations man.

In 1951, Trinity's president, G. Keith Funston, became president of the New York Stock Exchange and a few years later asked Bob to join him there. As Keith's personal assistant, Bob's previous skills and experience were immediately put to good use. He visited out-of-town offices of member firms, found out what kind of services they wanted, and when possible saw that the services were provided. He established a NYSE–member-firm newspaper, for example. He became moderately well liked by people in the investment business. Neither Keith nor Bob anticipated then what Bob's chief responsibility would later be—and how the exercise of that responsibility would cause many members to feel anger when Bob's name was mentioned.

In 1960, Keith made Bob associate director of the Member Firms Department, and Bob became partly responsible for supervising the financial condition of member firms—not yet a serious problem. In 1966, Keith made him a vice president of the Exchange and director of the Member Firms Department. As such he now became completely responsible for the financial soundness of member firms—which became a very serious problem indeed in 1969.

Why? Because the volume of trading—and accordingly members' commissions—declined precipitously from the record levels of 1968. From nearly 20 million shares on December 19, 1968, volume abruptly declined to 16 million the next day, and 13 million the day after that. And it stayed near or below that level, with few exceptions, for many months afterward.[2]

The abnormal volume of trading in the the early and middle sixties— and the boom in stock exchange commissions—had been caused in large part by two simultaneous wars: the Vietnam War and President Johnson's War Against Poverty. The federal government's spending on these wars put billions of dollars into the hands of consumers and investors— which the government did not take away in taxes.

Inflating the money supply did not push consumer prices up much, however, in the early and middle sixties because the Federal Reserve, then chaired by William McChesney Martin, raised interest rates.

But in fiscal 1968—that is, from July 1, 1967, to June 30, 1968—federal expenditures ballooned. The deficit reached a post–World War II record high of $25 billion. It was twice the previous post–World War II record deficit. Twenty-five billion dollars may seem small compared to deficits incurred in the eighties and nineties, but the dollar was worth much more in the sixties and gross domestic product was much smaller.[3]

The big jump in government spending without a commensurate tax increase scared not only economists but even members of Congress. They feared that interest rates couldn't be raised high enough to prevent an unacceptable rise in the rate of inflation. The economy was already producing nearly as much as it could, so most of the additional money in the hands of consumers would be used to bid prices up.

Congress and President Johnson panicked. The Congress passed and President Johnson signed a bill that increased taxes in fiscal 1969 enormously. That year the federal government collected more than it spent. And Federal Reserve Chairman William McChesney Martin raised interest rates even higher.

The higher taxes took money out of the hands of investors, thus reducing the demand for securities. At the same time, higher interest rates made stocks relatively less attractive than bonds. In 1965, lower grade corporate bonds had paid less than 5 percent. In November 1968, they paid 7 percent. And in succeeding months even more.[4]

Equally important, the higher taxes took money out of the hands of consumers, reducing the demand for the products and services corporations sell. Investors saw corporate profits fall slightly in 1969 and anticipated profits would fall even further in 1970.

It was virtually inevitable that the volume of trading on the New York Stock Exchange—and consequently the commissions members received—would decline. Individuals, pension funds and other institutional investors had less money to invest, and common stocks became less attractive, tarnished by lower corporate profits, the anticipation of even lower profits, and interest rates that increased the attractiveness of bonds.

Profits of member firms were further squeezed by high costs; many firms had increased their costs of operation in order to process the huge order volume of 1968. The volume of trading needed by the average firm to break even more than doubled from 1966 to 1969.

Very early in 1969, several firms approached bankruptcy.[5]

It was Bob's responsibility to monitor the financial condition of member firms and to do what he could to prevent any firm from becoming bankrupt. His first step was usually to order the partners of a near-bankrupt firm to get more capital.

Often this had been easy for one or more of the partners of a firm to do. Consider McDonnell & Co. in January 1969.

McDonnell & Co. had grown rapidly during the happy days of the early and middle 1960s. Murray McDonnell and his brother, Sean, had made an excellent team. Murray was a great salesman—brought in considerable business—especially from wealthy Irish Catholics. Sean was one of the best back-office heads. Murray was Mr. Outside, Sean Mr. Inside.[6]

But Sean died in June 1968 from a heart attack while jogging. To replace him, Murray brought in Lawrence F. O'Brien as president. Larry O'Brien was a highly paid lobbyist who had been an aide to John F. Kennedy when Kennedy was a senator and president. Larry was a politician, not an investment man, nor an accountant, much less a computer expert.

In other words, Murray McDonnell chose as Sean's replacement someone who could help him get accounts, not someone with expertise in solving back-office problems. Murray, like so many CEOs of investment firms of the time, underrated the competence needed to operate a back office efficiently.[7]

When Larry accepted the McDonnell & Co. presidency in late 1968, he did not realize he had been asked to become a top officer of a sinking ship. On the day Larry started work January 1, 1969—six months after Sean's death—McDonnell & Co.'s capital had declined to a dangerous level.[8]

Income had declined below expenses.

A large number of fails had also depleted the firm's capital. Often when McDonnell sold a stock to a customer, it was unable to deliver the stock to the customer promptly. Sometimes McDonnell's back office had not received the shares from the broker McDonnell was buying from. Sometimes McDonnell's back office had simply mislaid the shares. In either case, McDonnell was then forced to go into the open market and buy the shares so as to fulfill its sale to its customer, depleting McDonnell's capital.[9]

As a consequence, McDonnell's capital was far below the level that the New York Stock Exchange had established to protect investors. One rule stated that a member firm's liabilities should not exceed 20 times its capital. On January 1, 1969, McDonnell's liabilities had climbed to $118 million. And its capital had declined to only $2 million. Instead of a better than 20 to 1 ratio, its ratio was 55 to 1.

When Bob Bishop ordered Murray to get more capital, Murray asked his rich relatives—the Ford family—for money. He got some but not enough. So he borrowed $1.6 million from First National City Bank to bring McDonnell & Co.'s capital up to a level that satisfied Bob Bishop.[10]

As the months rolled by in 1969, more and more brokerage firms violated or came near to violating the Exchange's capital rules. Not only did the volume of trading stay low relative to the heady days of 1968—causing nearly half of all members to lose money on their commission business in 1969—but stock prices declined as well.[11]

The decline in stock prices impaired member firms' capital for reasons peculiar to the investment business. Many member firms made markets in stocks not listed on the Exchange. To do so they had to maintain an inventory of such stocks. When stock prices fell, so did the worth of a firm's assets.

Furthermore, much of the capital of many investment firms consisted not of cash, but of common stocks. Why? Instead of contributing cash to his firm, a partner could instead pledge common stocks. Many partners in investment firms did this because they hoped to, and often did, benefit from the stocks rising in price.

The principal purpose of the capital contributed by a brokerage firm's partners in those days was to meet emergencies. It was primarily a reserve to draw on if panicky customers acted like commercial bank depositors running to withdraw their money.

The capital contributed by the partners in many firms didn't need to be liquid because these firms used the cash that customers left on deposit with them as operating capital.[12] In the beginning of 1970, this cash on deposit totaled $2.8 billion.[13] Money market funds hadn't been invented in the sixties and seventies, so brokerage firms got the use of this money interest-free.

To sum up: The capital of most investment firms declined because so much of member firms' capital consisted of common stocks and because the firms necessarily maintained inventories of common stocks. When stock prices fell, so did the capital of most investment firms.

And stock prices did fall. From a closing level of 985 on November 29, 1968, the Dow Jones Industrial Average fell more or less steadily to 774 on March 20, 1970.

Investors were responding to actions taken by the Federal Reserve governors. Taxes had continued high—the deficit was only $3 billion—but galloping inflation, still responding to the sharp 1968 deficit, could not be reined in quickly. Consumer prices continued to rise at an unacceptable 5½ percent annual rate. So the Fed kept interest rates high; lower-grade bonds paid close to 9 percent during the early months of 1970.

As a consequence, many investors chose to buy bonds instead of stocks. More and more brokerage firms came close to bankruptcy as their costs exceeded their incomes.

Bob curbed the activities of 47 member firms in 1969 and threatened to curb the activities of dozens more.[14]

Behind the statistics were days and nights of horror for hundreds of partners of brokerage firms. Many had invested all their money in their brokerage firms. They had few other assets or none at all. They feared not only that they would lose all their own money, not only that they would be forced into immense debt, but that they would also lose the money that relatives, friends, and clients had lent their firms—people who had trusted them. They, who had always been looked up to, would be disgraced.[15]

One evening 30 years later, a self-made partner of one of these firms was asked in the main dining room of the University Club in New York to recall those days. He was a well-poised man, always well-contained. He had fought the Japanese in World War II without flinching. But as he started to recall those days and nights—when he talked about "Bob Bishop calling us at home just as we're about to go to bed to tell us that if we didn't get more capital by the next day, he would put us out of business,"—his eyes filled with tears, and he couldn't continue.

As more and more firms came close to collapse, Bob tried, and often succeeded, in preventing bankruptcies by ordering the partners to take steps that angered them. When the partners of a firm with a liabilities-to-capital ratio exceeding or approaching 20 to 1 did not raise sufficient capital, Bob often ordered the partners to close offices and/or reduce the number of their customers, and/or not underwrite any securities.[16] Bob thus reduced their hopes of profits.

Exchange members had a direct interest in preventing any of their fellow members from actually declaring bankruptcy. The effect would have been traumatic not only for the customers of the bankrupted firm but for the partners of other member firms of The New York Stock

Exchange as well. The news would cause customers who had left cash and securities with other firms to realize the risks they were taking.

An even more important incentive for well-managed firms to prevent the bankruptcies of poorly managed firms was this: The businesses of the firms were (and are) so intertwined that the bankruptcy of one firm could cause the bankruptcy of several other firms. A trade most often consists of one brokerage firm selling securities to another firm and vice versa, each on behalf of customers. If one firm fails to deliver the cash or securities it owes other firms, it could cause the bankruptcy of those other firms.

This had happened in 1873. The failure of Jay Cooke & Co. caused the demise of 57 other brokerage firms in a few weeks.[17]

Yet investors didn't rush to withdraw their money and securities from brokerage firms in 1969.

In January 1969, a *Wall Street Journal* story warned investors, "A spectre haunts Wall Street—and if the nation's 26.4 million shareholders are unaware of it, that's only because the securities industry finds it too frightening to discuss openly.

"The spectre is the possibility that troubles in handling high stock-trading volume could cause the collapse of some major brokerage houses in a financial chain reaction."[18]

This story didn't deter investors from leaving money and securities with investment firms because it was much too late. Investors could see that *high* stock trading volume was no longer a threat. The problem in 1969 was trading volume so low that many brokerage firms were not profitable.

Furthermore, many stockbrokers, at the behest of their managements, urged their customers to leave their securities with their firms so that the Central Certificate System could function more efficiently.

Investors who bought stocks on margin were required to leave the stocks with the firms that lent them the money, and many other investors left money and stocks with brokerage firms just for convenience. In 1970, Merrill Lynch, for example, held $18 billion worth of customers' securities in so-called safekeeping. Merrill Lynch's capital was a tenth of that—about $1.8 billion.

Some investors were "subordinated lenders"; they agreed to leave their money and/or securities with a firm and not withdraw it without, say, a six-month notice. The investors received interest on their capital on top of the dividends and interest they received on the securities.

Bob Bishop and his boss, Lee Arning, skillfully fenced with reporters, leaving them and investors ignorant of the terrifying dimensions of the truth:[19] If a firm went bankrupt, many of its customers risked losing not only much or all of the money they had left on deposit with the firm but also the securities they had left in the firm's "safekeeping."

Bob and Lee knew panic would make matters worse. If brokerage firm customers withdrew their assets, the capital positions of brokerage firms would be weakened even further. Like a run on a bank before bank deposits were federally insured, mob psychology could bring on the very result feared by individuals making up the mob—the loss of their money.

Bob and Lee often felt like the Dutch boy of the fable who put his finger in a leak in the dike and so saved Holland—except that they ran from leak to leak while at the same time deprecating the danger.

But no matter how alert Bob was to the financial condition of member firms, no matter how often he asked member firms to increase their capital, no matter how much he curbed the activities of over-extended firms, he was not always successful in what he aimed to do. The continuing decline in the volume of trading and in stock prices made it impossible to prevent several firms from becoming technically bankrupt.

As of March 1, 1970, more than half the 572 member firms of The New York Stock Exchange that dealt with the general public were in danger of bankruptcy.[20] They were losing so much money that, if they continued to do so, they'd be out of business in six months. Six of these firms were among the ten largest.

To prevent failing firms from declaring bankruptcy or liquidation, Chairman Bunny Lasker devoted his abilities, his considerable energy, and his power to arranging for weaker firms to merge with strong ones. In so doing he was following a practice of the thirties when a number of firms approached bankruptcy. E. A. Pierce & Co., for example, took over so many badly managed firms that it became the country's largest brokerage firm. Eventually E. A. Pierce & Co. itself became so weak that it had to be taken over by the much smaller Merrill Lynch & Co.

Bunny convened meetings of the Surveillance Committee, colloquially called the "Crisis Committee," not just once a week but several days during the week at The New York Stock Exchange and often weekends uptown at his elegant suite in the Carlyle Hotel.[21] The chairman of the Crisis Committee was 42-year-old Felix Rohaytn, a Lazard Freres partner since he was 32. Bunny and Felix sometimes made 150 to 200 telephone calls a weekend, urging mergers, seeking capital for weak firms, and calling governors to urge them to support measures they deemed desirable.

As a last resort to prevent bankruptcies, The New York Stock Exchange had set up a Special Trust Fund in 1963. It had then seemed big enough to liquidate any troubled member firm without loss to its customers: $10 million in cash, raised by a levy on New York Stock Exchange members, and $15 million in standby credit with banks.[22]

The Special Trust Fund became necessary because of an unintended consequence of the Glass-Steagall Act, passed in 1933. The act made it illegal for commercial banks to engage in the stock brokerage business. The framers of the act intended to protect commercial banks from the hazards of the investment business. But they unintendedly removed any incentive for commercial banks to rescue failing brokerage firms by supplying them with the ready money they needed to stay solvent. In fact, when a brokerage firm seemed likely to fail, commercial banks pushed for early liquidation to reduce their losses from unpaid loans.

In the panics of 1907 and 1929, commercial bankers had promptly rushed to the aid of failing brokerage firms.[23] Historians have portrayed J. P. Morgan and other commercial bankers as patriotic as they contributed and rounded up ready cash in 1907, but they were often saving subsidiaries of their own businesses from loss. Even commercial banks with well-managed brokerage subsidiaries would suffer from the bankruptcy of one large brokerage firm or several small ones as the banks' brokerage affiliates failed to receive the cash and securities that bankrupted brokerage firms owed them.

In 1970, no government organization protected investors who left their money and securities with brokerage firms the way the Federal Deposit Insurance Corporation had protected savers since 1933.

In June 1969 U.S. Senator Edmund S. Muskie had introduced a bill to establish a "Federal Broker-Dealer Insurance Corporation" that would protect investors the way the Federal Deposit Insurance Corporation protected people who left money on deposit with banks.

(Senator Muskie had been the Democratic Party's vice presidential candidate the year before and had hopes of becoming President.)

At about the same time, Representative John H. Moss had introduced a similar bill in the House.

But neither bill was voted on because of lack of support from leaders in the investment business.

In 1970, brokerage firms were on their own, yet most operated with minimum capital—thin and shaky.[24] Only the willingness of well-managed, financially strong firms to prevent the bankrupcy of poorly managed firms protected investors who had left cash and/or securities on deposit.

Mismanaged McDonnell & Co. again presented the most imminent danger early in 1970. The losses had continued, and when Murray McDonnell again asked his rich relatives to contribute money to his firm, his relatives refused.[25]

The bankers at First National City, afraid they would never get back the $1.6 million they had lent McDonnell, pressed for immediate liquidation of the firm.[26] As they observed the deteriorating situation, the sooner McDonnell was liquidated, the more likely they would be repaid.

But Bob Bishop feared, from his analysis, that if technically bankrupt

McDonnell actually declared bankruptcy, its customers would lose $10 million.

The "Crisis Fund" was virtually depleted. The previous year nearly $8 million had been taken out of the fund to prevent the customers of two insolvent firms—Gregory & Sons and Ammot Baker—from losing money and securities.

The members had contributed $5 million more to the Crisis Fund, but this too had been drawn on so as to liquidate several smaller firms without losses to customers.

So if McDonnell customers were not to lose money, members of the Exchange would have to contribute more money to the Crisis Fund. Which they did—contributing enough to liquidate McDonnell & Co. without loss to any of its customers: $10 million.[27]

In an effort to increase the incomes of member firms and so prevent further technical bankruptcies, commissions were increased. Effective April 10, 1970, investors paid a surcharge of $15 per order on stock transactions of 1,000 shares or less.[28]

But this minor injection of revenue was not nearly enough to prevent several more firms from becoming technically bankrupt. Hayden, Stone & Co., the firm that had fired Norm Swanton so as to retain the capital of the possibly crooked partner, was one of those firms.

In an effort to reduce the amount of money to be withdrawn from the Crisis Fund if Hayden, Stone were liquidated, Bunny Lasker suggested to Merrill Lynch CEO Donald T. Regan, that Merrill Lynch acquire Hayden, Stone.

But Don was not interested.

Bunny tried to get other firms to acquire Hayden, Stone. As did Felix Rohaytn, President Bob Haack, Lee Arning, and some officers of investment firms. Lee thought they had succeeded in arranging a merger with Walston & Co.,[29] a fast-growing, well-managed firm, originally headquartered in San Francisco that had moved its headquarters to New York City when it grew to become a national firm. Walston wanted the merger. It would then become the third-largest firm in the country.

But the Hayden, Stone stockbrokers revolted. They thought joining Walston & Co. would be a step down. More than any other firm, Walston & Co. had grown by attracting small investors willing to take big risks. One of its ads, for example, had simply been headlined "13 Risk Stocks"—and had gained thousands of replies. (A far cry from Merrill Lynch's "Investigate then invest" slogan of twenty years earlier.)

Hayden, Stone stockbrokers wanted to merge with a more conservative firm geared to serving upscale investors.[30] The average commission per trade would be bigger because the number of shares per trade would be higher. They also wanted to merge with a major underwriter or one that bought blocks of stocks that it distributed in small lots through brokers. Stockbrokers usually got twice the normal commissions on such orders.[31]

And some may also have been motivated by pride. Saying at a cocktail party that one is a stockbroker with Morgan Stanley or Paine Webber is likely to gain admiring glances. Saying one is a stockbroker with a little-known or little-admired firm is likely to result in a change of subject.

The Hayden, Stone brokers got their way. If Bunny had attempted to bully the merger through, many brokers would have defected taking their customers with them and thus making the merger unattractive to Walston.

Bunny helped Hayden, Stone merge with Cogan, Berlind, Weill and Levitt, Inc., a firm loaded with talent as later events would prove. Its back office was in excellent shape because it was run by Frank G. Zarb. He combined the expertise of a Norm Swanton with the winning personality of a salesman or successful politician. When Sanford T. Weill became CEO of Travelers in the 1990s, he made Frank CEO of Traveler's investment subsidiary, Smith Barney. The Levitt in the firm's name was Arthur Levitt, Jr. who would become chairman of the Securities and Exchange Commission in 1993. When he assumed office, he was spurred by Frank Zarb, who had become CEO of Smith Barney, to radically improve practices in the underwriting and distribution of municipal bonds.

The new, merged firm was named CBWL–Hayden, Stone, but soon the CBWL would be dropped as well as the comma between "Hayden" and "Stone." The reason: Even though Sandy Weill and the other officers of CBWL dominated, Hayden, Stone was much better known and was widely respected. Apparently, nobody outside the firm knew about the incident of the possibly crooked partner described in Chapter 1.[32]

CBWL, however, would not take on the liabilities of Hayden, Stone without a healthy contribution from the Crisis Fund. The merger cost Exchange members $9.8 million.[33]

The reports in the media about the near bankruptcy of member firm after member firm caused Senator Muskie to revive the bill he had introduced in 1969. His bill for establishing a "Federal Broker-Dealer Insurance Corporation" was poorly drafted by virtually any standard. It was mostly a paragraph by paragraph copy of the act establishing the Federal Deposit Insurance Corporation. In a few instances, the copiers even forgot to change the word "bank" to "broker-dealer."[34] None of the differences between the banking industry and the investment industry were taken into account.

At about the same time, Representative John H. Moss introduced a similar bill in the House of Representatives. Moss, who had been a real estate broker, was astounded when his staff informed him that the cash that investors left with investment firms was not escrowed, as it was in the real estate industry.[35]

At the Senate hearing on Muskie's bill held April 16, 1970, Don Regan,

CEO of Merrill Lynch, diplomatically but strongly opposed not just the bill but its concept. Senator Harrison A. Williams, Jr., Chairman of the Securities Subcommittee, asked Don, "Do you prefer self-regulation to the FBDIC?"[36]

Don answered with a flat, "Yes, sir."

Don Regan's opposition was understandable. The bill required brokerage firms to contribute to establish a fund to indemnify customers if a brokerage firm became bankrupt. If more money were required than was in the fund, the U.S. Treasury could be drawn on—with surviving brokerage firms being assessed to repay the Treasury.

How much each firm would be assessed to build up the fund was vague at this point—but it was clear that each assessment would be based on each firm's size. Merrill Lynch might be forced to pay nearly two million dollars to keep competitors in business.

Don used the Senate hearing as a forum for urging the Securities and Exchange Commission to apply tighter rules regarding the capital of investment firms. He objected to other firms stretching the use of their capital beyond the bounds of prudence, with the result that Merrill Lynch was taxed when they failed.

Many other powerful men in the investment business opposed Muskie's bill. The cost, after all, was considerable, limitless, and would fall on investment firms, not on taxpayers.

NYSE ex-Chairman Gus Levy, who still exerted considerable influence, opposed the bill. So did Crisis Chairman Felix Rohatyn.[37] Why should government bureaucrats be able to administer a rescue fund better than people in the investment business?

Many Senators and Representatives may not have liked the idea because it might give the appearance that the U.S. government would be bailing out the rich.[38]

And the Securities and Exchange commissioners and staff had their own ideas about what should be done—primarily that the SEC should have control.[39]

But those who felt that a government-connected insurance fund of some kind was necessary were not deterred. They elected Ralph D. DeNunzio chairman of a seven-man group charged to formulate a compromise plan. Ralph was CEO of Kidder, Peabody & Co., a highly regarded, sizable investment firm and vice chairman of the Exchange.

At a subsequent hearing on June 18, he delivered the draft of a bill that "meets, we believe, the important public interests of the Muskie bill. At the same time, however, the draft bill is designed to substitute and build upon the self-regulatory approach developed over the last 30-odd years. This is believed to be more efficient, to result in less cost, and to avoid a new tier of government regulation."[40]

He further stated, "the respective bodies of the New York and American Stock Exchanges have met and formally approved the specific plan proposed by the task force."

To emphasize that the purpose of the bill was to protect investors, not to save brokerage firms, "Federal Broker-Dealer Insurance Corporation" was changed to "Securities Investors Protection Corporation."

Now the problems were principally political. The views of the commissioners and staff of the Securities and Exchange Commission had to be considered. As did those of the staff of the Treasury Department. Senators and Representatives had hundreds of other bills to consider. Weeks went by without a bill being reported to the full Senate or House of Representatives. Would Congress—could Congress—pass a bill in 1970? Or would the whole process need to be repeated when a new Congress convened on January 1, 1971? Congress was going to be in recess from August 14 to September 9 and was slated to adjourn on October 14 for the 1970 election campaign. Whether a lame-duck Congress would return after the elections was questionable.

While the legislation languished, events showed how much investors needed some kind of government protection.

In July 1970, Bob Bishop had concluded that another big firm, Dempsey-Tegler, would declare bankruptcy with consequent loss to its customers unless the Exchange acted promptly.[41] He so reported to Lee Arning who in turn discussed the impending bankruptcy with Bob Haack, Bunny Lasker, and Felix Rohaytn.

Lee told Felix that the price tag for rescuing Dempsey-Tegler without cost to its customers would again be big—at least $9 million, perhaps $15 million. Dempsey-Tegler's books were in such bad shape, Bob Bishop couldn't tell.

At about the same time, Bob told Lee that in addition to Dempsey-Tegler, six other financially troubled firms needed to be liquidated.[42] Saving their customers would cost at least $20 million, perhaps $40 million.

Authorized outlays to liquidate these six firms plus Dempsey-Telgler might total $55 million—far, far more than the amount of cash left in the Crisis Fund, plus the standby credit!

Just by luck, a way was found to add to the Crisis Fund without imposing contributions on member firms or running to the government for help. (The *deus ex machina* resolutions of bad drama do sometimes occur in real life.) Years before the governors had approved the setting aside of several millions of dollars each year in another trust fund to erect a new, enormous home for the Exchange.

"What a dumb thing that would have been!" Lee Arning told the NYSE oral histories interviewer. "It would have been a white elephant. A huge building! The brokers would have needed roller skates to get around. Nobody was thinking of computers when the building fund was started."

The governors voted to transfer the $30 million in the Building Fund to the Crisis Fund—and the firms were liquidated without cost or much inconvenience to their customers.

But the experience was scary.

The strain on Bob Bishop was intense. He was like a soldier on the front line continually subjected to bombs, artillery shelling, and machine gun fire. He was the one who personally warned heads of firms that their firms were in danger of being suspended. It was he who signed the letters to heads of firms ordering them to take actions that reduced their incomes or that put them out of business. And after being assaulted by the head of a member firm for being too strict, he was then often assaulted by members of the Crisis Committee, especially Felix Rohaytn, for being too lenient.

Bob's stress in closely watching the financial conditions of the more than 500 member firms and in curbing the activities of 167 firms in 1970 was intensified by his being shorthanded. He had more than 200 people working for him, but they were not enough to keep track of all the troubled firms as well as was desirable.[43] The problems increased faster than people could be added and trained to handle them, even if cost were no object—which it wasn't. Bob Haack was constrained by the budget passed each year by the board of governors. The governors, many of whose firms were in financial difficulty, wanted to keep their contributions to New York Stock Exchange activities down.

Lee Arning, following Bob Haack's cost-restraing policy, even sent a memo to Bob Bishop, in the midst of serious problems, quibbling about a small amount Bob Bishop had put on his expense account.[44]

The strain on Bob Bishop was so great that, despite his courage as an Air Force pilot in World War II, he sometimes had difficulty maintaining his composure in meetings with Bob Haack and others.[45]

In August 1970, Bob Bishop reported to the Crisis Committee that two modest-sized firms were in violation of the Exchange's capital rule and had few prospects of getting more capital themselves.[46]

One was Charles Plohn & Co. Early in 1970, Plohn had absorbed the offices of another firm that needed to be liquidated, but in so doing had over-extended itself. To raise capital Charles Plohn and his associates had taken several extreme steps. The wife of the senior partner had sold a cherished collection of silver for more than half a million dollars and added the proceeds to the firm's capital.[47]

But Mrs. Plohn's sacrifice and other heroic measures were to no avail.

The other firm was First Devonshire Corp.

Money from the Crisis Fund was needed if customers of the two firms were not to lose money as the firms went out of business. However, the Crisis Fund was very nearly depleted, even with the $30 million from the building fund.

And many members were loath to contribute any more money to prevent bankruptcies of member firms. Votes by the governors proposing that members contribute more money to the Crisis Fund had become increasingly close. On one occasion Bunny Lasker delayed the vote until a favorable governor on his way from Washington could rush from LaGuardia Airport down the FDR Drive to the Governors' Room of The New York Stock Exchange.[48]

Bunny's phone calls revealed to him that some governors were especially loath to help customers of Plohn and First Devonshire because they felt that the partners of those firms may have been guilty of more than mismanagement.[49]

Even more important, several influential members of the Exchange, notably Andre Meyer, senior partner of Lazard Freres and Felix Rohaytn's boss, felt that precedents were being established that the Exchange would finance the liquidation of any member firm[50]—precedents that would be legally binding on all member firms to contribute many millions of dollars. To a cautious executive, the legal liability was frightening.

Consequently, for the first time, the governors refused to rescue a failing firm.

This gave Stanley Sporkin, who as the associate director of the Securities and Exchange Commission was responsible for overseeing the New York Stock Exchange, the opportunity he had been waiting for. In previous crises, such as those of McDonnell and Dempsey-Tegler, he had wanted to declare the firms bankrupt.[51] He may have wanted to punish incompetent managers. In the event of a bankruptcy all of the partners' personal assets would have been taken to satisfy creditors. He also may have felt that allowing one firm's partners to be financially destroyed would serve as a lesson to others and so prevent more bankruptcies.

But in each instance Bob Haack had been able to dissuade him from declaring a firm bankrupt by stating that the Exchange would then no longer supply the firm with any money. Investors would consequently lose sizable sums.

Now, however, Stanely could do what he had always wanted to do. He declared Charles Plohn & Co. and First Devonshire legally bankrupt.

On September 1, Robinson & Co., a firm of similar size (8,000 customers), filed for bankruptcy.[52] At first, this didn't worry Bunny Lasker, Felix Rohatyn, and other governors much. Robinson & Co. had resigned from the Exchange in July. Therefore, it was argued, Robinson & Co.'s problems were not the Exchange's concern.

But the firm's customers felt otherwise and sued the Exchange for the kind of financial help given customers of McDonnell & Co.; Hayden, Stone; Dempsey Tegler; and several other firms. Andre Meyer's fears about the Exchange's precedent-setting rescues were turning out not to have been far-fetched.

A few days after the Robinson & Co. bankruptcy, Bob Bishop reported to the Crisis Committee that another firm, Blair & Co., was close to bankruptcy.[53] Despite the unwillingness of the governors to vote money for Plohn, First Devonshire, and Robinson & Co., it was agreed that the 9,000 customers of Blair & Co. should be protected against any loss. The governors may have been intimidated by the bad publicity the Exchange was getting for ignoring the impending losses that the customers of Charles Plohn & Co., First Devonshire Corp., and Robinson & Co. would suffer.

They may also have felt they had already quieted Andre Meyer's fears by not financing the liquidation of every member firm. In any case, they decided to take $12 million out of the Crisis Fund to ease the liquidation of Blair & Co.

"Big Board Seeking Vast New Financing to Protect Investors," screamed a *Wall Street Journal* headline on October 1, 1970.[54] The liquidations of many member firms had necessarily been reported, as had the amount of money put in and taken out of the Crisis Fund. Adding the figures up made his conclusion logical.

The story infuriated Bob Haack. He stormed into the *Wall Street Journal*'s offices (which were only a few blocks from The New York Stock Exchange) accompanied by vice chairman Ralph DeNunzio and the Exchange's public relations head. Bob called the story "irresponsible journalism"[55] and denied that any more money would be needed to bolster member firms.[56]

He may have been sincere. The volume of trading had suddenly soared in September to 14.4 million shares a day from just over 10 million shares a day in most of the previous months. It appeared to him and many other Wall Streeters that the worst was over. Higher commissions from an increased volume of trading would solve all their problems.

Bob Haack couldn't have made a bigger public relations blunder. Suddenly a bigger threat to the reputation of The New York Stock Exchange appeared—one much bigger than Blair's liquidation or that of any other troubled firm. Goodbody & Co. was ten times bigger than Plohn, First Devonshire, and Robinson & Co. *combined*. It was the fourth largest firm, with 225,000 customers. And it needed many millions of dollars if it were not to become bankrupt.[57]

During the Spring and Summer of 1970, subordinated lender after subordinated lender had withdrawn his or her capital from Goodbody & Co. They were free to do so under Goodbody's by-laws with only 30 days notice. Consequently, Goodbody had continually come close to violating the Exchange's 20 to 1 liabilities-to-assets rule—or had actually violated it.

When Bob Haack stormed into the *Wall Street Journal*'s office, denying any more money would be needed for the Crisis Fund, he and Bob Bishop *et al.* thought Goodbody had been saved by a merger with a mutual fund firm,[58] but that fell through. Members of the Exchange didn't want to set a precedent by allowing an institutional investor to trade directly on the Exchange, eliminating the need for a stockbroker.

Bob Bishop told Bunny Lasker through Lee Arning that something drastic needed to be done—and done quickly.

Bunny called the senior partners of the 30 largest firms and all the living ex-chairmen of the Exchange into a meeting to consider the problem. He and former chairman Gus Levy had done this secretly before in emergencies, even before Plohn's problems. It was the heads of the big firms who had the real power in crises such as this, not the governors of the Exchange. This time, however, only the fact of the meeting (but not the details) was reported by the media.

Bunny described a terrifying situation. Goodbody would require many, many millions of dollars.

Just weeks earlier, the governors had quibbled about allocating a few million dollars to make it possible to liquidate Charles Plohn, First Devonshire, and Robinson & Co. without loss to investors. Yet the mood of this meeting of the leaders in the industry was "Goodbody could not be permitted to fail." Goodbody was too big. The effect on the investment business would be disastrous.

The alternatives differed little from those that had been considered in similar situations in the past. One member of the group suggested that Goodbody's branch offices and businesses be divided among a number of member firms, but in the ensuing discussion, it soon became apparent that this would take too long, if it were feasible at all.[59]

Someone suggested that several well-heeled firms—rather than all the members—get together and contribute capital to Goodbody.[60] This too was seen as impractical. It would be too complicated, financially and legally. Who would be in charge? How could the shares of each contributor be determined?

What about one, big, well-managed, well-capitalized firm taking over Goodbody? This seemed like a good solution to most of those present, but what firm would?

Merrill Lynch, Pierce, Fenner & Smith was the obvious candidate.

Bunny Lasker talked to Don Regan, but Don demurred. Among his objections: Merrill Lynch might be sued under the antitrust laws.

Over the next few days, Bunny, Felix Rohatyn, Lee Arning and other members of the Crisis Committee directly and indirectly approached 17 other well-capitalized, well-managed firms, but all turned the offer down.

The situation appeared hopeless.

Bunny went back to Don Regan. Only Merrill Lynch could save the investment industry from serious injury—an injury from which the investment business would take a long time to recover—and Merrill Lynch, because it was the biggest, would suffer the most.

Bunny also quoted the "failing firm" doctrine. Antitrust laws don't apply if the firm taken over would otherwise fail.

Don said he would agree only if two conditions were met. Merrill Lynch would make Goodbody viable and eventually merge with it, but if any of the 20 largest member firms were suspended or expelled because of financial difficulties, the deal was off.[61] Why did Don make this condition? Because if some other large firm were allowed to go bankrupt, the lack of public confidence in all investment firms would cause Merrill Lynch's revenues to plummet, handicapping its rescue operation. The drowning firm might drag its intended rescuer down with it. (And Don may have guessed that another large firm, one bigger than Goodbody, might soon be in financial difficulty.)

Don also required that the other members obligate themselves to contribute up to $30 million for any losses Merrill Lynch might suffer as a consequence of its rescue of Goodbody & Co.[62]

These conditions could not be agreed to by the governors alone. The Exchange's constitution would need to be amended by a vote of all the members. A few weeks later—on November 4, 1970—the members voted the amendment, and Merrill Lynch immediately lent Goodbody $15 million so Goodbody's capital would meet the Exchange's requirements.

The Goodbody incident, coming on top of Plohn, First Devonshire, Robinson & Co., and Blair, was frightening. What firm or firms were going to need rescuing next?

Both the Senate and the House had passed bills establishing SIPC, but the bills differed in many respects. A joint committee needed to agree on an identical bill.

"Getting to conference wasn't easy," Theodore H. Focht, special counsel to the House committee dealing with the bill, recalls. "It almost died in conference. Then it was a question . . . if we could get the conference report written and passed by both houses before Congress adjourned."[63]

Congress did vote to come back in November, and the conference report was delivered on time, but Congress had not come back to deal with SIPC but with several major appropriation bills, two controversial bills dealing with the Vietnam War, the super-sonic plane, welfare reform, and import restrictions.

An announcement by Chairman Moss on November 16, 1970, the day Congress reconvened, made passage of SIPC even more doubtful. He said he would not allow the House to vote on SIPC if SIPC was to be immediately drawn on for the liquidation of Plohn, First Devonshire, Robinson & Co., Goodbody & Co., or any other presently troubled firm.

"We don't want to be in the position where the immediate liabilities would wipe out the fund and require the use of the Treasury line of credit," Representative Moss said.[64]

Bob Haack had attempted to dissuade Moss from making that statement. Two days previously, Bob had reversed himself and had publicly announced that the Crisis Fund would need to be enlarged and that Plohn and First Devonshire customers would not lose any money.[65]

But this had not satisfied Moss. And it was too late to incorporate the kind of language Moss wanted into the bill. The lame duck session would end January 2, 1971.

So Chairman Bunny Lasker and Vice Chairman Ralph DeNunzio (who was slated to become chairman the following year) privately assured Moss that no firm currently in difficulty would draw on funds in the Securities Investors Protection Corporation if Congress created it. In so doing they were emphasizing statements made in the Senate hearings. Ralph had assured Senator Muskie in July: "If between now and the time of the adoption of this legislation there are firms that should be in violation of the net capital rules, the stock exchange will have to cope with that at that time and as it relates to a specific member."

Bunny and Ralph's private assurances were reluctantly accepted by Moss—and all seemed well. But two powerful senators—powerful enough to prevent passage of the bill—voiced last-minute objections. One was pressured to relent, but the other objector, Senator Proxmire, was obdurate. A commissioner of the Securities and Exchange Commission hurriedly wrote Proxmire a letter, promising the Senator that what he wanted would be covered by regulations issued by the SEC after the bill was passed.[66]

Proxmire also relented.

"The legislation almost didn't get passed," Ted Focht recalls.

President Nixon signed the bill at virtually the last moment, on December 30, 1970.

"It's a miracle that it became law," Ted recalls.

The passage of SIPC meant that the bankruptcy of one large or of several, even many, medium-sized firms could no longer cause The New York Stock Exchange to collapse.

It also made it possible for today's investors to leave securities worth sizable sums and sizable amounts of cash on deposit with many investment firms. SIPC insured only $50,000 worth of case and securities. But SIPC's covering of the basic risk—and its prevention of a cascade of bankruptcies—made it attractive for insurance companies to insure deposits in excess of those meager amounts. Today investors can leave $5 million in cash and/or securities with some brokerage firms without fear of loss.

The passage of SIPC also meant that millions of investors never knew—until now—how narrowly they had come to losing millions of dollars. And the American public never knew how narrowly The New York Stock Exchange—the heart of American capitalism—came to collapsing.

In fact, the danger to the survival of The New York Stock Exchange had actually been even worse—far worse—than has been described in this chapter. The next two chapters, for the first time, reveal the extent of that danger.

4

The Desirability of Permanent Capital[1]

Jim Lynch feared late in 1970 that he would be without a job and at the same time owe Chemical Bank $130,000. Jim's fears were accentuated by his having no assets other than his mortgaged home and no rich relatives who could give or lend him money. Furthermore, a wife and two young children depended upon him for support.

He would have been even more terrified if he had known that the senior partner of his firm had put him more than a hundred thousand dollars deeper into debt.

How could he have allowed himself to get into such a desperate situation? He was neither a gambler nor a womanizer, but, in fact, frugal, as well as a devoted husband and father, and a boring confessor to his priest.

The answer lay in how the partners of Glore Forgan Staats, Inc. behaved in 1968, 1969, and 1970.

In 1968 they acted as if the firm's record profits of that year would go on forever.

They raised virtually everyone's salary—handsomely.

The firm opened a sumptuous sales office on Park Avenue in New York City, opposite the Waldorf-Astoria.

New, palatial headquarters for the Western region were built in Los Angeles.

Stockbrokers in San Francisco, Chicago, La Jolla, and elsewhere were moved into larger, more splendid quarters. The new Cleveland office was furnished with such rare and expensive antiques that its opening was featured, not in the Cleveland Plain Dealer's financial section, but in its style section.

Much larger, more elegant space was leased at 95 Wall Street to house the firm's headquarters.

In addition, as previously described, Norm Swanton had incurred a big capital expenditure with new computers and upped monthly costs by expanding the back office staff.

Payrolls, rents, mortgage payments and other expenses soared.

Perhaps expenses of such magnitude would not have been made if Maury Stans had been concentrating on his duties as CEO. He was diverted from his Glore Forgan responsibilities by his raising money to help Richard Nixon be elected President. He formally left the firm to become Secretary of Commerce in November 1968.

Perhaps Jim would also not have found himself in such a perilous situation if Maury's successor as CEO had been a different kind of person.

The task of finding a replacement for Maury as CEO fell to Russ Forgan, the firm's chairman. He himself was too old for the strain imposed on a CEO. He could have been CEO when Glore Forgan & Co. merged with Wm. R. Staats, but declined.

Three top executives in the firm were well equipped to be CEO, but all three declined. Harry Colmery, the head of Glore Forgan's Western region liked living in Los Angeles and so did his wife. Why work in damp, cold New York City when one can live in continual warmth and much sunshine?

The head of the Midwest region also declined. He and his wife were enmeshed in Chicago society. He was so well regarded by Illinois Republicans, they had considered nominating him as U.S. Senator.

The nominal number two man in the firm, Vice Chairman Charles J. Hodge, who occupied himself mostly with investment banking and trading, considered becoming president a step down.

Besides, being a CEO of a brokerage firm may be prestigious, but it's not so creative as investment banking nor as exciting as trading. All the possible CEOs within the firm looked upon being CEO as mostly housekeeping.

A search firm was retained, but it failed to produce an acceptable candidate.

Russ mentioned the firm's problem to an old friend, Hans Stauffer, founder and chairman of Stauffer Chemical Company (later merged into Cheseborough-Ponds). Hans told Russ he had exactly the right man for the job, Archie E. Albright, Jr., a partner in Kuhn, Loeb & Co., one of Wall Street's major investment banking firms at the time.

It is difficult to assess Hans' motives in recommending Archie, who had only a year's experience in the investment business. Previously, Archie had been executive vice president of Stauffer Chemical. Hans had not thought Archie sufficiently competent to ever become CEO of Stauffer Chemical—and had told Archie so. That was why Archie had quit and gone to Kuhn, Loeb.

It may be just that Hans liked Archie very much.

Archie was in some ways typical of the kind of man who gets ahead in business by being liked by superiors for his personal characteristics.

"Archie looked like he stepped out of central casting for a CEO," Norm Swanton recalls. "Very handsome, well groomed, articulate."

Archie's dark brown hair was always neatly in place, its part never marred by an errant wisp.

His resume made him look good as well. He had graduated magna cum laude from Wittenberg College and had two law degrees from Yale.

But . . . "I never saw him make an important decision the whole time he was Glore Forgan's president,"[2] one high-ranking Glore Forgan executive recalls.

This avoidance of decision-making was apparently part of his character. Every day he wore what appeared to be the same dark blue suit, so dark as to be almost black, a white shirt, and the same tie with a muted pattern. He owned seven of these suits and bought identical ties half a dozen at a time from Sulka's. (Armand Assante, playing the mock hero of a satirical 1997 movie, *Fatal Instinct*, had a similar wardrobe.)

Maury Stans may have been the only Glore Forgan executive to assess Archie correctly. Maury was not the type of man who is taken in by appearances. Before going to Washington, Maury had interviewed Archie—and voted against hiring him. But when Maury was asked to name an alternative, he couldn't, so even Maury assented to Archie becoming CEO of Glore Forgan Staats, Inc. in November 1968.

And to be fair, bad luck hit Archie hard within months of his becoming president. Suddenly Glore Forgan Staats, Inc. needed more capital. Maury had taken his capital with him. Maury's attorneys had advised him that it would be illegal for him as Secretary of Commerce to own stock in a brokerage firm. No one in the firm wanted to buy Maury's stock, and he couldn't legally sell it in the open market. (This was two years before Bill Donaldson, Dan Lufkin, and Richard Jenrette forced the NYSE to make that possible.) So Maury cashed in.

Then the sole remaining partner related to the super-rich Marshal Field family—Marshall Field IV—died. His will directed that his money be withdrawn and put into the Field Foundation.

And Glore Forgan lost money in January and February 1969 as the volume of trading plummetted.

Bob Bishop told Archie to add $6 million to Glore Forgan Staats' capital.

The wealthy partners, such as Russ Forgan, were reluctant to contribute significant sums. What is more, they were all elderly. They would retire soon, withdrawing their money; if they contributed capital, the capital problem would only be postponed.

An obvious solution was to assess each partner a sum proportionate to his position. And that's what Glore Forgan Staats' board of directors voted to do.

The head of the Western division was assessed $350,000, for example. Jim Lynch, Norm Swanton, and similarly ranked officers were assessed $100,000 each.

For most of the partners, the assessment posed no problem. They were independently wealthy or their families were.

If Jim Lynch were to continue as a partner of Glore Forgan Staats Inc., he would have to borrow $100,000. It was easy in the first months of 1969. The loan officers at Chemical Bank (which later merged with Chase) were eager to lend the money. The bankers at Chemical as well as men at most major banks were as optimistic about the future of the investment business as men in the investment business itself. Bankers made similar loans to Norm Swanton, other Glore Forgan partners, and partners of other firms, besides loaning money directly to firms.

For the money which Jim and Norm borrowed from Chemical and then lent to Glore Forgan Staats, Inc., Jim and Norm received subordinated notes. "Subordinated" means everybody else gets paid off first in a bankruptcy. Each also received stock in Glore Forgan Staats, Inc.—stock that would be worthless if Glore Forgan became bankrupt.

The $6 million took Glore Forgan off the list of firms Bob Bishop worried about—for a while.

The losses of the first two months of the year proved not to be aberrations. The Federal Reserve's tightening of the money supply curbed trading volumes and held stock prices down. Glore Forgan lost money month after month.

In October 1969, Jim, Norm, and everyone else in the investment business was given false hope when the NYSE trading volume surged upward to near its 1968 level and stock prices stopped falling. But the respite was only temporary. Volumes and prices fell the following month and continued low for the rest of the year.[3]

Glore Forgan lost money every month in 1969, as did many other firms.

Bob Bishop came close to restricting Glore Forgan's activities in 1969, but Glore Forgan's capital stayed within the NYSE's boundaries for two reasons: (1) Jim, Norm and the other partners had contributed capital early in the year, and (2) because Glore Forgan did not need to establish so big a reserve against fails as many other investment firms.

Jim and Norm, like the partners in most firms in 1970, became increasingly worried. The stock market slid downward with few halts—and the volume of trading continued at a level unprofitable for many firms—10–12 million shares a day.

Some Glore Forgan partners, anticipating that conditions would not get better soon, decided to leave the firm, taking their capital with them. Glore Forgan's New York regional salesmanager was typical although perhaps more astute than most.[4]

While flying on a business trip from New York to New Orleans via Altanta late in March 1970, he thought about the way Glore Forgan priced the shares of voting stockholders when those stockholders resigned: at their book value at the end of the quarter. If he resigned immediately, his shares would be priced at their value as of the end of 1969. If he waited until after March 31, 1970, to resign, his shares would be priced much lower—at their March 31, 1970, value. In Atlanta, before boarding the connecting flight, he went to a public telephone, dictated a resignation letter to his assistant, and asked her to sign the letter for him. She had often done so. As a consequence, he received several thousand dollars more for this shares than if he had waited until after he returned from New Orleans to resign.

Glore Forgan's executive vice president also resigned as did several other lower-ranked stockholders, further reducing Glore Forgan's capital.

"Rats deserting a sinking ship!" muttered the head of Glore Forgan's Midwest division, but the "rats" could have retorted that they had been betrayed by inept management and were acting like prudent businessmen. And that the Midwest chieftain didn't have their worries because he was independently wealthy.

Glore Forgan's capital was so reduced by the withdrawals of capital by departing stockholders, by declining stock prices, and by operating losses, that Bob Bishop did what he had previously threatened. He restricted the firm, forbidding it to advertise or open any new offices or underwrite offerings of securities.

For Glore Forgan, a continued restriction of underwritings could mean the end of the firm. Many of the most successful account executives would leave, going to another firm that enabled them to offer their customers opportunities to invest in new offerings. (Remember the revolt of the Hayden, Stone stockbrokers against merging with Walston, described in Chapter 3?)

But if raising capital had been bothersome back in 1969, it was impossible in the early months of 1970.

All the top officers of Glore Forgan recognized that only one alternative remained: Glore Forgan must merge with another firm—one that could provide it with financial support.

All this occurred before the Exchange governors allowed member firms to sell shares in their firms to the general public. These events do more than show in detail how very necessary permanent capital can be to the survival of an investment firm. They show how capitalism in general could not have flourished as it has without the separation of the function of investors from the functions of administering a business. Every now and then a sizable corporation owned only by members of a family has flourished, but these are exceptions. The machinery needed for the Industrial Revolution could not have been brought without the creation of the investor-owned corporation.

Furthermore, an investor-owned business operated by hired, professional managers is more likely to be better managed. Can you imagine those Elizabethan capitalists who got together and financed the voyage of a ship to the East Indies deciding that the most wealthy of them would be captain? Of course, there are exceptions. The Ford Motor Company, for example, was long owned by the Ford family and successfully managed by Henry Ford and then Henry Ford II. But isn't a CEO hired for his competence more likely to make key decisions correctly than a CEO who gained this power because he or she has the most money? Furthermore, an employee-CEO can be more easily fired if he or she proves unequal to the challenges faced by the business.

5

Negotiating a Merger[1]

To tide Glore Forgan over, Russ Forgan personally lent the firm half a million dollars. This satisfied Bob Bishop, and he lifted the restrictions. But it was understood by Archie Albright, Jim Lynch, and the other partners that this was only a short-term loan, made principally so Glore Forgan could manage two upcoming underwritings.

Russ and other top partners felt out their friends to see which firms would be willing to merge with Glore Forgan. Shearson Hammill & Co., a large brokerage firm with 63 offices in the United States and abroad plus an excellent securities research department, showed a willingness to merge—indeed, proved to be an eager prospect.

An agreement was reached but not signed.

To celebrate the merger, Russ invited Robert C. Van Tuyl, Shearson's chairman, to lunch with him at the ultra-exclusive Recess Club. Russ brought Jim Lynch and another Glore Forgan officer with him. Van Tuyl brought two of his top officers.

Minutes after they sat down, a waiter, unbidden, placed a martini in front of Russ. Unless Russ had an engagement elsewhere, Russ lunched at the Recess Club every day. The waiters knew him well. The martini was specially made to Russ's instructions.

As soon as the waiter brought Bob Van Tuyl and the others drinks, Van Tuyl raised his glass in a toast, saying, here's to Shearson Glore Forgan.

A startled look came over Russ's face

In a courteous, yet firm voice, Russ said that the firm's name should be *Glore Forgan* Shearson.

Van Tuyl put his glass down, unsipped.

The Shearson–Glore Forgan merger never took place despite the advantages to each firm.

Van Tuyl was motivated by pride, Russ mostly by financial acumen.

What's in a name? Plenty! If the new firm were called Shearson Glore Forgan, its profits would be less than if it were called Glore Forgan Shearson. Why? Because of a reciprocal arrangement between a group of prestigious investment firms, called "majors," short for "major underwriters," that has been assailed as collusion.

Consider a typical underwriting of, say, bonds by a long-established corporation with a good reputation:

The corporation selects an investment firm, say, Morgan Stanley, to underwrite the new issue.

Morgan Stanley's syndicate manager invites other investment firms, say 50, to join the syndicate which will underwrite the bonds, sharing the risks and the profits.

The syndicate manager plays favorites. Each syndicate manager would usually like to get as many bonds as he can for his firm to underwrite because the perceived profits outweigh the perceived risks, but the Morgan Stanley syndicate manager allots two to three times as many bonds to about 20 favored firms than to the remaining 30.

When any of these 20 favored firms—the majors—itself originates an underwriting, its syndicate manager also favors the same 20 or so firms and discriminates against the rest.

Sound "anti-trust"? It has been tested in the courts and found to be legal. The majors earn their privileges by themselves originating a good number of high quality deals.

Glore Forgan was a major, but Shearson Hammill was not. Forgan knew that if the Shearson name came first, the other major underwriters would consider the firm dominated by the Shearson people and so not treat it as a major underwriter.

And so, because of Bob Van Tuyl's pride, the Shearson merger was off, and the Glore Forgan officers resumed their search for a suitable merger partner.

The practice of majors favoring majors continues today, and some of the majors of 1970 are still majors as of 1999: Allen & Co.; Goldman Sachs; Lazard Freres; Lehman Brothers; Merrill Lynch; and Morgan Stanley. Others, such as Dillon Read and Smith Barney have merged with other firms, but their valuable names continue as part of the combined names.

Russ's talks with Clark, Dodge & Co. a modest, well-capitalized firm that specialized in institutional accounts, foundered on the same question the proposed merger with Shearson did: whose name would come first?

The giant brokerage firm of Francis I. duPont & Co. seemed a logical merger partner not only to Russ and other officers of Glore Forgan but to Bob Bishop, Lee Arning and other officials of The New York Stock Exchange. DuPont was the third largest brokerage firm with 325,000 customers and over 100 offices in the United States and abroad. It was even larger than Shearson, and, like Shearson, not a major underwriter, so each side would have something to offer the other.

Francis I. duPont appeared to be not just financially sound, but "strong, vigorous and viable"[2] in the words of Wallace C. Latour, the firm's senior managing partner, when he appeared days earlier before the Senate subcommittee considering the enactment of SIPC. According to his written statement, "Our capital funds stand at over $60 million, more than enough to meet our needs and to protect our customers. Our capital ratio, a key indicator constantly scrutinized by The New York Stock Exchange, is currently below 1:15, which is well below the Exchange requirement of 1:20."

He also said that no problem regarding the processing of orders "exists in any serious way."

Later developments would indicate that his statements were not accurate. (He may have been misinformed by a fellow partner.) But the partners of Glore Forgan had no reason not to believe him. And if they had, they would have said to themselves, as one recalled their thinking: "Look at all that duPont money. The duPont family is one of the wealthiest families in the world. It's unthinkable that they'd let a firm carrying their name fail."[3]

Russ prodded Archie Albright to talk to "Wally" Latour. Russ knew Edmond duPont, the top, controlling partner at Francis I. duPont and a grandson of the founder, from their days at Princeton together. They were about the same age. But Russ, probably because he was too proud, didn't want to approach Edmond duPont directly.

Wally did not have the CEO title, but most people in the firm reported to him directly or indirectly. Only the heads of operations, finance, and partnership relations by-passed him, reporting directly to Edmond duPont.

Self-confident Wally, 46, had been sucked upward to a dominating position at duPont just a few months earlier by a sudden vacuum at the top. He had left Merrill Lynch in 1962 to become duPont's syndicate manager and one of several partners. (Unlike Glore Forgan Staats, Inc., Francis I. duPont & Co. was a legal partnership.) After a while, Wally was put in charge of the underwriting group, supervising not only the syndicate manager but the distribution of underwritten securities to account executives within the firm.

An old prep school buddy—a very close buddy—of Edmond duPont's had been chief operating officer. When they both were accepted at Princeton, duPont and his buddy bought identical sport cars and drove them to the college. Told that they couldn't keep the cars, they scornfully drove away and spent the year enjoying themselves in Europe.

But by the late sixties, duPont's buddy drank so much during the working day that Francis I. duPont may have been the worst-managed large firm on Wall Street. Its capital fell so low in 1968—a year of prosperity for most firms but also a year of mounting fails—that in October Bishop had restricted the firm, forbidding it to advertise, forbidding it to add additional account executives, forbidding it to open new offices.

Edmond duPont had bolstered the firm's capital by obtaining contributions from his relatives, and Bob Bishop had removed the restrictions in January 1969. But for many months duPont led all other investment firms in the number of complaints from customers. In March 1970, the NYSE fined the firm $110,000 for failure to promptly answer customers' complaints.

This last was too much for the partner in charge of legal affairs, Edwin B. Peterson. Short, rotund, in his fifties, Peterson had been brought up in Ridgewood, a lower-class, mostly German section of Queens. It was a short, fast subway ride to the corner of Wall Street and Broad Street, so, like many of the young men in his neighborhood, he went to work for The New York Stock Exchange right out of high school. Unlike most of his fellow workers, however, he attended Pace University at night, and worked his way up the NYSE hierarchy. He became so knowledgeable about securities that, even though he had no law degree, few lawyers knew as much as he. Francis I. duPont hired him. At duPont he proved his worth several times, on one occasion cleaning up a two-million-dollar commodities mess.

Ed Peterson pointed out to Edmond duPont the damage the drunken CEO was doing to the firm, convincing Mr. duPont to dismiss his old buddy. (No one in the investment business except his old buddy called Edmond duPont by his first name, much less "Ed" or "Eddie".) As Mr. duPont looked around for a replacement, he found he did not have a wide range of candidates to choose from. Most ostensible candidates for the job were highly placed not so much for their capabilities as for their relationships with duPonts through blood or marriage.

Ed Peterson was an exception, but he did not have people-managing skills.

Milton A. Speicher, another non-relative right under Edmond duPont, wouldn't make a suitable CEO either. He was in charge of accounting, relationships with the duPont partners and lenders, as well as other financial matters. Milt, like Ed Peterson, had achieved his position by merit and by working hard and often late into the night. He was a long-time duPont employee, and nobody outside the duPont family—indeed, few inside—knew the duPont family finances so well. Heavy, short, wispy-haired, he affected a cultured accent, thus conforming to the class discrimination prevalent at the time.

But Milt didn't possess people-managing skills either. He was especially close-mouthed, never answering an unspoken question. And Milt was in his late sixties.

What is more, neither Ed Peterson nor Milt Speicher had the urge to direct a large organization, giving people orders, instead of consulting with them. Ed and Milt had staff, not command, personalities.

Wally Latour, in contrast, had a take-charge personality and knew how to manipulate people. He was also an attractive choice for Edmond duPont because Wally came from a wealthy family and had upper-class manners, attitudes, and speech. He was the only possible successor.

Wally, like Archie Albright at Glore Forgan, was intelligent (a Phi Beta Kappa graduate of Princeton), good-looking (though his red hair was thinning), and could be charming whenever he wanted to be—which was most of the time.

Wally was well-liked by those who knew him socially. He had been elected president of the Westchester County Tennis League when he was much younger. He was one of the best players at the prestigious Bronxville Field Club.

He and his wife were termed "a lovely couple," by an interviewee who knew them both well.

After talking to Wally, Archie reported back to Russ and the other top officers. Wally acknowledged that duPont was in trouble, Archie said, but Wally predicted that marrying Glore Forgan's major underwriter status with duPont's giant distribution system would result in a successful firm.

Russ Forgan pushed the possible merger in talking to the other partners saying that the people at Francis I. duPont were the type of people Glore Forgan should talk to.

So Russ met with Edmond duPont, surprising him by acting as if he would be doing Mr. duPont a favor, stressing how much Francis I. duPont would benefit from Glore Forgan's major underwriter status.

Perhaps Russ's attitude annoyed Edmond duPont. Negotiations stalled. Glore Forgan officers talked with other firms, including Laidlaw & Co. and A. G. Becker, but negotiations petered out for lack of enthusiasm on both sides.

Lee Arning—whose usual charm had helped cause Bob Haack to raise him to a near-top position at the Exchange—became exasperated. As a schoolboy, Lee had seen from the inside the numerous bank failures of the 1930s. His father had been a banker and had been appointed by the Secretary of Treasury as a conservator—an executive who took over failing banks and tried to save them.[4]

Lee knew the customers of Glore Forgan had no concept of the risks they were taking—no concept of the risk because they had been informed, correctly, that investment firms had better solvency records than banks.

Yet the risks that Glore Forgan customers unknowingly ran were considerable. If the brokerage firm became bankrupt, its customers could lose all or part of their "free credit balances"—that is, the money they had left on deposit with the firms. Customers might also lose all or some of the stocks and/or bonds they had left for "safekeeping" with the brokerage firm.

Lee told Archie Albright near the end of May 1970, "You must get more capital. And you must get it fast."

Lee also pressed Edmond duPont to merge, but both sides continued to procrastinate.

Lee became uncharacteristically dictatorial. He told Archie Albright, "You will merge with Francis I. duPont or I will suspend your firm!"

He spoke similarly to Edmond duPont.

So the top officers of both firms agreed to get together again sometime when it was convenient for all of them.

The next day Lee phoned Archie and exploded when he heard how casually his order had been treated.

"You will meet before the end of the month!" he shouted, which was only a couple of days away.[5]

So the top partners of the two firms arranged to meet on Saturday, May 30, 1970—the only day when they could get together. Jim Lynch was included. He was the firm's secretary and general counsel and had recently been elected administrative vice president with overall responsibility for compliance, internal audit, personnel, administrative services and advertising.

That morning, Jim drove from his home in New Jersey to the upper east side of New York City, picked up Archie, and continued up to Wally's imposing home in Bronxville, New York to discuss the merger. They arrived about the same time as Russ.

Jim, Archie, and Russ were all wearing business suits and ties, but both Edmond duPont and Wally Latour were wearing slacks and sports shirts, Jim noted as he walked into the house. Mr. DuPont, in his mid-sixties, his fine features tanned, acted as if he were the host, even though it was Wally's home. In a cultivated, prep school accent, Mr. duPont greeted Russ warmly as an equal, but was curt and distainful when he greeted Archie and Jim.

Mr. duPont was usually shorter than the man he talked to, and so, perhaps, he was making sure by his manner that he would be emotionally looked up to. Or perhaps he had discovered at an early age that snobbery resulted in his being treated by others the way he wanted to be treated.

Or perhaps he considered himself superior just because his family was super-rich—not an illogical conclusion since he had belonged since birth to the class with the most power.

Most of the time Edmond duPont did not behave like an active, involved manager. That was his chum's and then Wally Latour's job. Mr. duPont usually took the entire summer off.

One must sympathize with Wally's problems in dealing with Mr. duPont who had a short attention span. He didn't like to have matters explained to him in detail. Making matters even more difficult for those who worked for him, he didn't like to hear bad news. Managing him required a skill that few executives have.

Wally Latour had it.

Often men like Mr. duPont are treated with extra respect while at the same time are secretly despised by those upon whom they depend for information and the management of their affairs. That Wally Latour secretly despised Edmond duPont seems likely inasmuch as Wally voiced his disdain of Edmond duPont from time to time to his confidants.

When Jim was introduced to Edmond duPont, Jim was so intimidated by Mr. duPont's manner that then and ever afterward, he, like everyone else, addressed Edmond duPont as "Mr. duPont," even though Mr. duPont immediately called Lynch "Jim."

Wally, slim and athletic, was confident and charming, although he indicated surprise that Jim was there, muttering that he didn't know any lawyers were going to attend.

Soon two more Francis I. duPont partners arrived, Ed Peterson and Milt Speicher. Both wore business suits and ties. Lynch knew and admired them both. He had worked with them during his days at the Association of Stock Exchange Firms.

As Jim looked around, he noted that everyone seemed happy. Stock prices had been dropping more or less steadily for 18 months, but they had gone up and up and up every day for the three days prior to the meeting, probably in anticipation of lower taxes the following year.

In addition, fails for all NYSE member firms had been steadily dropping—had been less than one billion dollars in April—enabling two actions to be taken that would increase revenues.[6]

The governors of the Exchange had ordered that the normal closing hour of 3:30 be resumed effective May 1, which could increase the volume of trading and hence brokerage commissions.[7]

The Federal Reserve had reduced initial margin requirements to 65 percent effective May 6.[8] Ever since 1968, speculators had been required to ante up 80 percent of the cost of any stock they wanted to buy. The reduction in initial margin requirements increased the interest brokers received. Speculators could borrow 35 percent of the cost of their investments instead of just 20 percent. The reduction in initial margin requirements also was bullish. Speculators could buy more stocks with the same amount of money, thus increasing the demand for stocks.

Everyone at the meeting was jovial except for Jim Lynch who, typically, concealed his feelings. Already annoyed at being forced to spend Saturday away from his wife and two young children, he became impatient. Instead of getting right down to business, Edmond duPont and Russ Forgan reminisced about their days at Princeton. Mr. duPont told Russ, to appreciative laughter, the story of the two identical sport cars.

Wally and Archie, as equals, talked to each other, mostly discussing tennis. The others talked about golf.

Jim had no interest in sports and despised conspicuous consumption.

After more than half an hour of chit-chat, the group got around to discussing the merger in a sunny breakfast room. The two older men, Russ and Mr. duPont, sat off to one side in comfortable chairs; the other five sat at a rectangular, glass-topped table. As if to indicate that this was not an adversarial meeting, Wally and Archie sat next to each other on the same side of the table. The other three sat opposite.

Jim soon realized that all assumed that the firms would merge, the only question was how. Lee Arning's shotgun was figuratively pointed at them all.

Jim also saw that Mr. duPont and Wally were the most powerful people there, already signaled by their dressing casually in a business situation.

Wally, with his bright intellect and charm, dominated the meeting, with Archie doing most of the talking for the Glore Forgan side. Jim, Milt, and Ed Peterson were consulted from time to time. They usually spoke up on their own initiative only when they thought it imperative. Early on, when Jim tried to volunteer a statement, Archie's body language told Jim he should speak only when spoken to.

When Wally suggested that "duPont" precede "Glore Forgan" in the new firm's name, Russ Forgan did not object. The enormous wealth of the duPont family and the success of the other business with the family's name made the duPont name even more prestigious then than now. E. I. duPont de Nemours was the largest chemical company in the world and at that time also owned a controlling interest in the largest automobile manufacturer in the world, General Motors. The other majors would welcome to their classifications a firm that combined duPont's wealth and prestige with Glore Forgan's experience and skills.

Archie, Russ, and Jim had assumed the new, merged firm would be a corporation (like Glore Forgan Staats, Inc.) not a partnership (like Francis I. duPont & Co.) In the event of bankruptcy, the owners of a corporation lose only the money they have invested. The owners of a partnership, in contrast, face unlimited risk. If a partnership becomes bankrupt, all the general partners are liable for the firm's debts without any limit. They can lose their other investments, their savings, their homes, their furniture, even their automobiles. They can be plunged into deep debt as well.

Milt Speicher, however, confided a peculiar reason for not incorporating the combined firm.

Many duPont partners had little capital of their own, Milt explained. They had borrowed the money they had invested in the firm, often from members of the duPont family. The duPont partnership, as was the custom at most NYSE firms at the time, paid interest to each partner on the money he had invested, about 8 percent. The share of the profits a partner received was in addition to that interest.

Some partners simply passed along the 8 percent interest to those whose capital they had borrowed (called "pledgors"). Others partners made a little profit, giving the pledgors, say, 7 percent, and keeping 1 percent.

These "pledge" accounts posed a problem, Milt explained. They couldn't be paid off. Francis I. duPont didn't have enough capital.

Furthermore, few pledgors were likely to consent to accepting stock in a new corporation in exchange for their pledges. Why should they accept what would seem to them to be the uncertainty of owning common stock? Being owed the money would seem safer.

In addition, many of the pledgors were financially unsophisticated and had no understanding that their money was at risk. It was better to let sleeping dogs lie.

Close-mouthed Milt may not have told the group all he knew—that a change to the corporate form would necessitate such a thorough investigation that duPont's financial condition would be revealed as far, far worse than its balance sheet showed. Even though its balance sheet had been approved by an outside accounting firm.

Jim remembers his fears of the partnership form being quieted by his being told that duPont's brokerage business was profitable—which it may have been. Jim was told that the millions of dollars duPont had lost in 1969 resulted in large part from two weeks of disastrous trading in government bonds, a one-time fluke.

So Archie, Russ and Jim assented to the partnership form—something Jim would later rue—and to the partnership being called F. I. duPont, Glore Forgan & Co.

As the negotiations droned on into the middle of the afternoon, Jim became increasingly irritated. He was hungry. Wally served only coffee, and Jim's breakfast had been light.

Both sides eventually agreed that Edmond duPont, Wally Latour, Ed Peterson, and Milt Speicher would continue in their powerful positions. Russ was content to be named honorary chairman of the board of directing partners. In effect, he retired. He was to become a limited partner—that is, he agreed to leave some capital in the firm and get interest on that money, but he would not assume the risks of a general partner nor would he share in any of the profits.

Archie got two titles: vice chairman of the board and chairman of the executive committee. And he was to be in charge of investment banking.

Charley Hodge, vice chairman of Glore Forgan Staats, was to be demoted to being just another member of the executive committee.

Jim was to become secretary of the executive committee. Whether he was to be a voting member or not was not discussed. Jim was also given immediate responsibilities. He was put in charge of "slotting"—that is, suggesting who should fill what position in the new firm. Jim was also named to the advance team which would work out the details of the merger.

Wally demanded that the heads of Glore Forgan's three regions outside the East be removed from the executive committee unless they moved to New York—something Archie, Jim and Russ knew none of them would do. Harry Colmery and the Midwest regional head had been asked to become CEO of Glore Forgan when Maury left the firm, but both had refused because they didn't want to live in New York.

Wally also demanded that the regional heads be removed from their regional positions. Three of the most powerful men in Glore Forgan— two who had been actively considered for the presidency—were to be reduced to office managers! They were, however, expected to be active in investment banking.

Wally further demanded that all Glore Forgan office managers report directly to him—just as the more than 100 duPont managers already did. No management consultant would have submitted an organization chart with so many people reporting to one person. Seven is the rule of thumb maximum.

Wally additionally insisted that their Sam Gay, not Glore Forgan's Norm Swanton, be put in charge of the back office and be put on the executive committee—despite Norm's accomplishments and smooth-running operation.

Archie, Russ and Jim agreed not only to all this but to Glore Forgan's records being fed into duPont's computer system. It would be duPont's back office that would process orders for the combined firm.

Edmond duPont soothed everyone's capital concerns by lending Glore Forgan several hundred thousand dollars to tide Glore Forgan over until the merger was consummated.

The meeting ended with the general feeling that the two firms would merge but that much remained to be decided.

Wally Latour had got what he wanted—power and elevation of the firm he managed to major underwriting status—something that as a former syndicate manager he especially prized.

Edmond duPont had got what he wanted—increased prestige for the firm bearing his family's name. And Russ, Archie and Jim thought they had got relief from their money worries and would soon be freed from the nagging of Lee Arning and Bob Bishop.

The allotment of responsibilities made at the merger meeting at Wally's home indicates the value to an executive of being at such a meeting. The participants tend to parcel out the responsibilities and rewards among themselves, besides organizing the firm the way they want. If, for example, Harry Colmery had been at the meeting, it would have been harder for Wally to downgrade him. Harry might have persuaded the others to his point of view or might even have made the merger impossible.

Many aspects of the negotiations indicate the value of having a third party present who is experienced in mergers and who obviously has no ties to either side. A third party might have been able to shame the CEO of Shearson, Hammill or of Clark, Dodge into agreeing to putting Glore Forgan's name first. He (or she) could have argued the benefits of putting profits before pride with an objectivity recognized by both parties. The same arguments coming from Russ Forgan could appear to the CEO of the other firm as mainly egotistical rationalizations.

A third party would probably have advised against—or at least strongly demurred at—the absurdity of more than 100 office managers reporting to one man.

A third party would probably have advised against humiliating Harry Colmery and the Midwest regional chieftain by reducing these valuable executives to mere office managers.

A third party would probably have looked at the conditions of the back offices of both firms and have recommended that the proven capable manager, Norm Swanton, be made head of the back office of the combined firms.

A third party might have strongly advised against the partnership form for the combined firm, with all the dangers that entailed—as will be seen in a subsequent chapter.

And a third party would probably have prevented the merger from occurring at all if he or she had been present at the meeting to be described in the next chapter.

Today an objective third party is more likely to be present because the firms are more likely to be publicly owned. Consequently, the principals are more likely to regard themselves, not as owners free to indulge their egos, but as professional managers. Furthermore, what they negotiate will be carefully scrutinized by stockholders and the media. Having third, objective party present enhances the chances of any merger being objectively advantageous to the stockholders of both firms.

The intense professionalism of executives of present-day brokerage firms is indicated by the change in drinking at lunchtime. In the sixties and early 1970s, drinking at lunch, as Russ Forgan did, was common, and lunch was often a leisurely pleasure at an exclusive, members-only club. Today executives drink at lunch only on special occasions. One firm has a rule: If you drink at lunch, take the afternoon off. Lunches are often a quick bite at the desk. And the members-only clubs, one by one, have nearly vanished. And a way of doing business is gone forever.

6

Obstacles to the Merger

As Jim drove back to New York with Archie from the merger meeting at Wally's home, Jim voiced some reservations about what had been agreed to, but Jim had no answer when Archie asked him to suggest an alternative.

On Monday, a meeting of the Glore Forgan executive committee was convened. Some were present in person, some tied in by phone.

When Archie described the proposed terms of the merger, all who had not been at Wally's home were indignant. Unalterably opposed. Harry Colmery, the West Coast regional manager, said he was going to have great difficulty preventing the top brokers in his offices from leaving. They looked down on Francis I. duPont as a "wire house." This was a derogatory term meaning that all it did was connect passive brokers in distant offices to The New York Stock Exchange. Glore Forgan Staats in contrast was a tightly knit organization whose brokers actively sold stocks the firm underwrote or acquired in large blocks. (Remember how the intended merger of Hayden, Stone with Walston, described in Chapter 3, was derailed by the Hayden, Stone brokers?)

In addition, Harry felt his office managers were not going to like reporting directly to Wally.

Archie parried thrusts against the merger with wordiness that could be reduced to what he had earlier said to Jim: Suggest an alternative.

The meeting broke up without a decision.[1]

Over at Francis I. duPont, Edmond duPont and Wally Latour easily persuaded the other top duPont partners that the merger would be advantageous. The partners salivated over the possibility of duPont becoming a major underwriter.

The next day, Norm Swanton appeared before a rump meeting of Glore Forgan's board of directors.[2] Around the polished table in the firm's new, elaborate board room at 95 Wall Street sat Russ, Archie, Jim and about a dozen other Glore Forgan directors with offices in New York. The regional managers were not present.

Norm had not been told that the merger with duPont was a near certainty. Nor had he been told that the proposed merger with Shearson had no possibility of being consummated.

Norm had investigated Francis I. duPont & Co.—looked behind duPont's balance sheet to see if it reflected reality—and was appalled at what he had discovered.

Norm demonstrated to the board—he thought "without any doubt"— that the proposed duPont–Glore Forgan merger would be a disaster. If duPont's back office were the surviving operation, Glore Forgan's records would need to be re-recorded *by hand*, a tremendously time-consuming task. And duPont's back office was in even worse condition than Glore Forgan's had been before Norm's reorganization. The orderly edifice of records Norm had painstakingly erected would be reduced to rubble.

Norm tried to explain this—asked that at least the two back offices be run independently until a new, third system could be set up. Jim supported him, but Archie brushed this idea aside. If we merge with duPont, said Archie, "the tail can't wag the dog."

The discussion continued for hours.

"If we liquidate," Norm warned, "all we can lose is our capital. DuPont is hopeless."[3]

About 9:30 P.M. a secretary entered and said Mr. Latour and Mr. duPont had arrived. Archie asked her to show them in. Edmond duPont entered first, now wearing an expensive, European-style suit, accompanied by Wally, wearing a comfortable, light-weight suit. Norm went over the figures again, but Edmond duPont's demeanor caused Norm to doubt that the wealthy scion grasped their significance. Mr. DuPont seemed impatient, nervously pressing the top of a ball point pen he held in his hand so that it audibly clicked.

The discussion soon degenerated into an animated confrontation between patrician Wally and immigrant Norm. Wally sneeringly challenged Norm's assertion that duPont was technically bankrupt. Norm hotly responded from across the polished table. Each got angrier and angrier. No one else could get a word in.

At one point, according to Norm, athletic Wally lunged so far over the table that it crossed Norm's mind that he was about to be struck.

Only the patriarchal presences of Russ Forgan and Edmond duPont prevented the meeting from degenerating further.

When Norm and Wally exhausted themselves, staring hatefully at each other, Edmond duPont rose majestically and said that he didn't know whether what Mr. Swanton said was true or not, but that he had just come over to tell the directors of Glore Forgan that he had just got off the phone with his family and they were sending up twenty million dollars in capital, if that was all right with the directors.

The Glore Forgan partners stared for a moment, then erupted into smiles, laughter, cheers, and self-congratulatory remarks. They thought it wonderful to have a potential partner who could write a check for millions of dollars.

Only Norman was despondent. He doubted the duPonts would put in enough money to save the firm. He estimated that Francis I. duPont's liabilities exceeded its assets by $50 million, if valid accounting methods were used.

Waves of rage and frustration alternately washed over Norm as he thought of the waste of his efforts and the enormous number of fails that would occur. He began to cry. With tears streaming down his face, he muttered obscenities to himself.

"I've got to get out of here," he shouted to the happy, uncomprehending partners. "I resign!" and he strode out of the room.

He went into his office and started to pack his belongings. Archie and Jim entered a few moments later.

Archie urged him to calm down and told him that he would be head of operations in the combined firm.

Jim was shocked, recalling that Archie had already agreed that Sam Gay would occupy that position. Norm, however, obviated the need for Jim to speak up.

Norm, the idealist, looked at Archie in astonishment. Norm slowly realized that Archie thought he had been deviously putting on an act, that he was really concerned only about his personal future, not that of the firm.

Norm wordlessly turned his back on Archie, packed his personal belongings and left—left not only Glore Forgan but the country, returning to where he was born—Ireland—to get far, far away from the firm he had labored so hard to save.

But before he left, he decided he would write a memo—"It was a little testy," recalls Norm, "just so everybody would know that there's a forty or fifty million dollar hole in duPont. I sent it to all of the officers. Archie sent somebody around to collect every copy of this memo so it didn't get out."[4]

Norm's self-exile to Ireland was cut short by a telegram from Bob Bishop asking him to come back right away. Bob Bishop wanted Norm to monitor the impending merger and the performance of other member firms as a consultant to the Exchange.

Norm complied.

Norm, as he came to realize later, had lost his innocence and reached the kind of position for which he was temperamentally suited. He would become very successful as a consultant to investment firms and later head his own venture capital company.

Wally had wanted to keep the intended merger secret but was thwarted by Archie's inexperience. Unfamiliar with the gossipy nature of Wall Street people, Archie foolishly sent an internal memorandum on the proposed merger to all Glore Forgan's account executives. On Tuesday, June 2, a *Wall Street Journal* reporter called Wally, who was forced to confirm that duPont and Glore Forgan planned to merge on July 1, 1970.

The same week the reporter called Wally, Bob Bishop called Archie, asking him when the papers describing the agreement were going to be sent to the Exchange.

Archie thoughtlessly replied that he hadn't thought about it.

Bob was furious. From what Archie had said previously, Bob thought that agreement had been reached, but the truth was that considerable dissension still existed among members of Glore Forgan's executive committee.

Bob said he wanted to see the papers and the pro forma capital structure of the put-together firms right away.

Archie airily replied that the drafting of the papers hadn't even begun—that he and the others concerned still had a lot of decisions to make.

Bob replied so cuttingly that Archie hurriedly called Jim in and told him to get to work coordinating the drafting of the agreement.

The legal and tax problems were enormous. That month, Jim left for work at 6:00 A.M and returned home at 10:00 or 11:00 at night. Weekends included.

In developing the merger agreement, Jim worked closely with William J. Casey, Glore Forgan's house counsel. Bill Casey and Russ Forgan were buddies; they had worked closely together in France during World War II when they were in the OSS (Office of Strategic Services),[5] the precusor to the CIA (Central Intelligence Agency). Casey would become Director of Central Intelligence during Ronald Reagan's Presidency.

The merger agreement stated that the merged firm would be a partnership called F. I. duPont, Glore Forgan but that a subsidiary corporation, called duPont Glore Forgan, Inc. would handle investment banking and retain certain assets and liabilities of Glore Forgan Staats, Inc.

Jim and other Glore Forgan Staats, Inc. officers would become partners in F. I. duPont, Glore Forgan without contributing any capital to the partnership.

When some junior Francis I. duPont partners heard this, they were incensed, especially those who had borrowed money in order to become partners. Why should ex-duPont partners share any of the anticipated huge profits from the brokerage side of the business with ex–Glore Forgan executives who would not be putting any money into the partnership?

On the other side, some of the Glore Forgan Staats, Inc. partners opposed the merger for a different reason. duPont Glore Forgan, Inc. had been setup primarily at the urging of Wally Latour to protect duPont partners from the effects of a pending lawsuit against Glore Forgan Staats, Inc. At issue was Glore Forgan's proper underwriting of securities issued by Revenue Properties Inc.

"Wally and the others were extremely fearful," Jim Lynch recalls, "that if they took everything that was in Glore Forgan Staats, Inc. into the partnership and we lost the Revenue Properties' case, they might be wiped out."

By setting up duPont Glore Forgan, Inc. only investors in that specific firm would lose money. Among these investors were the holders of the subordinated notes in Glore Forgan Staats, Inc.

"Holy shit!" cried one holder of subordinated notes, "You're taking all the business away from Glore Forgan Staats and just leaving the subordinated notes there all by themselves!"[6]

Jim quieted the holders of the subordinated notes somewhat by pointing out that they were protected against another eventuality: If F. I. duPont, Glore Forgan collapsed and the Revenue Properties case was successfully defended, the subordinated note holders would be protected. They would have first claim on the assets of duPont Glore Forgan, Inc.

Eventually the voting stockholders of Glore Forgan Staats who had been absent from the merger meeting at Wally's home did not so much agree to the merger as agree not to oppose it. Harry Colmery's consent was the most tentative. He worried about how well the back office of the merged firm would function. He tried to raise capital from a West Coast source so as to maintain Glore Forgan's independence, but without success.

All the squabbling and any indications that the merger might not be a tremendous success were kept from the general public, from investigative reporters, from members of Congress (especially Senator Muskie and Congressman Moss), and indeed from other people in the investment business.

Prospects seemed so rosy that a medium-sized, well-heeled firm, Hirsch & Co., asked to join the merger.

Like so many other firms, Hirsch had been losing money month after month. The reasons were typical: The back office needed updating, but the partnership structure and the partners' ultra-gentlemanly treatment of each other, which had been admirable and no handicap for nearly two hundred years previous, made reform impossible.

"There was so much wrong [with the back office]," recalls one Hirsch partner,[7] "that I wouldn't know how to explain it. We needed somebody to come into the firm of unquestioned ability. I had a couple of people in mind, one was a high officer of Manufacturers Hanover Bank—a friend of mine. I never even got a chance to talk to him. I couldn't talk to him without the knowledge and consent of the other partners, but that was not forthcoming."

Why not? Because the partner presently responsible for supervising the back office would be offended!

Even an invitation to merge from Bache & Co., which had a well-managed back office, had been turned down because one of the three senior partners objected. The objecting partner wouldn't even give his partners his reason, yet the two senior partners would not over-ride him.

Like so many partners in brokerage firms at the time, the senior partners had no sense that managing a business required certain distinct talents.[8]

For example: As the losses mounted, the junior partners of Hirsch grew increasingly worried and dismayed at the way the senior partners were managing the firm. Eventually, they nominated one of their number, Gilbert Bach, to communicate their concern to the senior partner entrusted with the day-to-day management of the firm.

Gil walked into the managing partner's office and after a few preliminary remarks, politely but firmly demanded that something be done.

The managing partner responded by simply picking up a portfolio from his desk and handing it to Gil, suggesting that Gil tell him what to do.

Gil was taken aback. He was a star at institutional sales and syndicating, but he knew little about the rest of the firm. And he was realistic enough to know that he didn't have the required expertise or experience. But what other alternative was there?

"I'll take a shot at it," he said.[9]

Gil and the other junior partners looked at the detailed figures and discovered that Hirsch & Co. was in even worse condition than they had thought.

Gil revived the possibility of the Bache merger, but the hold-out partner continued to object to Bache—but not to merging with some other firm.

Suddenly, without warning, the managing partner told Gil and the other junior partners that Hirsch was going to merge with Francis I. duPont and Glore Forgan.[10]

One of the senior partners had heard about the proposed Glore Forgan–Francis I. duPont merger, and thinking that the merged firm would be powerful and profitable, asked Lee Arning if Hirsch could be included.[11]

The offer was gleefully encouraged by Lee Arning and accepted by the managements of Francis I. duPont and Glore Forgan Staats.

Some of the Hirsch partners held a grudge against Glore Forgan and so were not enthusiastic about the proposed merger. Here's why: In 1967, Jim Lynch, as general counsel for Glore Forgan had negotiated a consent agreement with Stanley Sporkin, chief prosecutor of the Securities and Exchange Commission, that had resulted in reducing Hirsch & Co.'s income. By the consent degree, Glore Forgan agreed to stop accepting payments from Investors Overseas Services for certain services. (More about this in a later chapter.) Stanley then applied the consent decree to all brokerage firms dealing with Investors Overseas Services, of which Hirsch & Co. was one.

But when the Hirsch partners who were annoyed at Glore Forgan considered the lack of a sensible alternative, they didn't seriously object.[12] (Remember that Archie Albright retorted similarly when Jim or any other partner raised objections to Glore Forgan merging with Francis I. duPont: Do we have an alternative?)

Gil Bach, however, felt he had to find an alternative. He thought the new firm would be managed only a little better than Hirsch had been. What is more, a limited Hirsch partner told Gil he thought that most of the duPonts didn't care much about the brokerage firm and couldn't be depended upon as rescuers. He based this conclusion on a personal friendship with a member of the duPont family. They went fishing together."

The limited partner decided to semi-retire. Gil arranged to join Loeb Rhoades & Co.

No partner, however, vetoed the proposed merger and so most of the partners of Hirsch & Co., along with their much-desired capital, agreed to join the soon-to-be-formed firm. A few, like Gil, joined other firms or retired.

But now Jim, who knew much that others didn't, began to have doubts about the wisdom of his becoming a partner in the new firm. Norm's presentation had disturbed Jim even though he thought Norm had been exaggerating. Jim had later heard horrific corroborating tales of duPont's back office from other sources. And the *Wall Street Journal* published a story on June 18 showing that Francis I. duPont's operating loss for the first quarter of the year was 23 percent of its revenues.

The unlimited liability that a general partner assumes, which he well understood as a lawyer, also bothered him. Any partner is responsible not only for the debts of the firm but for any debts or obligations incurred by any other partner in the course of business.

If he resigned now, he would get back the $100,000 he had lent Glore

Forgan Staats, Inc. and so be able to repay Chemical Bank that amount. He would still owe Chemical Bank the $30,000 he had previously borrowed to buy Glore Forgan Staats stock—now worthless. But that would be it, he thought. He wouldn't risk losing $100,000 and very much more if the merged firm collapsed.

He decided not to become a general partner of the contemplated new firm.

When Edmond duPont heard of Jim's decision, Mr. duPont asked Jim to come to his office the following morning at 8:00 A.M. Mr. duPont was now paying far closer attention to the management of the firm than he ever had before.

Mr. duPont knew Jim's judgment was highly regarded by his associates. If Jim refused to become a partner, several other key employees would refuse to become general partners and leave the firm. The merger would be imperiled.

Jim recalls Mr. duPont saying that Jim was going to be part of the management of this firm and that Jim couldn't be part of the management unless he were a general partner.

Jim along with Mr. duPont's son, Peter, and another relative would ultimately run the firm, Jim recalls Mr. duPont hinting.

When this didn't persuade Jim, Mr. duPont went further. Jim recalls Mr. duPont saying that he would personally guarantee Jim against any loss, but Jim must not tell anyone else that he had made this guarantee.

Mr. duPont's offer appeared to Jim to have no downside and plenty of upside potential. Besides, it was flattering. Jim accepted.

Jim did not feel he needed to get Mr. duPont's promise in writing. Mr. duPont was fond of saying his word was his bond. Moreover, people in the investment business, then and now, need to depend on each other's verbal promises. Often there is no time to put a contract in writing, even though millions of dollars may be involved. Anyone in the investment business who does not keep his word will not be in the investment business long.

Confident that Mr. duPont would keep his word, Jim agreed to stay on.

Sam Gay, duPont's back office manager, however, agreed to remain with the firm for several weeks after the merger only after Edmond duPont gave him a guarantee similar to Jim's in writing.[13]

Richard J. McDonald, in charge of duPont's over-the-counter department was, like Jim and Sam Gay, skeptical of the wisdom of becoming a general partner in the new firm.[14] Fails were even more of a problem for OTC stocks than for stocks listed on The New York Stock Exchange.

Thirty-six in 1970, sandy-haired with startling blue eyes, Richard had gained fame early in his career at duPont when an account executive; he had converted a spectacular percentage of prospects who responded to duPont's advertising into customers.

Richard was one of several up-and-coming duPont executives offered general partnerships to protect them in the triage that would necessarily occur after the merger. Unless they were partners, they might be edged out by voting stockholders of Glore Forgan with lesser ability.

Richard's skepticism was further weakened by the example of two high-powered executives who were leaving First Boston, one of the three most powerful major underwriters at the time, to become duPont partners.

But Richard had no money to invest. Like Jim, he could get money to put into the firm only by borrowing, but he didn't like the idea of going to a bank and asking for a loan.

"If you want me to be a partner," he told his boss, "the firm will have to lend me the money."[15]

Edmond duPont approved of the loan, and Richard agreed to become a partner.

Other executives, not so wary as Richard McDonald and Sam Gay, agreed to become general partners by putting in cash or borrowing from a bank.[16]

All seemed well.

Nobody—not even Jim Lynch—knew all that had gone on in attempting to merge Francis I. duPont with Glore Forgan and Hirsch. Each had the kind of incomplete knowledge exemplified by the blind men examining the elephant.

And, of course, reporters and the public knew even less.

This is true of many mergers today: Many difficulties are overcome— or are not overcome—that few people know about. And often some key facts are hidden from the participants.

Today audited reports of investment firms can usually be relied upon for accuracy, even though their assets and liabilities continually change in value. It is the audited reports of other kinds of businesses that so worried SEC Chairman Arthur Levitt in 1999 that he began to tighten the rules.

7

How and Why Ross Perot Saved The New York Stock Exchange from Possible Collapse

All seemed well—till Wally Latour got a call from Bob Bishop. Bob had reviewed the pro forma balance sheet of the combined firms and decided that F. I. duPont, Glore Forgan & Co. would not have sufficient capital to meet The New York Stock Exchange's standards. He told Wally he would not approve the merger unless the firm's capital was increased by several million dollars.

Bob was not overly concerned about issuing this order.

Edmund duPont had often said to Bob, Lee and others that in an emergency, he was sure his family could be counted on.[1] Bob didn't know that Edmond duPont had sustained this illusion by secretly borrowing millions of dollars on behalf of all the partners of Francis I. duPont from an insurance company—and that both wells were now dry.

Where would the new money come from?

Why should anyone who knew the facts be willing to risk millions of dollars by lending or investing in a combination of firms that, *prima facie*, had been so badly managed?

And even if the money could possibly be raised, could it be raised in time?

Because of his belief that the duPont family could—and would—contribute any capital that was needed by any company bearing the family name, Bob didn't know how close he was coming to causing the collapse of The New York Stock Exchange by his ukase. If the money were not found within days, he would be forced to take actions which would result in the liquidation—or possibly the bankruptcy—of Francis I. duPont & Co. That in turn would have caused hundreds of other firms, owed money and securities by Francis I. duPont to become bankrupt as well. And consequently The New York Stock Exchange might have collapsed.

This danger offered H. Ross Perot an opportunity. He wanted to get into the investment business to bolster the earnings of Electronic Data Systems (EDS).[2] Each year from 1964 to 1969, EDS had doubled its earnings from the year before. But Ross could see that EDS had virtually reached the limit of the pastureland on which it had fattened.

The repeated doubling of the earnings had been largely based on the establishment of Medicare in 1965. Blue Cross and Blue Shield organizations across the country had been flooded with complicated forms and they couldn't keep up. Bill collectors had hounded senior citizens for payment of bills for which senior citizens had not been reimbursed. Senior citizens, in great numbers, had bombarded Congress with complaints.

Blue Cross–Blue Shield of Texas, Inc. had been an exception. It had been a model of efficiency and responsivess. With Texas Blue Cross–Blue Shield as an example, Ross had been able to add one Blue Cross–Blue Shield organization after another to EDS' customer list.

But by 1969, not only had the number of Blue Cross–Blue Shield prospects dwindled, some were displacing EDS with other computer companies. Once EDS got a computer system running efficiently, customers tended to resent EDS's high fees. Social Security officials asked to see EDS's books, for example, because they felt EDS mark-ups were exhorbitant. EDS experts didn't seem to contribute much once EDS had set up a system that solved the customers' problems. The machines seemed to run themselves. Once an EDS contract ended, customers tended to look for a lower-cost competitor or to achieve even lower costs by operating the computers themselves. Furthermore, by 1969, EDS had lost several of its non-health customers.[3]

Ross had decided to apply the pattern that had worked so well in the health industry to other industries. He would gain the computer operating business of one company in an industry, make it a shining example of efficiency and profitability, and use it as an example to get additional accounts in the same industry.

Three industries were chosen: brokerage, insurance, and utilities. Ross and his close associates had set to work to study how they could gain entry into these industries.[4]

Ross had talked to Ken Langone, the investment banker who had taken EDS public. Ross had asked Ken who was the best person he and his associates could talk to so as to learn about the back office operations of brokerage firms. Ken suggested Lee Arning.

On Saturday night, November 9, 1969, just as Lee was dressing for dinner, Lee's telephone rang. It was Milledge A. Hart III, Ross's cousin and president of EDS. He asked Lee to come down to Dallas the next day, Sunday.

Lee listened intently to Mitch. Lee was excited by more than the prospect of EDS's expertise in computers reducing the enormous number of fails in the industry. He also envisioned Ross or EDS contributing sizable amounts of capital to the investment business. Fails had jumped from less than $1.5 billion in September to nearly $1.9 million in October.[5]

Ross and EDS seemed to Lee like the U.S. calvary coming over the hill, trumpet sounding. Concealing his eagerness, Lee agreed to come.

Ross, Mitch and their associates "picked my brains clean," Lee told the NYSE oral histories interviewer (described in the Preface). When Lee described the general operating picture to them, they were amazed that "every member firm was going its own way in terms of order processing, customer statement formats, clearing entries, machine programs, margin calculations, etcetera."

Ross and his associates could hardly believe that every one of the departmental functions was different from firm to firm. It was so absurdly inefficient.

"I also utilized the opportunity to fill them in on what I thought the opportunities were on Wall Street," Lee recalls. "I told them that while we had a lot of problems, and we had a lot of firms in less than the healthiest of financial condition, we were also going through one of the worst market intervals in recent history; that the securities marketplace was one that simply had to grow, and that there was a place for newcomers."

On the ride back to the airport late that evening with Mitch Hart, Lee agreed to arrange "a meeting for Ross Perot and our Crisis Committee to explore opportunities."

At that meeting at The New York Stock Exchange early in 1970, "Perot's first pitch was he wanted to handle the clearing operation of the New York Stock Exchange," Lee recalled in 1984. "His overall concept was unerringly accurate. There was a need in Wall Street for uniform procedures, uniform systems, and to move away from the independent structures that were in existence where there was no compatibility."

But entrusting such a fundamental process to a firm inexperienced in the securities business could result in a catastrophe. So Lee had tried to help Ross get the back office business of individual brokerage firms— without success.[6] It may be that no firm wanted to entrust its back office to anyone without experience or much knowledge of the investment business.

It was at the stage in Ross Perot's search for investment business that Francis I. duPont & Co. needed several million dollars so it could merge with Glore Forgan Staats, Inc..

The catalyst that turned these two needs into a mutual benefit was a Francis I. duPont partner named Rudolph A. Smutny. He had previously been president of a medium-sized firm, but had been forced out by his fellow partners because of his overly aggressive personality. That previous firm was Pressprich & Co., the investment firm that had underwritten the first offering of the stock of Electronic Data Systems Inc. Since switching firms, he had been trying to get EDS as an underwriting client for Francis I. duPont.[7]

Ross, however, had close ties to Kenneth A. Langone, the investment banker at Pressprich who had actually handled the underwriting in 1965. They had become close friends. So getting Ross to switch his business to duPont would require some doing. One way, Rudy thought, would be to do Ross a favor. He discovered an ingenious way to help Ross through F. I. duPont, Glore Forgan's need for liquid capital.

Technically Francis I. duPont rented its computers from a wholly-owned subsidiary, Wall Street Leasing. This arrangement reduced the taxes duPont partners paid each year on any profits. When duPont was profitable, the rent payments transferred income from the partnership to a corporation where the tax rate was lower.

Rudy suggested that EDS buy Wall Street Leasing from Francis I. duPont for several million dollars and continue to lease the computers to Francis I. duPont. The deal would supply Francis I. duPont with the additional liquid capital it needed to meet Bob Bishop's demand. At the same time, it would give Ross Perot's firm a foot in the door. Nothing more. The back office would continue to be operated by Francis I. duPont people—but if the combined firm's back office foundered, EDS would be right there to get the data processing business.

Consequently, when Rudy Smutny proposed the deal to Ross and to Wally, both sides eagerly agreed.

The deal didn't increase Francis I. duPont's net worth, but simply made duPont's capital more liquid—which satisfied Bob Bishop.

The little agony involved in this financial sleight-of-hand may have lulled all concerned into a false sense that future financial problems, if any, could be solved with equal ease.

The details of the duPont–Glore Forgan–Hirsch merger agreement were rapidly settled, and the draft of the merger agreement was approved by Glore Forgan's board of directors. But the executives that the management wanted to stay with the firm had to be persuaded to vote for the merger and to stay with the combined firm.

Jim was assigned this task. He sped across the country to get signatures: 10:00 A.M in San Francisco, 4:00 P.M. in Los Angeles on June 25, 3:00 P.M. in Chicago on June 26, 4:00 P.M in New York on June 29.

Most partners were easy to persuade. They had read glowing stories in the *Wall Street Journal, Barron's* and elsewhere lauding the contemplated merger, all written by reporters who had no way of knowing the perils involved. Envious comments by members of other firms, who also did not know the true facts, eased Jim's task. The new firm would be the third largest investment firm, behind Merrill Lynch and Bache, and would be a major underwriter while Bache was not. How could F. I. duPont Glore Forgan not be a big money maker? Why wouldn't its partners become rich—very rich indeed?

Because Jim had promised not to reveal Edmond duPont's guarantee that Jim would not lose any money if he became a partner and the firm failed, Jim felt like a Judas goat when he talked to the other partners about the pros and cons of the proposed merger. Jim soothed his conscience by emphasizing the risk of unlimited liability that every partner would assume. And he made sure that the holders of the subordinated notes understood that their notes would immediately be redeemed in full if they resigned. They could get out whole while the getting was good.

Nearly all the partners that the top management wanted to stay did stay.[8] As one of them reminisced, "You're merging two firms together. You've got two people for every job. Some people were going to have a job and some people were *not* going to have a job. The key people had to be partners. If you didn't sign, you were going to be unemployed. At the time, there weren't a lot of extra jobs around because so many firms had merged. There were a lot of people out of work. Where would you go? What would you do?

"Beside, we all felt there was no way the duPont family was going to let their name be dragged into a bankruptcy court. They would always step up and make the company whole and solvent, we thought."[9]

To ease the transition, all the Glore Forgan voting stockholders sold their stock—which technically was worthless—to Jim for a dollar. Jim was thus for a few days the sole owner of Glore Forgan Staats, Inc. (This was to cause Jim grief with his personal income tax for the next nine years. The IRS refused to consider it a technicality. Why wasn't all this stock income to Jim?)[10]

On July 6, 1970, full page advertisements in the *Wall Street Journal* and the *New York Times* announced the merger of Francis I. duPont & Co., Glore Forgan Staats, Inc. and Hirsch & Co. to form F. I. duPont, Glore Forgan.[11]

No one except those concerned has ever known—until now—that the merger of F. I. duPont–Glore Forgan–Hirsch was almost aborted at the last minute by a shortage of capital. Nor has anyone known, except those concerned, that if it had not been for Rudolph Smutny's ingenuity and Ross Perot's eagerness to get investment firm business for EDS, Francis I. duPont & Co. might have been forced into bankruptcy, with dire consequences for The New York Stock Exchange—perhaps even its collapse.

8

How The New York Stock Exchange Came Closer—Much, Much Closer—to Collapse the Second Time

A few weeks after the merger advertisement appeared, Richard Mc-Donald discovered he couldn't sell over-the-counter stocks to other firms. They were reacting to some unfortunate experiences: After they contracted to buy over-the-counter stocks from F. I. duPont, Glore Forgan, the actual securities were not delivered or were delivered inexcusably late.

Richard decided to complain to Peter duPont, Edmond duPont's son—fair-haired both actually and metaphorically—who headed up the back office. Sam Gay, the back office head whom Wally had insisted supersede Norm Swanton, had quit as previously agreed upon.

When Richard marched into Peter duPont's office, he looked around and saw pile after pile of computer print-outs stacked on desks, chairs, tables, and window ledges.[1]

The back office debacle predicted by Norm Swanton had occurred. duPont had used IBM computers; Glore Forgan had used the incompatible RCA Spectra.

EDS was not to blame. EDS only owned some of the computers through Wall Street Leasing; it operated none.

The stock market couldn't be faulted. Low volume, combined with a somewhat improved Central Certificate System, had enabled most other firms to reduce their fails.

Richard talked to Jim Lynch, who decided something had to be done. He couldn't, however, count on Archie Albright, the former Glore Forgan CEO, for any help.

Archie had begun behaving erratically,[2] perhaps because of the back office mess, perhaps because he was depressed.

After the merger was finalized, he was seldom consulted by Wally, even though Archie was titled chairman of the executive committee.

And Archie was, in Jim's opinion, over his head in his other position, head of investment banking. Several ex–Glore Forgan executives, especially the former regional chieftains, were superior investment bankers. Archie had brought in a few small chemical companies as clients, but that was all.

"Archie wouldn't show up for meetings and nobody knew where he was,"[3] recalls Harry Colmery. And when he did show up he was often listless.

Jim had dinner with two of the former Glore Forgan regional heads while both were in New York to discuss what should be done. They hadn't seen the fails figure for July, but they knew the number and dollar volume of the fails would be excessively large. They hadn't yet seen the profit and loss statement for July either, but they knew the loss would be big as well. (It would turn out to be $2.5 million.) They agreed that the back office could only be made efficient by retaining an outside computer firm to manage it.

The next day they discovered that Wally Latour was way ahead of them. When Wally had defended Francis I. duPont against Norm Swanton's attacks (as described in Chapter 6), it is likely that Wally had been somewhat aware of the deficiencies of duPont's back office—aware not because he had dirtied his hands in the back office's mechanics but as a result of the numerous complaints he received from duPont's office managers.[4]

Norm had angered Wally probably because Wally was forced to defend the mess left by Edmond duPont's old buddy. Further, Wally—a former syndicate manager—probably wanted Glore Forgan's major underwriting status, and Norm had threatened achievement of that goal.

When Jim talked to Wally, he discovered Wally had already talked not only to EDS but—despite the Wall Street Leasing deal—to another computer service bureau with excellent experience, Automatic Data Processing, Inc., usually referred to as ADP. It was headed by Frank Lautenberg, who would be elected a U.S. senator from New Jersey in 1990 and be re-elected, even though a Democrat, in the Republican landslide of 1994.

Both ADP and EDS sent delegations to New York who made presentations to Edmond and Peter duPont, Wally, Ed Peterson, Jim, and other executives of the firm in New York. A foggy[5] Archie Albright attended. (He resigned from the firm effective August 30, 1970.)

The contrast between the presentations and what followed later may indicate much about Ross Perot's way of getting accounts.

Mitch Hart, president but not CEO of EDS, headed the EDS team. Ross

Perot didn't even appear. And Mitch Hart talked mostly in generalities, describing what EDS had done for Texas Blue Cross.[6]

Mitch Hart's presentation ignored two basic principles in trying to make a sale of this kind. First, the CEO of the firm trying to make the sale should be present. The prospect thus feels that his account will get top level attention.

More important, prospects want to know as specifically as possible what the selling firm will do for them. What the selling firm has done for others is best used just as proof that the selling firm can carry out the promises it makes.[7]

The ADP delegation, in contrast, was led by the future Senator himself. He specified in a polished audio-visual presentation what ADP would do for F. I. duPont, Glore Forgan, backing his promises up with information about ADP's experience in processing payrolls.

Jim, some other former Glore Forgan executives, and Ed Peterson voted to retain Automatic Data Processing. All the former Francis I. duPont executives except Ed Peterson favored EDS.[8] They may have felt an obligation to Ross Perot because of the Wall Street Leasing deal.

Several days were spent discussing which firm to choose. The delay gave Ross time do what he had often done in the past: Beat out his competitors in an unorthodox way.[9]

When he was a salesman for IBM, he showed one prospect what could be accomplished with a computer by staying up all one night and feeding new data into it when the computer completed a run. He slept intermittently on a cot next to the computer.

He sold Southwestern Life Insurance Company a huge computer by finding a government agency that would buy otherwise idle time on the computer, thus making the computer an apparently economical buy.

After forming EDS, he got the key Texas Blue Cross–Blue Shield account by first getting an assignment with the organization as a personal consultant. He was on both sides of the deal when EDS got the account.

Unlike most salesmen, Ross Perot may seldom have made a one-on-one sale because his prospect identified with him. Ross probably would not have become the success he did if, for example, he had been forced to sell non-specialty steel. Ross is morally strict. He doesn't smoke or drink, swear, tell dirty jokes, or consort with women of easy virtue. In trying to make sales, Ross spent little or no time trying to get prospects to like him. He usually got right down to discussing what he was selling. When he made a sale, he usually won with polite but almost bullying logic. His sales to health organizations were often achieved by scaring his prospects—telling them how bad their businesses would be if they failed to retain EDS.

When Ross realized he might lose the contest with Frank Lautenberg's firm for the F. I. duPont, Glore Forgan account, he made an offer it was difficult for the brokerage firm's partners to refuse. He offered to put 100,000 shares of EDS stock into the firm as subordinated capital.

Frank Lautenberg was given a chance to match Ross Perot's unorthodox offer but declined.

When Jim and Ed Peterson heard about Ross's offer, they looked at F. I. duPont, Glore Forgan's income statement. They saw the $2½ million July loss.[10] Although they didn't know how other firms were doing at the time, they would not have been surprised to learn the sad fact that F. I. duPont, Glore Forgan was in worse financial condition than any other NYSE firm. They grudgingly but promptly assented to taking Ross up on his offer.

Thus EDS got the account, not because of EDS's expertise or salesmanship, but because Ross Perot used his money as a sweetener. (ADP's orthodox method of getting business, however, would benefit ADP in the long run. By 1998, ADP would be processing more than 15 percent of the retail equity transactions in the United States and Canada.)

In August 1970, Wally signed an eight-year contract with EDS under which F. I. duPont, Glore Forgan promised to pay EDS at least $8 million a year for providing all of F. I. duPont, Glore Forgan's electronic data processing requirements.[11]

Ross seemed to have taken the first big, essential step in his plan of applying EDS's health industry pattern to the brokerage business.

And F. I. duPont, Glore Forgan seemed to be on its way to being financially sound with no back office problems.

In September 1970, the firm broke even.[12] Commissions had jumped as the volume of trading on The New York Stock Exchange rose from the 10 million share days of the previous three months to more than 14 million shares a day.[13]

F. I. duPont, Glore Forgan's capital had also been bolstered by a steadily rising stock market.

But Jim's sense of relief lasted only a few weeks.

When Jim got the profit and loss statement for October 1970, he saw that F. I. duPont, Glore Forgan had lost a million dollars. The volume of trading on the NYSE had fallen to under 12 million shares a day[14] in October—an unprofitable level for many firms, and especially for F. I. duPont, Glore Forgan.

EDS had somewhat improved the back office, but there was only so much that could be done with Wall Street Leasing's now old-fashioned computers. Furthermore, EDS fees were high—just as they had been for Blue Cross–Blue Shield organizations. For F. I. duPont, Glore Forgan to be profitable, the volume of trading needed to be at least 14 million shares a day.[15]

Bob Bishop saw F. I. duPont, Glore Forgan's liabilities-to-capital ratio severely worsening and so informed Lee Arning, Bob Haack, Bunny Lasker, Felix Rohatyn and other members of the Crisis Committee.

They were concerned but not deeply.

"The duPont family had always come to bat and put in additional capital," Lee Arning told the NYSE oral history reporter. "Edmond said he was going down to Wilmington the next day, the next week. Finally Bob Haack went with him and laid it on the line."

Bob Haack chose an unusually inappropriate time to ask Lammont duPont Copeland, Sr., chairman of E. I. duPont & Co., the giant chemical company, for money. Copeland's son and namesake was nearing bankruptcy proceedings which would cost the duPont family tens of millions of dollars.[16]

An angry Bob Haack returned to New York empty handed.

Bob Bishop was among the many people surprised at the attitude of the duPont family; Edmond duPont had so often and so earnestly stated that the family would never let the firm down.

Bob Bishop, Lee, John, Bob Haack, Felix, and Bunny were probably more than surprised. They were probably terrified. F. I. DuPont, Glore Forgan's declaring bankruptcy had previously been, in their minds, only a theoretical possibility.[17]

The destruction of The New York Stock Exchange suddenly became a real possibility. (Remember this is 1970, before SIPC had been enacted.) If F. I. duPont, Glore Forgan went bankrupt, Don Regan would abandon Goodbody & Co., as Bunny Lasker and the governors had agreed he could. Goodbody & Co. would then go bankrupt. At any one time F. I. duPont, Glore Forgan and Goodbody owed other firms many millions of dollars in cash and securities. Their bankruptcies thus would cause the bankruptcy of many other firms. This would so tarnish The New York Stock Exchange that being a member of The New York Stock Exchange would become a liability instead of an asset to the surviving firms, and most would resign.

On November 5, 1970—the same day the governors voted to contribute a likely $30 million to Merrill for taking over Goodbody—Bob Bishop ordered Wally Latour to do something with F. I. duPont, Glore Forgan's capital which was only possible because of the way many (but not all) NYSE firms were capitalized. Securities held by a NYSE member firm and in its subordinated accounts were not credited at their full market value in calculating NYSE capital requirements. The reason: in an emergency the securities might actually need to be sold at lower prices than their prices on the books. These so-called "haircuts" varied, depending upon a stock or bond's liquidity, but usually were about 30 percent. Converting a sufficient number of securities into cash would technically increase F. I. duPont, Glore Forgan's capital by almost a third.

So Bob Bishop ordered Wally to sell securities in the accounts of subordinated lenders for cash.[18] Wally delayed. Bob insisted. And Wally gave the necessary orders to Richard MacDonald and others.

"That's when I knew the firm was in real trouble," recalls Richard McDonald who, as head of over-the-counter trading at F. I. duPont, Glore Forgan, handled the actual selling of the OTC securities in the partners' accounts. "We liquidated all the partnership holdings. We got down to Treasury bills on which there was only a 5 percent haircut, picking up very little extra capital. We liquidated everything."[19]

Before the securities in a subordinated acount were sold, the lender was warned and given a chance to substitute cash and take back the securities. A lender could thus avoid paying a capital gain on the sale of a common stock—which would usually be necessary because the securities had been held for so long that they had substantially appreciated. Inflation had multiplied the prices of many stocks—even those of companies that had made only modest profits.

Well-off lenders usually substituted cash, but many others could not. They were forced into debt in order to pay the capital gains tax. Some who did not own the stock themselves—who had borrowed the stock from a duPont relative or a friend—were forced into personal bankruptcy.

Among the securities that could be sold to bolster F. I. duPont, Glore Foran's capital position were the 100,000 shares of EDS stock that EDS contributed to F. I. duPont, Glore Forgan's capital. Their sale was highly desirable because converting them to cash would boost their capital-requirement value by more than 30 percent. But at the same time, getting the price at which the stock was carried on F. I. duPont, Glore Forgan's books—even getting a price close to it—could not be obtained just by entering an order to sell. The price quoted was for 100 shares, 200 shares, or so—not for 100,000.

The problem of selling the 100,000 shares came to Lee's attention. He talked to Ken Langone.

Coincidently, Pressprich was about to offer 500,000 shares of EDS for sale through a network of brokerage firms—in Wall Street jargon, "a secondary offering." Ross may have needed the cash, in part, to replace Wall Street Leasing's old IBM computers and Glore Forgan's RCA Spectra with IBM 360s.

Lee asked Ken Langone if he could sell another 100,000 shares of stock.[20]

Ken replied in his usual breezy, confident way that he could.

So Lee told him, very confidentially, that F. I. duPont, Glore Forgan had some capital problems and had 100,000 shares of EDS they'd like to sell.

Ken, like nearly everybody on Wall Street except the few in the know, didn't realize until then that F. I. duPont, Glore Forgan was in financial trouble.

"Look, Lee," said Ken, "This is not my deal. This is Perot's deal. I'm the underwriter, but it's his call. I'd suggest you go down and talk to him."

By this time, however, it had become apparent that selling out all the subordinated accounts, including the EDS stock, would not boost F. I. duPont, Glore Forgan's capital sufficiently to meet the NYSE requirements.

F. I. duPont, Glore Forgan's capital position was far worse than its own reports—and those of Bob Bishop's staff—had indicated. A preliminary report of a surprise audit by an independent accounting firm begun on September 27, 1970, showed that, even after converting the partners' accounts to cash, the firm was short an estimated $5 million from meeting the NYSE capital requirements.

How could the accountants differ so? The net worth of an investment firm is difficult to establish even in the best of times partly because of an unusual characteristic of the investment business. An investment firm's principal assets and liabilities—stocks and bonds—are continually changing hands as the firm buys and sells securities. And the worth of those assets and liabilities is continually changing as well. Their prices change not just from week to week, not just from day to day, not even from hour to hour, but from second to second. Consequently, audits made at different times always give different results. In a rapidly changing market, the results can be radically different.

Add to this the condition of the back offices of investment firms which were little improved in 1970 from the conditions in the sixties described in Chapter 2: Many of the back office people were inexperienced in operating, adjusting and repairing computers. Skilled workers were few. And attracting capable people was difficult because of the low pay.

Consequently, the reports of auditors were often just good—or bad—guesses. But whatever their validity, the reports had to be relied upon and appropriate actions taken.

As a consequence of the most recent audit, Lee queried Ross not only about his attitude toward the selling of 100,000 shares of EDS stock, but whether he would lend F. I. duPont, Glore Forgan the $5 million it needed.[21]

While Ross was thinking this over, Bob Bishop got the final results of the audit. F. I. duPont, Glore Forgan & Co. was short, not just $5 million, but $10 million.

So Ross was asked to ante up twice the original amount.

Ross was astonished[22] at the big jump in so short a time—not just thousands of dollars but millions! His scorn[23] for people in the investment business intensified.

Why should he put more millions into a company that was run so badly? Wouldn't he just lose more?

He refused to lend F. I. duPont, Glore Forgan the money it needed.

Bunny, Felix and Bob Haack were horrified when Lee told them this. More than ever before, their worst imaginings seemed liable to become terrifying realities.[24]

They knew no firm or combination of firms would lend F. I. duPont, Glore Forgan $10 million. Nor would any profit-minded investor be likely to even consider risking his money in such a mammoth, losing business. The *Wall Street Journal* had uncovered some confidential statistics, and recently published them, showing that predecessor Francis I. duPont & Co. had lost $41 million in 1969. Donaldson, Lufkin & Jenrette, in contrast, had made $38 million, and its stock was actively traded.[25]

And the Crisis Fund was virtually depleted.

Bunny couldn't ask the governors to vote to ask the member firms to tax themselves again. He had only just been able to persuade the governors to ask the members to contribute a possible $30 million to prevent the bankruptcy of Goodbody & Co. What is more, Bunny had also just revealed to the governors and the members that the Dempsey-Tegler liquidation—which they had already voted to liquidate in an orderly manner—would require several millions more than originally estimated—perhaps $9 million more.[26]

If Dempsey-Tegler cost twice what was originally estimated, wasn't it likely that just $10 million wouldn't be enough to save F. I. duPont, Glore Forgan?

The number of members voicing their antagonism to the entire concept of the Exchange rescuing failing firms—and the intensity of their opposition—had increased.

To make matters more desperate, even if Bunny could convince the governors to vote to ask the members to tax themselves again, the money would never arrive in time. The heads of the large firms and opinion-leaders among the governors would have to be to persuaded individually and privately. Certain rules of the New York Stock Exchange would need to be complied with. The governors would have to pass a resolution asking the members to vote on making a contribution. And the entire membership of the Exchange would have to vote in favor of the making the contribution. About a month usually elapsed between the members of the Crisis Committee agreeing that the Exchange should ask the members to tax themselves and the money actually becoming available.

A month! By that time, the SEC's Stanley Sporkin would do what he had threatened to do time and again when an investment firm was technically bankrupt.[27] He would declare F. I. duPont, Glore Forgan bankrupt. Time and again in the past, Stanley had only been persuaded not to declare a *technically* bankrupt firm *legally* bankrupt by Bob Haack's promise that the failing firm would be saved by The New York Stock Exchange. Now Bob Haack could not make that promise.

What about the U.S. government as a savior?

Members of Congress were reluctant even if they could have acted on time. As noted in a previous chapter, John M. Moss, Chairman of the House Subcommittee on Commerce and Finance, said on November 16 he would not allow the House to vote on the SIPC bill if SIPC was to be immediately drawn on for the liquidation of Plohn, First Devonshire, Robinson or any other presently troubled firm. And even if Congressman Moss and Senator Muskie could have been convinced to include F. I. duPont, Glore Forgan in SIPC's coverage—only a theoretical possibility— a month or more would pass before the House and Senate could pass a bill creating SIPC and the bill be signed by the president. F. I. duPont, Glore Forgan would be forced to declare bankruptcy long before that unless it received an injection of $10 million.

Disaster threatened the investment business and perhaps even the American economy as never before.[28] As previously described, commercial bankers had promptly rushed to the aid of brokerage firms in the past—they had an incentive to do so—but in 1970, commercial bankers were anxious to get money *out* of brokerage firms, not put any money *in*. No banker would think for a moment of lending F. I. duPont, Glore Forgan any money.

So with commercial bankers no longer sufficiently concerned, the Congress unable to act in time if at all, and F. I. duPont, Glore Forgan too risky a venture for any profit-minded investor, the situation was awesomely desperate. If F. I. duPont, Glore Forgan didn't receive $10 million within a few weeks, the governors would be forced by their own rules and those of the Securities and Exchange Commission to suspend F. I. duPont, Glore Forgan, which would force the firm into bankruptcy. Merrill Lynch, per Don Regan's agreement with the NYSE, would abandon its rescue of Goodbody. The half million or so customers of two big investment firms—Goodbody and F. I. duPont, Glore Forgan—would lose many millions of dollars, probably billions.[29]

The bankruptcy of F. I. duPont, Glore Forgan and Goodbody would also force dozens of other firms to whom F. I. duPont, Glore Forgan and Goodbody owed cash and securities to declare bankruptcy. Panicked customers of other firms would withdraw their cash and ask that stock certificates be sent them, aborting the nine-month-old Central Certificate System. Banks would not renew many of their loans to marginal, even sound brokerage firms, forcing some to liquidate. Many well-capitalized firms would resign from The New York Stock Exchange so as to escape paying the many millions of dollars they would be assessed; Morgan Stanley, Kuhn Loeb, and Dillon Read had already threatened to do so. The New York Stock Exchange would vanish not just because membership would no longer attract investors but also because membership was hazardous to any firm's financial health.

Stock prices would plummet because people with money would refrain from buying stocks. Lower stock prices and lower volumes would cause more firms to become bankrupt, whether they were members of the Exchange or not. Raising capital for growing companies might become impossible for months, certainly difficult and more costly for years.

Bunny Lasker talked to Ross Perot. They knew each other well. They had worked together, both raising money for Richard Nixon's 1968 campaign. Despite Bunny's pleading, Ross refused to put any more money into F. I. duPont, Glore Forgan.

So Bunny telephoned the President of the United States and told him how near The New York Stock Exchange was to collapsing.

It was easy for Bunny to call Richard Nixon.

"Bunny was at the White House all the time," says Ken Langone.[30] Bunny had raised so much money for Nixon, the President couldn't refuse Bunny's calls.

As Nixon listened, he had good reasons of his own to be terrified. The Republican party had just lost—in the November 3, 1970 elections—nine seats in the House of Representatives, plus 21 state governor contests.[31] These losses Nixon ascribed in part to the economy. He was already so worried about the high level of unemployment, he was thinking of firing his economic advisors.[32]

Equally important, the collapse of The New York Stock Exchange would encourage enemies of the free market system as well as other Nixon opponents at a critical time. In September, the Soviet Union had been detected trying to sneak atomic weapons into Cuba in violation of the agreement reached by President Kennedy following the Cuban missile crisis. In October the Weathermen had bombed and demolished buildings in several cities and universities.

Communist parties now controlled one third of the world—which was more than the British Empire had at its height.

The Communists had just gained an important victory in South America. On November 3, heretofore non-Communist Chile had elected a Communist president despite the CIA's support of the opposition with several million dollars.[33]

Opponents of the Vietnam War were harassing Nixon almost everywhere he went; rocks, eggs, and vegetables had been thrown at him in California.[34]

If The New York Stock Exchange—the heart of capitalism—collapsed, the enemies of capitalism, of the United States of America, and of Richard Nixon would be encouraged—especially the North Vietnamese. They and their supporters in the United States and elsewhere would become even more confident of the rightness of the Communist cause. Getting the North Vietnamese to negotiate a peace would be further delayed.

But there was no official way Nixon could help Bunny prevent the demise of F. I. duPont, Glore Forgan. No legal pretext could be established for the President of the United States, or the SEC, or the Federal Reserve or any other government body to supply F. I. duPont, Glore Forgan with several million dollars. The President could order the Army to take over a failing or strike-bound manufacturing corporation or even a retailer like Sears Roebuck, using national defense as an excuse, but he couldn't legally supply it with money. Only Congress could do that—as it did with Chrysler. And taking over a failing investment firm would require money. Furthermore, the Democratic-controlled Congress was strongly antagonistic to the Republican President, as would soon be seen as the Watergate scandal developed. For Nixon to take any illegal action using government funds to rescue what would be viewed as his rich supporters was unthinkable.

Only a super-rich patriot could prevent the collapse of The New York Stock Exchange and subsequent economic disaster.

As a result of Bunny's call to Nixon, Attorney General John N. Mitchell called Ross. When Ross wouldn't budge, soon-to-be Secretary of the Treasury John Connally called, as did Presidential assistant Peter M. Flanigan, and other top government officials.[35] All urged Ross to supply F. I. duPont, Glore Forgan with the needed capital.

Ross Perot is unusually patriotic, as befits a graduate of the U.S. Naval Academy. Plus Ross has altruistic impulses that go beyond patriotism. When he sees a need, he has difficulty not trying to fulfill it. When he learned that New York City could not afford to buy the best kind of horses for police work—Tennessee Walkers—he bought a dozen and had them shipped, free, to New York City. When he learned that American prisoners of war were starving in Vietnam, he chartered two planes, loaded them with food, and tried to land them in Vietnam—unsuccessfully. Examples of his helping employees in need of surgery or other medical care abound.

But Ross did resist the calls. Wouldn't he look like a fool if he put more millions into F. I. duPont, Glore Forgan and it failed? He still got credit for a "noble effort" after he failed to feed the starving prisoners of war, but if he lost $10 million on top of the stock he had previously lent duPont Glore Forgan, wouldn't he just look dumb?

Anyway, wasn't it likely to turn out that much more than $10 million would be needed?

Ross told Attorney General John Mitchell that there were a lot of people more capable than he of putting up the necessary money. Ross asked that he be put at the bottom of the list and that Mitchell work on the other people.

John Mitchell made about a dozen fruitless calls, came back to Ross and told him that only he could prevent the impending financial, economic, and political calamity.

Who the Attorney General had approached nobody knows, but it's worth asking: Why did no other member of the super-rich ride to the rescue of Wall Street? Some were Democrats and so couldn't be expected to respond favorably to an appeal by a Republican administration. Many Republicans, especially those in the East, hated the President who had originally been backed by Western oil entrepreneurs. The Fords couldn't be expected to help since they had refused to save McDonnell, their relative's firm. But where were the other billionaires and centimillionaires who professed devotion to the public good?

Perhaps the super-rich families to which John Mitchell appealed were warned against it by their financial advisors.[36] (Few of the inherited super-rich make their own investment decisions.) The advisors certainly couldn't be persuaded that it would be a sensible investment. And they would have to liquidate some profitable, sound investments and pay capital gains taxes in order to free up money to save F. I. duPont, Glore Forgan.

In 1995, studious readers of the *New York Times* would get a glimpse of how advisors to the inherited super-rich are more concerned about the profits they can make for their clients than their clients are. Stories about the bankruptcy of Rockefeller Center showed how advisors to the Rockefeller family imposed stiffer terms on the Japanese bank that bought 80 percent of Rockefeller Center than David Rockefeller would have supported if he'd started paying attention in time. It's traditional for courtiers to be "more royal than the king."

Many, perhaps all, of the super-rich and their advisors may also have been deterred from contributing money to save F. I. duPont, Glore Forgan by each super-rich family tending to have its own brokerage firm—one to which it directed most of its brokerage business and in which it would often have a capital stake. Perhaps each member of the super-rich that John Mitchell called felt that if the duPonts wouldn't save their own firm, why should they?[37]

Furthermore, each super-rich advisor may have felt that the family who employed him would profit rather than lose from the demise of F. I. duPont, Glore Forgan. With a giant competitor out of the way, the families' brokerage firms might do better over the long term. If their personal firms got into financial difficulty, the super-rich could and would rescue them. The greater the danger, the more the family advisors would want to reserve their families' capital to rescue the firms in which the families had a stake.

The deterioration, even the demise, of The New York Stock Exchange would not affect the super-rich personally. The growth of the economy would be slowed, but this would not affect the super-rich families much. Most of the super-rich are more concerned with conserving their wealth than in increasing it. The super-rich do give some of their wealth away, but tend to do so in more personally gratifying ways, such as endowing a hospital or supporting their favorite university.

Back in November 1929, President Herbert Hoover tried to get those with economic power to save the nation. He called to the White House a number of influential businessmen of great wealth, including Pierre duPont and Henry Ford, and warned them of the disaster that lay ahead unless they came to the rescue of the nation. He asked them not to cut wages, not to lay off workers, and to increase construction of factories. The dozen or so super-rich men present agreed unanimously—yes, unanimously!—to do as Hoover asked them. And then *did precisely the opposite*. Each acted to protect his own interests by reducing wages, laying off workers, and deferring construction projects.[38]

Many super-rich were also unlikely to respond to a plea from Richard Nixon because they disliked, even hated him. He was a Californian. His political career had been largely financed by Western oil men. Most of the super-rich lived in the East. And he had beaten one of the Eastern super-rich, Nelson Rockefeller, for the Republican nomination for President.

It seemed clear to everyone concerned that if Ross Perot did not save F. I. duPont, Glore Forgan, nobody would. The firm would become bankrupt with consequent disasters.

John Mitchell so stated emphatically to Ross.[39]

Pressed, Ross more or less consented but, like a skilled judo wrestler, turned the Attorney General's pressure back on him.

If the Federal government wanted so much for Ross Perot to rescue the firm, why shouldn't the Federal government help out financially? Of course, the government couldn't appropriate money directly, but it could indirectly.

Here's how: Ross wouldn't put cash into the firm, nor would he put in EDS stock. Instead, he would borrow money, using EDS stock as collateral, buy municipal bonds, and deliver the tax-exempt bonds to F. I. duPont, Glore Forgan as subordinated capital. Thus Ross would not only get interest as a subordinated lender (which would be more than he was paying on the borrowed money), but he would also get tax-free interest on the municipal bonds, plus the dividends on the EDS stock! And on top of all that, he would subtract the interest he paid on the loan from his taxable income![40]

There was only one obstacle—the reason something like this had not been done before. An IRS regulation forbids a taxpayer to deduct interest on money borrowed to buy municipal bonds. The IRS wants to prevent anyone from profiting by borrowing money and using the money to buy municipal bonds when the interest rate on municipal bonds is high enough to make such arbitrage profitable.

While the regulation is clear, applying it to individual cases sometimes is not. Suppose a taxpayer mortgages his home and immediately uses the proceeds to buy municipal bonds. He clearly cannot deduct the interest on his mortgage from his income tax. But suppose a taxpayer who already has a mortgage on his home—has mortgaged his home years before—buys municipal bonds. He can still deduct the interest on his mortgage even though he could have used the money to reduce the mortgage on his home.

Even more confusing are margined brokerage accounts which include both stocks and municipal bonds. How much of the money the investor has borrowed from the brokerage firm should be considered as used to buy municipal bonds? All? Some? None?

Even so, what Ross Perot proposed flagrantly violated the IRS regulation, but to the Attorney General of the United States it was a cheap way to get Ross to rescue F. I. duPont, Glore Forgan and prevent a national calamity. He ordered the IRS to send Ross Perot a letter exempting him from the interest-deduction regulation.[41]

The letter didn't come. And it didn't come, despite many calls to the IRS. Were the bureaucrats at the IRS miffed at this clear evasion of a regulation and so were maneuvering to avoid following a directive?[42]

Whatever the motives of the IRS bureaucrats, the days ticked by between the notification of F. I. duPont, Glore Forgan's violation of capital requirements and the date by which its capital needed to be in compliance.

Eventually Ross Perot went personally to the IRS office in Washington and demanded the letter. The bureaucrats told him—*told a multimillionaire who was trying to save the American economy from disaster*—that it would take a while.

He said he'd wait.

He sat in the office of the IRS until the letter of exemption was eventually handed to him.[43]

Ross also imposed other conditions for his lending F. I. duPont, Glore Forgan $10 million.

First and foremost, he wanted to control the firm. Why should he hand $10 million over to demonstrably inept executives without being able to direct or replace them?

Second, the firm had to become a corporation. He certainly didn't want to become a partner and be liable to an unlimited extent.

Third, the partners of the firm had to raise $5 million that would be added to the firm's capital.

Neither Jim nor any other former ex–Glore Forgan Staats executive objected to Ross Perot gaining control of the firm. In fact, they welcomed it. But a cabal of former Francis I. duPont partners was outraged. They would not give up so much of the firm's potential profits as well as control of the firm to Ross Perot.[44] And the firm being a partnership, all their signatures were necessary for the deal to be legal.

Days went by with both sides adamant, with Edmond duPont quietly supporting the resisting partners. Because of the laws governing partnerships, unless every partner of F. I. duPont, Glore Forgan agreed to Ross Perot's terms, the firm would become bankrupt and a disastrous series of events would follow.

An angry, fearful, impatient Bunny Lasker decided to try a different tack.

He phoned Edmond duPont before 9:00 A.M. while by chance Jim Lynch was in Edmond duPont's office. (In these critical days, even Mr. duPont was coming to the office early.) Bunny told Mr. duPont to come over to The New York Stock Exchange immediately. The Exchange was only a block away from F. I. duPont, Glore Forgan's offices at One Wall Street, yet Edmond duPont demurred.

Bunny insisted.

Mr. Dupont hung up, turned to Jim, and said that Jim should come with him because he was a lawyer.

As soon as they entered Bunny's office at The New York Stock Exchange, Bunny's face showed his anger.

Glaring through his black-rimmed glasses, towering over the much shorter Edmond duPont, Bunny beat his long fingers against the edge of his desk as he spoke his thoughts directed at Mr. duPont.

Goodbody was just about saved and SIPC was nearly through Congress, shouted Bunny, much like a Marine drill sergeant correcting a derelict recruit. Bunny said over and over that he was not going let Mr. duPont torpedo the Perot acquisition. Swearing, he told Mr. duPont to get his partners in line and agree to Ross Perot's terms.[45]

When Bunny concluded, he didn't say, "Dismissed!" but came close.

Edmond duPont had probably never been talked to so harshly in his entire life. He meekly left, followed by Jim.[46]

Edmond duPont told the resisting cabal of ex–Francis I. duPont partners that he was giving up control of the firm and thought they should all agree to Ross Perot's terms. The revolt collapsed.

It appeared that only details needed to be attended to.

To allow time for all the legal and accounting work that needed to be done before F. I. duPont, Glore Forgan could be incorporated, Ross agreed to lend the firm $10 million for 90 days. At the end of the 90 days, Perot could convert $1.5 million of the loan into 51 percent of the stock of the corporation. As part of the agreement, the partners of F. I. duPont, Glore Forgan said they would raise $5 million on their own.[47]

Thus Wally Latour was able to announce to reporters on November

25, 1970, that F. I. duPont, Glore Forgan would receive a $15 million capital infusion[48] ($10 million from Ross Perot, $5 million to be raised by the F. I. duPont, Glore Forgan partners).

The announcement caught the media by surprise. The media had known and reported the selling out of subordinated accounts earlier in the month, but Wally had assured them then that those sales solved F. I. duPont, Glore Forgan's need for liquidity.

Reporters like Richard E. Rustin of the *Wall Street Journal* and Terry Robards of the *New York Times* did the best job any reporter could then and throughout this period, but it was impossible for them to know how vitally necessary Ross's investment was to the survival of F. I. duPont Glore Forgan.[49] And, indeed, to the survival of The New York Stock Exchange itself. Wally never admitted there was a serious crisis. He justified Ross Perot's putting capital into the firm by saying, "We wanted to have such a large influx of capital that nobody could raise any questions about the financial condition of the firm."[50]

It seemed that F. I. duPont, Glore Forgan had been saved, and that consequently, The New York Stock Exchange was saved. SIPC would be passed, and Congressman Moss would never know that he had been misinformed when Bunny and Ralph deNunzio assured him that no other firm was in danger of bankruptcy.

But was F. I. duPont, Glore Forgan really saved? The agreement had been announced—but not signed.

Bunny Lasker and his cohorts never knew about a telephone call Sam Freedman, a trusted EDS employee in New York, made to EDS headquarters shortly after Wally Latour's announcement. Only a very few people have ever known about his ominous call.[51]

Sam had been looking at the figures behind the figures that the management of F. I. duPont, Glore Forgan had supplied Ross Perot.

Sam was horrified at what he discovered.

When Mitch Hart, in Dallas, answered the phone, Sam, in New York, asked to be switched to Ross Perot.

Mitch told him that Ross was in New York.

Sam said he had to speak to Ross Perot right away.

Mitch called Ross who said he could give Sam an hour that afternoon.

Sam hadn't expected to get an audience so promptly. He didn't yet have his report in the shipshape form ex–Naval officer Ross Perot always demanded.

Sam called Ross directly and said he couldn't be ready until the evening.

Ross said he didn't know if he could see Sam then.

Sam responded firmly that Ross had better see him—that the matter was very serious indeed.

Ross asked what he meant.

Sam·said he really didn't want to talk about the matter over the phone.
Ross agreed to see Sam in Ross's suite at the Waldorf-Astoria at 6:00
P.M.

Sam pressured typists to get the report ready on time.

When Sam and two associates, carrying loaded briefcases, stood before
the Waldorf reception desk inquiring the number of Ross Perot's suite,
they heard a fire alarm sound.

Pandemonium!

Disheveled hotel guests poured out of crowded elevators into the
Christmas-decorated lobby. Among the guests was an angry Ross Perot,
clad only in an undershirt and pants. His feet were bare.

The emergency soon ended, and the four men went up to Ross's suite.
As they entered, Ross upbraided Sam, asking him what was so disastrous.

Sam told him F. I. duPont, Glore Forgan wasn't worth saving.

Ross sat on an armchair in undershirt, pants and bare feet, read the
report, and listened to Sam who was dressed in the EDS uniform—dark
suit, white shirt, narrow tie, black laced-up wing-tip shoes. What he read
enraged Ross. He repeatedly pounded the arm of the chair, asking rhe-
torically whether Edmond duPont and Wally Latour and Milt Speicher—
all of them—had lied to him![52]

Sam replied that he could only tell Ross that the figures were false—
that the figures didn't reflect the true financial condition of F. I. duPont,
Glore Forgan. Whether Mr. duPont, Wally, and Milt knew it or not, Sam
said he didn't know.

But what could Ross Perot do? He had promised the President of the
United States that he would rescue F. I. duPont, Glore Forgan. And the
media had already been told he would contribute $10 million to F. I.
duPont, Glore Forgan's capital.

Furthermore, the price of EDS stock had been declining—probably
because security analysts anticipated EDS revenues flattening out—and
Ross needed the revenues from F. I. duPont, Glore Forgan to resuscitate
the price of EDS common stock, even perhaps to maintain its price.

If F. I. duPont, Glore Forgan went out of business, EDS would lose
the revenues it was getting from the investment firm, which were about
20 percent of total EDS revenues.

The publicity would make the financial facts seem even worse. *Fortune*
magazine and other publications had glorified Ross. If he gave up, the
media would denigrate both him and EDS. Some reporters might become
vicious—as they sometimes do when they feel they have been misled.

Furthermore, any continued decline in the price of EDS stock would
damage the morale of many EDS employees. Ross didn't pay EDS employees much, but he rewarded many with options to buy EDS stock,
thus causing them to identify their own futures with the company.

Of critical importance: if Ross allowed F. I. duPont, Glore Forgan to become bankrupt, the first victory in his strategy[53] for conquering the investment business as he had conquered the health industry would be reversed.

On December 15, 1970, Ross and all the partners of F. I. duPont, Glore Forgan signed the agreement.

The next day Bunny Lasker joyfully told reporters, "I think we can safely say that we are aware of no major firm that is in danger at the present time."

Bunny thought he was telling the truth.

The media never found out about Ross Perot's lucrative, legally questionable municipal bond deal with the Federal government. Wally had truthfully told reporters at the time that Perot's loan would take the form of "either cash or high-grade fixed income securities, like U.S. Governments." And the media couldn't be expected to guess that there was a story behind those words and cross-question Wally or Ross Perot on the matter.

The media eventually discovered that President Nixon had had a hand in saving F. I. duPont, Glore Forgan but never knew about John Mitchell's role and the search for other saviors besides Ross Perot. Not until now has the public been told how very, very close the third largest Wall Street firm and consequently The New York Stock Exchange itself came to collapsing in 1970. Nor has the public known about the farcical scene in which the economy of the United States was saved from cyclonic disaster by the successful bullying of a member of the inherited super-rich. And only Sam Freedman and his close friends have known that Ross Perot had been warned by Sam of the immensity of the risk he was taking.

This story might lead one to speculate that top business leaders and government officials are keeping similar dangers—in international finance, for example—from the media and the general public today. One might speculate, in fact, whether some dangers have been avoided without the media and the general public knowing they ever even existed.

Not only were the media kept in the dark about the circumstances surrounding the nearly catastrophic collapse of F. I. duPont, Glore Forgan, the media also never knew of the near catastrophe that followed and how it was prevented. That near catastrophe is described in the next chapter.

9

How a Giant Investment Firm Very Nearly Went Bankrupt in 1971, Potentially Causing Investors to Lose Millions of Dollars Despite the Existence of the Securities Investors Protection Corporation

Immediately following Wally's November 25, 1970, announcement that F. I. duPont, Glore Forgan would get a $15 million capital infusion—$10 million from Ross Perot, $5 million to be raised by the investment firm's partners—many outsiders thought Ross Perot had accomplished a great coup: gaining the right to control the third-largest investment firm by lending the firm a relatively modest sum.

But in December outsiders got some hint that Ross might have made a bad bargain. A story in the *Wall Street Journal* revealed that F. I. duPont, Glore Forgan would lose at least $16 million in 1970, stating, "The deficit looms as the largest on record for a brokerage house."[1]

The story also revealed that a duPont relative and another partner had together withdrawn more than $5 million in capital at the beginning of 1970.

And then the reputation of the firm was tarnished in mid-December— thereby affecting its ability to attract and keep customers—by the indictment of a senior officer on charges of insider trading. He was Charles J. Hodge, who had been vice chairman of Glore Forgan Staats, Inc. and a god-like figure to many Glore Forgan employees including Jim Lynch.

The insider-trading scandal made headlines day after day because it involved the biggest bankruptcy to date in U.S. history—that of the Penn Central Railroad. (More about this is in Chapter 12.)

Yet many outsiders, including most people in the investment business, continued to be optimistic about the future of F. I. duPont, Glore Forgan—and would continue to be so for several months to come. *Fortune* magazine would call Ross Perot "a dominant figure on Wall Street" and note that his "stake in the firm could be worth around $150 million in five years."[2]

There was much they didn't know or recognize as important.

They didn't know Sam Freedman had told Ross that F. I. duPont, Glore Forgan wasn't worth saving.[3]

They didn't know how badly F. I. duPont, Glore Forgan was organized and managed.[4]

They did know through the December *Wall Street Journal* article that several F. I. duPont, Glore Forgan partners were withdrawing their capital, but didn't recognize the seriousness of those actions. These partners had given the required six-months notice back in May, June, and July 1970, and so were free to withdraw their capital in December 1970 and in January and February 1971. Their withdrawals could total more than $30 million![5]

And outsiders couldn't have been expected to anticipate the combination of other events that would again imperil the survival of F. I. duPont, Glore Forgan, threatening its hundreds of thousands of customers with losses amounting to many millions of dollars. Cash and securities in "safekeeping" at other firms were covered by the Securities Investors Protection Corporation, but not the cash and securities on deposit at F. I. duPont, Glore Forgan. This lack of coverage was a result of the promise (described by Chapter 3) by Ralph DeNunzio to Representative John Moss to get SIPC passed: that any firm in financial difficulty prior to the passage of SIPC would not be covered by SIPC.

Shortly after the November 25 announcement of the agreement giving Perot an option to control the firm, a disgruntled Ralph W. Williams, manager of duPont Glore Forgan's Atlanta office, and an equally disgruntled Jerome K. Rosenstein, manager of the Miami Beach office, called Mitch Hart, the president of EDS and told him they wanted to talk about the future.[6] They knew Mitch from discussions with him about the firm's back office.

Thirty-seven-year-old Mitch Hart was a man of few words. He often answered questions with a simple "yes" or "no" without any explanation for his answer.

He told Ralph and Jerry Rosenstein he had too many other things to do.

Of course, as president of EDS he did. Further, he was not eager to get involved in the running of F. I. duPont, Glore Forgan. In fact, he may have been secretly dismayed[7] at Ross's spending money to shore up F. I. duPont, Glore Forgan that could otherwise have been spent improving EDS operations.

Jerry retorted that he and Ralph Williams represented the two largest offices in the Southeast—and that if they left the firm, F. I. dupont, Glore Forgan wouldn't have any offices at all in the Southeast.

That spurred Mitch into action. He flew to Atlanta, listened to them, became alarmed, called Ross Perot from Ralph Williams' office and advised Ross to talk to Jerry and Ralph.

Ross agreed. Ralph and Jerry flew to Dallas and told Ross about several errors of commission and omission in the management of F. I. duPont, Glore Forgan, telling him that Wally Latour had often made promises that he never carried out.

Even though Ross had no legal control over F. I. duPont, Glore Forgan—his option to take control was not effective until March 15, 1971—he immediately assumed command.

He demoted Wally Latour to head of institutional sales. (Wally would quit a few months later to become a director and senior vice president of Bache & Co.)

Ross appointed 64-year-old Harold A. "Chuck" Rousselot, head of the firm's commodity division, to Wally's top management position.

Ross demanded that Charley Hodge be promptly fired, which was understandable since the charges of insider trading against him damaged the firm's reputation. Jim Lynch was assigned this distasteful task. Jim tried to postpone Charley's going till after Christmas but was told to do it right away.

Ross deposed Edmond duPont from his position as senior partner but allowed him to continue as a member of the board of managing directors.

Ross made John C. Allyn the senior partner effective January 4, 1971. It seemed a logical appointment at the time. John had a far bigger stake in F. I. duPont, Glore Forgan than anyone else except Edmond duPont.

Ross also made several other organizational changes including the elimination of the ridiculous reporting of all office managers directly to the CEO. Instead a regional system was established.

In late January 1971, the firm's partners were forced to admit to Ross Perot that they couldn't raise the $5 million they had promised to contribute to the firm's capital. They had explored every source they could think of. They had sought money from banks, other investment firms, Pepsi-Cola and other corporations, as well as numerous individuals. But the widely reported insider trading scandal involving Charley Hodge and the Penn Central Railroad scared potential investors and lenders away.[8]

"At the same time" Bob Bishop would later write in a confidential memorandum[9] "another accounting firm was engaged to perform a fresh audit of the firm, in which the accountants were joined by an EDS task force and Exchange examiners. As the new audit proceeded, the extent of the firm's basic capital impairment began to appear far larger than the most pessimistic of earlier estimates. EDS had succeeded in straightening out current operations, but previously undiscovered past items kept being uncovered. By early February, the estimates of the total amount of capital needed to maintain the firm's capital ratio of 10:1 had ballooned from $10 million to as much as $40 million.

When Ross Perot got the facts, he faced a dilemma. Wouldn't he be thought a sucker—indeed *be* a sucker—if he poured more millions into F. I. duPont, Glore Forgan? Might not the firm go bankrupt regardless of what he did?

But he had promised the President of the United States he would save F. I. duPont, Glore Forgan, and he hated to quit trying.

Ross decided he would put more of his millions into F. I. duPont, Glore Forgan only if he and a few associates at EDS, such as Mitch Hart, were given 100 percent of the stock when F. I. duPont, Glore Forgan was incorporated.

It seemed to Ross—and was conceded by a few others in the firm, including Jim Lynch—that all the partners' equity had been wiped out by past losses. If the partners had no equity in the firm, why should they share in future profits?

Ross also demanded that the partners be responsible for the current debts of F. I. duPont, Glore Forgan. This amounted to $65,000 for Jim Lynch, larger amounts for Harry Colmery and similarly ranked partners, lesser amounts for lower-ranking partners.

Partners who were independently wealthy or had rich relatives, such as Harry Colmery, would be able to just hand in a check, but many partners had saved little and had no rich relatives. They faced the possibility of being in debt for years.

Jim decided to talk to Edmond duPont, recalling that Mr. duPont been fond of saying his word was his bond. But when Jim Lynch brought up Edmond's assurance that Jim would suffer no loss if he continued with the firm, Edmond was non-committal. Later Edmond's lawyer told Jim that Edmond didn't feel bound by that promise once Ross assumed command.[10] Jim had never before recognized so strongly the validity of Machievelli's advice: "Put not your trust in princes."

Jim, Harry, and virtually every other partner of F. I. duPont, Glore Forgan would have been even more dismayed if they'd known about the $3½ million Edmond duPont had secretly borrowed on the partnership's behalf. When that came to light several years later, Lynch discovered he and other similarly ranked partners were each liable for half a million dollars each!

Ross's demand that he and his associates get 100 percent of all future profits while ignoring F. I. duPont, Glore Forgan's debts turned some formerly acquiescent partners into antagonists. They saw themselves reduced to mere employees. They saw themselves giving up all hope of becoming super-rich. And some, now that they had a taste of the way

Ross managed, resented foregoing their freedom to exercise their expertise as they thought best.[11]

Faced with this intense, widespread opposition, Ross indicated he was going to cut his losses, not exercise his option to buy 51 percent of the shares of F. I. duPont, Glore Forgan, and would ask that the 90-day $10 million loan be repaid when it became due on March 15, 1971.

What a sudden and unexpected reversal of fortune for Bunny Lasker, Felix Rohatyn, Bob Haack, Ralph DeNunzio, Lee Arning and Bob Bishop! For a few weeks, their worries had seemed to be over. Goodbody had been saved. SIPC had been passed and signed on December 30, 1970. And few governors opposed asking the members to contribute the relatively few millions of dollars needed to back up the deal Ralph De-Nunzio had made with Representative Moss for The New York Stock Exchange to rescue First Devonshire, Charles Plohn, and Robinson & Co. It had seemed that their big worries were over.

Now, if F. I. duPont, Glore Forgan failed to receive at least $30 million—the $10 million Ross could withdraw on March 15 plus the $20 million or more recently required—the governors would be forced by their own rules and those of the Securities and Exchange Commission to suspend F. I. duPont, Glore Forgan. This would force the firm into bankruptcy.

But how could Bunny ask the governors to vote to have the members contribute that much money on top of the more than a hundred million dollars they had already contributed and were committed to contribute?

Bunny and his cohorts kept up a brave front. They hid the precarious condition of F. I. duPont, Glore Forgan from the media and the public.[12] Bob Haack did reveal some facts to the SEC commissioners and the newly formed board of SIPC, but, in Bob's words, "reiterated our strong hope that the firm could be salvaged." Remarkably, none of the bureaucrats leaked the facts to the media. So again, those who lent money to investment firms, other investors, and the press were kept in the dark. Only a few insiders knew that F. I. duPont, Glore Forgan was again in danger of bankruptcy.

Bunny talked to Don Regan who now wore two hats. He was not only CEO of Merrill Lynch, the industry's largest firm, but was also a member of the board of SIPC. Bunny suggested to Don Regan that Merrill Lynch take F. I. duPont, Glore Forgan over, but Don refused. He had his hands full absorbing Goodbody into Merrill Lynch. And no other firm would or could absorb F. I. duPont, Glore Forgan, Bunny knew from his experience with Goodbody. Goodbody had been big—had been the fifth largest wall street investment firm—but F. I. duPont, Glore Forgan was even bigger—the third largest!

As a member of the board of SIPC, Don Regan debated with the other members of the board and with Ted Forcht, who had joined the staff of

SIPC, whether SIPC should supply funds that would result in the liquidation of F. I. duPont, Glore Forgan without loss to its customers or other firms.[13]

The dilemma the board members faced was this: On the one hand, SIPC was only established because Ralph DeNunzio had promised John Moss that SIPC funds would not be used in instances such as this. On the other hand, the unaided bankruptcy of F. I. duPont, Glore Forgan would force dozens, perhaps hundreds, of other firms into bankruptcy because of their inter-relation with F. I. duPont, Glore Forgan. It might be cheaper and certainly less damaging to the economy of the United States if SIPC just liquidated F. I. duPont, Glore Forgan in an orderly manner. If not enough money was in SIPC—which was likely—they could, according to the terms of the law, call on the U.S. Treasury to supply any additional funds which would be necessary.[14]

The days rolled by without action being taken.

A week before the March 15, 1971, deadline, Bunny assembled the heads of several firms with excess capital and asked them either individually or as a group to supply F. I. duPont, Glore Forgan with the needed $30 million. None were willing.

He tried a second time with a bigger group of firms and got them to agree to supply the $5 million on which the F. I. duPont, Glore Forgan partners had defaulted.

But this was now far too little to convince Ross that he should supply many millions more unless he and his EDS associates completely owned F. I. duPont, Glore Forgan.

Within days of the March 15 deadline, a compromise was reached with all the partners save one: The F. I. duPont, Glore Forgan partnership would be converted into a corporation in which Ross and his EDS associates would own all the common stock, but the firm's partners would share in the profits according to an elaborately detailed schedule.

The one partner who could prevent the entire agreement from being consummated was John Allyn, the man Ross had just put in the senior partner post. Because of the nature of the partnership, his signature to the agreement was essential.

Like Edmond duPont, John had inherited an investment firm, but he had managed that firm, A. C. Allyn & Co., successfully and made money in other ways, principally in real estate. He owned the Chicago White Sox as well as considerable Chicago real estate. Chicago-based A. C. Allyn & Co. had done considerable commodity business; it was the merger with A. C. Allyn & Co. that had made Francis I. duPont's commodity business bigger than that of any other firm.

If Ross took over the firm, John Allyn wanted, not just part of the profits—a bonus like an employee—but some of the common stock.

Ross refused.[15]

The board of SIPC, more by default than by action, decided to do nothing.[16]

Bunny Lasker and the rest of the Crisis Committee were back in the same position they were in November 1970 when a cabal of partners backed by Edmond duPont would not agree to Ross's terms for lending the firm $10 million. (Except that the amount needed, however, had multiplied, and SIPC now covered the customers of other firms that would be bankrupted by F. I. duPont, Glore Forgan's failure.)

John Allyn, however, could not, like Edmond duPont, be bullied by Bunny into doing something he didn't want to do.

If John refused to sign—which seemed virtually certain—F. I. duPont, Glore Forgan would be forced to declare bankruptcy. And F. I. duPont, Glore Forgan was not covered by SIPC because the firm had been in trouble prior to the passage of the act establishing SIPC. The loss of millions of dollars by hundreds of thousands of investors would have hard-to-imagine economic and political repercussions. Lawyers could point out that customers of F. I. duPont, Glore Forgan had not been explicitly assured that their money and securities were insured by SIPC. But the legal niceties would not matter. F. I. duPont, Glore Forgan customers would be outraged.

The anger of customers of relatively tiny Robinson & Co. had been frightening enough when Bob Haack stated that The New York Stock Exchange would not reimburse them frightening enough to cause Congress to hold hearings and for the Crisis Committee to backtrack.

At the minimum, the example of what would happen to the customers of F. I. duPont, Glore Forgan would discourage millions of people from investing in securities. Obtaining capital would become more costly for corporations. Politicians favoring the free-market system would be silenced, and politicans who wanted to tightly regulate or socialize businesses would gain powerful popular support.

What is more, Communists all over the world—in Vietnam, in the Soviet Union, in China—would gain faith that their system was superior. The hot war was still on in Vietnam, and the Cold War would last another 17 years.

Russ Forgan called Maury Stans in Washington—Maury was now Secretary of Commerce—and discussed the problem with him. (Jim Lynch listened on an extension.)

"I know John Allyn very well," Jim recalls Maury saying. Maury and John were both from Chicago; John had been a big contributor to the Republican Party and Nixon's 1968 campaign.

Maury called John, urging him to agree, but John replied that he wasn't going to let that son-of-a-bitch take all the profits. John said he'd lost enough money and deserved some common stock.

Maury suggested John might be given an option to buy common stock under certain conditions, but John refused even that.

Maury called Russ back and told him of John Allyn's refusal.

Russ replied that the situation would be settled one way or another a few days later at a meeting of the board of directing partners. The 15th of March (when Perot's note came due) was fast approaching.

Russ told Maury the specific date, time, and place of the meeting.

Maury said he would see what he could do.

The board met as scheduled in the board room at One Wall Street. Jim Lynch attended in his capacity as general counsel. John Allyn glared at Russ and Jim with unconcealed hostility; everyone else attempted to be friendly. John was a maverick in appearance as well as in action. Edmond duPont and Russ Forgan wore expensive, well-tailored suits; John wore an off-the-rack, ill-fitting sports coat. Edmond and Russ spoke in Eastern, upper-class accents, John in a Midwestern twang. (Class distinctions are discussed further in a later chapter.)

John said he didn't appreciate the pressure that had been put on him and emphasized he wasn't going to vote for the agreement.

As if cued in a bad melodrama, Edmond's secretary came in, "almost ashen," Jim recalls. She whispered in Edmond's ear.

Edmond, his eyes wide, said she had to be kidding. He got up and told John that he had to come with him into his office right away.

They left. Edmond returned shortly, alone, and said to Russ that if Russ thought John was angry about Maury calling, to wait until John came back from this phone conversation—that it was the President.

Richard Nixon had plenty of other worries besides F. I. duPont, Glore Forgan and The New York Stock Exchange in March 1971. Just a few days before, some offices in the Senate side of the Capitol building had been bombed, probably by the Weathermen. Nixon had to deal with the negative publicity that had resulted from the militarily successful invasion of Laos in January. First Lieutenant William Calley, Jr. was on trial for murdering 22 South Vietnamese civilians as part of a military operation. Polls put Nixon's handling of the Vietnam War at an all-time low. He had to decide what to do, if anything, over the closing of the Suez Canal. Henry Kissinger was threatening to resign. The Lockheed Aircraft Company would go bankrupt unless Nixon did something to save it— which he could do in the well-recognized interests of national defense.

John did not return from his telephone conversation with Nixon. Instead Edmond's secretary reappeared through the boardroom's doorway, carrying a letter. John Allyn had dictated it to her after he finished talking to Nixon. John had then left without saying good-bye to the other board members.

Edmond read the letter to the awed executives. In it, John Allyn agreed to Ross's proposal.

Ross was speedily told that all the partners had agreed informally to the terms that had been worked out, but now there was too little time to get formal agreements prior to March 15, much less turn the partnership into a corporation. All the agreements were oral. Given what had gone on before, a last minute hitch might develop. More than a hundred signatures needed to be obtained.

Ross agreed to a seven-day extension.

Bob Haack invited all the partners of F. I. duPont, Glore Forgan, all the subordinated and other lenders, and all the pledgors to meet at The New York Stock Exchange at 7:00 P.M. on March 17. The meeting was attended by Bunny Lasker, Felix Rohatyn, and Lee Arning. Bob Haack was blunt. He told his audience that the alternative to agreeing to the proposal worked out with Ross Perot "is for all of you to lose everything."[17]

Chuck Rousselot spoke optimistically, describing the firm's recent sales achievements and profitability, but he bluntly and honestly stated that the pledge accounts had been wiped out.

The group was told that they had only one day to consider the proposition. If they delayed, the deal was off.

Many of those attending signed their approval before leaving. All the others signed in time the next day. What alternative did they have?

The greatest possible disaster that could have occurred on Wall Street seemed to be again averted.

Many of the pledgors had not attended the meeting, even though invited. Jim was directed to phone all the non-attending pledgors and give them the bad news. Many of the pledgors were elderly duPont relatives with little knowledge of finance even though they were living on the interest and dividends from their investments. They had lent the money thinking it absolutely safe, happy to get the 7 percent or 8 percent interest.

Jim often had difficulty getting pledgors to understand what had happened. He recalls talking to duPont widows and elderly maiden relatives and typically getting a timid response indicating they didn't understand what he was telling them. Typically they would querulously ask whether they would still get monthly checks.

Jim had to tell them they would not.

The truth was that the pledgors had been getting interest to which they were not entitled for many months. Their capital had been lost at the time of the Glore Forgan and F. I. duPont & Co. merger, if not before. But Jim didn't tell them that. Why make them feel worse?

Most of the partners of the firm, however, were euphoric. John J. Trask, whose investment in the firm ranked right after that of Edmond duPont and John Allyn, said that outside of the capital squeeze, he was more bullish on the firm than he had been for the thirty years he had been with the firm, and that he had been pretty darn bullish. He thought without a doubt that they had a wonderful operation going.

He spoke too soon.

Only a few days after the agreement had been signed, the special accounting team consisting of EDS people, a new accounting firm, and members of Bob Bishop's staff reported that the $40 million additional Perot had agreed to put into the firm was not enough.

The previous negotiations had been between Ross and the F. I. duPont, Glore Forgan partners. The New York Stock Exchange officials had only acted as mediators. Now the negotiations were directly between leaders of The New York Stock Exchange and Ross.

Fortune favored the negotiators—Bunny, Felix and Ralph. The figures they and Ross looked at for December 1970 and January and February 1971[18] made F. I. duPont, Glore Forgan seem like a less risky, possibly highly profitable venture. The figures also indicated that members of The New York Stock Exchange were better able to afford being taxed again to save a member firm.

Interest rates had continued their downward trend in December 1970 as the Federal Reserve attempted to pull the economy out of the recession. Stock prices and the volume of trading had climbed. In fact, more shares were traded on The New York Stock Exchange in December 1970 than during any previous month in Wall Street's history[19]—a daily average of 15,241,000 shares—bringing the total number of shares traded for the year to a record high as well.

Stock prices had continued to rise through the early months of 1971.[20] The volume of trading on The New York Stock Exchange reached a new monthly high in January 1971 of more than 17 million shares per day, and another new high in February of more than 19 million shares.

F. I. duPont, Glore Forgan's 1,750 stockbrokers had opened more than 8,100 new accounts in January and 8,200 new accounts in February.[21] There had never been anything wrong with the sales side of F. I. duPont, Glore Forgan. In fact, its marketing—and that of its predecessor firms—had been outstanding. Part of the problem had been that the firms' advertising and stockbrokers had produced more orders than the firms' back offices could handle.

And now its order processing was shipshape. Despite the surge in volume, EDS had reduced the firm's fails to a nominal level.

F. I. duPont, Glore Forgan had made half a million dollars in January, and another half million in February and seemed likely to be twice as profitable in March.[22]

The improved condition of most member firms made Bunny now feel that he could get the governors to vote favorably on conditionally contributing money to aid the merger. And the improved condition of F. I. duPont, Glore Forgan made it appear less risky to Ross.

Ross agreed to ante up $40 million and the Exchange agreed to indemnify him for any amount over that, up to $15 million, if and when needed to keep the firm's liabilities-to-capital ratio within the Exchange's limits.[23]

Again an enormous number of investors who had thought their money and securities were safe had been saved from losses. Again The New York Stock Exchange had been saved from disgrace. Again the economy of the United States had been saved from immeasurable damage in a Perils-of-Pauline fashion.

And again much was accomplished in secret. The public and historians have never known about the immense damage to the economy that was avoided nor how narrowly that danger was avoided. John Allyn's obstinacy and Richard Nixon's role have been well-kept secrets. The reason? It has never been in the interests of anyone involved to disclose what happened—not John Allyn, not Richard Nixon, not Ross Perot, not anybody in the government or at F. I. dupont, Glore Forgan. Nobody.

When it's not in anybody's interest to disclose what is going on at the high levels of business, the public is seldom informed—even, or perhaps especially, when the public interest is in dire peril.

In this instance, continued secrecy would have deprived the public and historians of a valuable example of how the free market system, in order to function properly—perhaps even to survive—needs *extra-legal* help from government officials from time to time.

10

The Importance of Management Style

When Ross Perot was negotiating for control of F. I. duPont, Glore Forgan in late 1970 and early 1971, he had sometimes talked as if he were willing, even anxious, to withdraw entirely from the investment business. But his actions contradicted his bargaining posture. From December 15, 1970 on, he assumed the responsibility for managing F. I. duPont, Glore Forgan. And no one said him nay.

Ross decided the firm needed to be managed very differently from the way it had been in the past, a reasonable attitude considering how ineptly Maurice Stans, Archie Albright, the senior partners of Hirsch, and Edmond duPont cum Wally Latour had failed to meet the challenges of the previous five years.

Hadn't Ross become one of the richest men in the world managing EDS the way he thought a business should be managed?

Ross began by doing what top partners of Glore Forgan and of most other firms had neglected. He visited the back offices. In fact, he was ten years ahead of his time in practicing the "walking around management" that Thomas J. Peters later popularized.[1]

Ross Perot breezed into department after department, affably talked to everyone, listened intently, and dictated notes to a lieutenant, deferential at his side.

The next day, departmental officers, like Richard McDonald who headed over-the-counter trading, got a list of orders.[2]

Unfortunately, U.S. Naval Academy graduate H. Ross Perot acted like a captain assuming command of a naval vessel, not like the CEO of an investment firm. Many of the orders given department heads were picayune, such as specifying the level to which the blinds should be drawn.

Again Ross had a sound precedent from his own experience. IBM, where Ross had been a great success before founding EDS, had been successfully managed in a semi-military, trifles-are-important fashion.

Richard McDonald, who had worked at IBM too, recalls how F. I. duPont, Glore Forgan was under Ross: "You could never leave anything on your desk at night. Everything had to look neat. It ended up just like we did at IBM. We stuffed everything on the desk chair and shoved the chair under the desk. So everybody's desk top was neat. Underneath were piles of papers."

When Ross visited the firm's West Coast offices, he was appalled to see stockbrokers dressed in casual clothes, golf bags nestling against desks. He was appalled, not only by the appearance, but by many brokers leaving early in the afternoon.[3]

Ross didn't appreciate that West Coast brokers work different hours because of the three-hour time difference with the East, getting to their desks at 6:00 A.M. When he tried to reform their habits, his orders were promptly countermanded by Harry Colmery, who knew that many of his most productive brokers would leave if Ross's orders were carried out.

In an effort to get brokers to get more customers and do more business with the customers they had, Ross attempted to use the inspirational sales management techniques that had proven so successful at EDS and at IBM. He held pep talks for F. I. duPont, Glore Forgan brokers, revival style, over the firm's nation-wide intercommunication system and at huge gatherings in Dallas.[4]

This approach seemed to work for a while. He had stockbrokers enthusiastically singing comradely songs at meetings. But the stockbrokers most favorably influenced were the younger ones who had to hustle to find new clients. Less enthusiastic, even cynical, were older stockbrokers who obtained new clients by referral, who could be more like investment advisors, and whose clients entered orders in thousands of shares at a time.

What is more, the enthusiasm younger stockbrokers generated in the meetings was probably worn down by the continual rebuffs that are part of cold-calling.[5]

Ross never seemed to catch on that stockbrokers, especially ones that are already successful, differ psychologically from the kind of people EDS hired. EDS employees were relatively easy to imbue with team spirit—to be aroused to put in extraordinary efforts on the company's behalf. Each had been carefully selected for his need to identify with an entity bigger than himself. Most had happily served in the armed services.

Stockbrokers, in contrast, tend to be leaders themselves. They are successful persuaders. Most recognize the techniques when someone tries to use emotion-satisfying arguments on them. They recognize when their material interests coincide with those of the organization they belong to—and when those interests diverge. Most stockbrokers felt then and feel now that they are in business for themselves. They regard themselves, like managers of Burger King fast-food outlets, as franchisees. And managements of most successful brokerage firms behave toward stockbrokers like franchis*ers*. In fact, in a series of disputes with the Labor Department in the 1960s, many brokerage firms contended that their brokers were "independent contractors."

Ross relied too much on rhetoric and not enough on cash. He continually voiced his anger over stockbrokers leaving the firm for higher payouts by competitors, complaining that he was running a whorehouse.[6]

When Ross saw that paternalism failed, he talked to Jim Lynch (even though Jim was not at that time technically the firm's legal counsel) about using legal methods to prevent brokers from leaving. But Jim had to tell him that legally brokers could sell themselves to the highest bidder.

For EDS, Ross had developed a way of hiring people that had worked very well indeed: Prospective executives were interviewed accompanied by their wives. This had worked well because EDS employees worked long hours and were away from home for days at a time. By being part of the interview, the wives understood and supported this. Ross believed that an employee with a complaining wife would not—could not—perform at his best. Ross often made extra, personal efforts to keep EDS wives on his side. He sent them presents from time to time, and sometimes handed them checks in person. In hiring a man, he made sure his wife would respond favorably to this paternalism, but in hiring investment executives, this approach sometimes backfired.

Example: Bob Ginsburg, one of the most competent back-office executives on Wall Street, was considered for a high-level job. So Mr. and Mrs. Ginsburg were flown down to Dallas for an interview.[7]

They were ushered into an office and asked to sit down before the chief interviewer and his staff. The chief interviewer began his questioning of Mrs. Ginsburg by asking her when she first toilet-trained her child.

Mrs. Ginsburg looked at Bob, and he at her.

She said to Bob, are you going to leave or am I?

They got up and left.

Ross made what would seem to have been a sensible, even brilliant, decision when he chose an energetic, near-genius, Morton H. Meyerson, as his deputy. Mort was the vice president of EDS who had been in charge of installing EDS systems at F. I. duPont, Glore Forgan. His IQ was so high, he had completed the EDS training course in less time than anyone else ever had—even though his major courses at the University of Texas had been philosophy and art.[8]

A born and brought up Texan, Mort's appearance did not match that of the movie stereotype. He seemed shorter than average because he was pudgy. He dressed the same somber way Ross had commanded that all men at EDS dress—a dark suit, a white shirt with a narrow tie—except that instead of the laced-up wing-tip shoes he wore loafers, perhaps in a desperate effort to preserve some individuality.

Like all of Ross's followers, he was a hard worker, often calling meetings at 8:00 A.M.

Both Ross and Mort expected employees to live up to a higher moral standard than was necessary for business purposes.

Example: Several months after Ross and Mort began running the firm, a long-time Glore Forgan executive, we'll call Quincy because he prefers to remain anonymous, queried Mort about an eminently qualified employee who had not been promoted.[9]

Mort cryptically said he, Quincy, knew what the problem was.

"What are you talking about?" a puzzled Quincy responded.

Mort told Quincy that the unpromoted valuable executive, who was married, was having an affair, something Quincy vaguely suspected but had decided was none of his business.

The Perot code says that anyone who is sexually dishonest will be financially dishonest[10]—a conclusion not supported by any research.

"What am I going to tell him about why he's not going to be promoted?" asked Quincy.

Mort replied that he didn't care what Quincy told him. Mort said Ross was very straight-laced.

"How did Ross find out about it?" asked the amazed Quincy.

Mort replied that all executives had been checked out, including Quincy, telling him that he and Ross knew more about Quincy than Quincy did himself.

The not-promoted executive—who had been one of the most valuable executives in the firm, bringing in considerable investment banking business—soon left for another major firm.

After an initial spurt of attention, Ross spent most of his time in Dallas. Ross, like a naval captain, expected Mort, his second-in-command, to run the investment firm from day to day. But the arrangement had its drawbacks. In the Navy, the executive officer almost always knows what his captain would do in any given situation. Managing an investment firm, unlike managing a battleship, requires solving many unforeseen and unforeseeable problems.

"When you asked Mort for a decision," recalls Richard McDonald, "you always felt he had to check with Ross before deciding."[11]

Harry Colmery concurs: "Those guys were scared to death of Perot. All of them. If you said to Mort or any of the others, 'You want to go across the street to have a beer?' they'd have to get Perot's approval."[12]

The most competent F. I. duPont, Glore Forgan executives were the most aggravated by these delays. In the investment business, big, important decisions involving sizable sums often need to be taken promptly to be meaningful.

When Harry Colmery got fed up with the way the firm was being run, he voiced his dismay to Mort Meyerson, who suggested Harry see a man on the EDS legal staff.

Perhaps the right kind of soothing talk might have improved Harry's morale, but the lawyer used precisely the wrong kind of talk. So Harry, certainly one of the most valuable executives at the firm, a man who had turned down the Glore Forgan presidency, resigned.

On the positive side, the new computers and systems Mort Meyerson had installed for processing the firm's orders were excellent. They put the firm's back office five years ahead of its competitors in speed and accuracy.[13]

"But," Jim Lynch recalls, "these systems were expensive. We had one of the highest prices per ticket on Wall Street." *Ticket* is back office Wall Street jargon for an order.

At the same time, the revenue from each ticket was relatively low. One reason: Some of the brokers with big accounts had left, presumably annoyed at Ross's policies. Another reason: Ross and Mort failed to take the steps necessary to attract orders from institutions.[14]

The high, fixed commissions preserved by Bunny Lasker benefited brokerage firms that catered to pension funds, mutual funds, etc. Institutions were the most profitable kind of customers because a large order costs the same or little more to execute than a small order.

Even mass-oriented Merrill Lynch had seized on the big profits institution-sized orders offered. Don Regan, seeing the trend, had ordered the head of Merrill Lynch's research department to beef up his department so that Merrill Lynch could compete with Donaldson, Lufkin & Jenrette, CBWL-Hayden Stone, and other institution-oriented firms. The research head, trained in Merrill Lynch's cost-conscious ways, failed to hire the very best analysts. When Don saw that little progress was being made, he scolded the research head and told him to take the rubber band off his bank roll.[15] The research head complied, and shortly thereafter *Institutional Investor* magazine ranked Merrill Lynch analysts as among the best, benefiting Merrill Lynch's bottom line.

But Ross and Mort were still learning the investment business. They made no special effort to entice institutional investors. The firm's customers continued overwhelmingly to be individuals, many with only modest sums to invest.

Ross soon fired Benn & MacDonough, Inc., the advertising agency that had helped bring Glore Forgan Staats more business than the firm's back office could handle. Ross was under the impression that advertising was easy. Any competent executive could create an ad, his actions seem to indicate.

Years previous, when one of the executives at EDS had wanted to retain an agency to create a recruitment advertisement, Ross commanded the executive to write the ad himself.

The executive did so, and EDS was deluged with responses[16]—which seemed to justify Ross's directive. Any experienced headhunter could have told Ross that he would have been better off placing an advertisement that carefully selected prospective employees with appropriate credentials and attitudes. The responses would have been far fewer, but EDS would have saved thousands of dollars in interviewing time.

Ross upped F. I. duPont, Glore Forgan's advertising budget, and a big-name agency with little experience in investment advertising was retained.

While Ross was attempting to make F. I. duPont, Glore Forgan an example that other firms would follow, the stock market was behaving like a flirtatious woman who accepts an ardent suitor's diamonds but has no intention of granting the suitor's desires.

As described in the previous chapter, when Ross had been negotiating to take over the firm during the first three months of 1971, stock prices and the volume of trading had increased, and F. I. duPont, Glore Forgan had been profitable.

Agreement was reached, orally, late in March but the agreement was not signed. While legal problems were being worked out, stock prices teasingly rose further.

On May, 15, 1971, duPont Glore Forgan, Inc. was officially formed, and the coquettish stock market frowned on Ross. Stock prices and volumes went down in May, and in June, and in July.[17]

In August, duPont Glore Forgan missed an unusual opportunity to supply its brokers with thousands of much-needed quality leads.

The opportunity was presented by President Nixon surprising the nation with his New Economic Policy in a televised speech on Sunday night, August 15:

The United States was reneging on its promises to redeem paper dollars held by foreign nationals with gold, just as it had reneged in 1933 on the same promise to U.S. citizens. The United States was no longer even on a modified gold standard.

All imports were to be taxed 10 percent.

Taxes were to be reduced for U.S. corporations manufacturing machinery and equipment in the United States.

And wages and prices were frozen.[18]

The policy resulted from a deterioration in international trade, rising unemployment, and Nixon's desire to insure his reelection in November 1972.

Secretary of Commerce Maurice F. Stans had stated on June 25, 1971, that the United States "has been losing, and is continuing to lose its competitiveness in world markets."[19] The United States no longer led the world in exporting manufactured goods, he said. Germany did.

The United States was suffering its first trade deficit since 1888. More money was flowing out of the United States than was coming in. This required, under international agreements then in effect, that the United States ship out enough gold to compensate.

In the week of August 9, 1971, a representative of the United Kingdom had asked the U.S. Treasury to send his country $3 billion in gold.[20]

Nixon could have complied with the British request, but if every foreigner asked for gold, he would be embarrassed. At the then current of gold, foreigners held paper dollars worth more than all the gold in the U.S. Treasury.[21]

Over the weekend of August 13–15, Nixon and his advisors had concocted his New Economic Policy. It was designed to postpone all the nation's economic problems—unemployment, inflation, the unfavorable balance of trade—until after the November 1972 election.

The suddenness and far-reaching nature of the changes made many, if not most, decisions about how to invest obsolete, besides creating great uncertainty. People were used to thinking of paper money as a substitute for gold or silver. The idea of money whose value was determined by what it could buy and other economic forces was worrisome to say the least. One effect would be to cause the price of gold to climb more or less steadily from $35 an ounce. This was bearish for stocks because some of the money that investors used to buy gold would not be used to buy stocks.

Taxing imports 10 percent could be anticipated to increase the earnings of domestic companies that competed with foreign companies by enabling them to sell more goods and services. They wouldn't, however, to be able to raise prices because prices were frozen. This was bullish for some companies, bearish for others.

Earnings of corporations manufacturing machinery and equipment in the United States could be expected to benefit, and consequently the prices of their stocks.

Within minutes after Nixon completed speaking on Sunday evening, the advertising agency that Ross Perot had fired (Benn & MacDonough) began creating an ad that capitalized on this event. Copy and layout for the ad were placed on the desk of the advertising manager of one of duPont Glore Forgan's competitors, Walston & Co., the morning after Nixon's speech. Walston was one of the nation's largest brokerage firms with offices from coast to coast. (More about Walston later.)

In the ad, Walston's research department offered to review investors' portfolios to take advantage of investment opportunities created by Nixon's announcement. Walston also offered to help investors protect themselves against the dangers the policy created.

The effect of Nixon's New Economic Policy was so uncertain and complicated—and consequently fearsome to many investors—that the ad, placed in the *Wall Street Journal*, produced many thousands of leads for Walston brokers to follow up—leads of the kind duPont Glore Forgan brokers needed and wanted badly. The Walston ad was weeks ahead of similar ads eventually placed by a few competing brokerage firms.

Spurred by Nixon's announcement, stock prices and the volume of trading rose temporarily but declined in October and November.[22]

In December 1971, however, Nixon's New Economic Policy combined with back-to-back deficits in the federal budget for the years ended June 30, 1971, and June 30, 1972, began to affect the economy and the stock market in a positive way.

Never before had the economy been so stimulated—not even during Johnson's Vietnam War–cum–War-on-Poverty years: a $23 million deficit in 1971 and a $24 million deficit in 1972.

Fewer people were out of work as gross national product zoomed up. Yet the rate of inflation, held down by the price and wage freezes, declined in 1971 and stayed down in 1972.[23]

Stock prices rose more or less steadily. The volume of trading rose significantly. A record daily average of 16½ million shares would be established for 1972.[24]

Most brokerage firms prospered, but duPont Glore Forgan, Inc. did not.

The failure of Ross Perot's management style to produce profits for duPont Glore Forgan in the 1970s proves the validity of the attitude of most business managers today. As American business has shifted from a largely industrial economy to a largely service economy, military-style management has proven to be increasingly obsolete.

Teamwork is necessary in any endeavor involving a sizable number of people. In the military, teamwork is often achieved by blind, unquestioning obedience to orders. The willing obedience to those orders is often engendered through inspirational leadership and by the joy felt by all in being part of something bigger than their individual selves.

In a service business, teamwork is engendered by communciation— by unfettered talking and writing, not just to the supervised, but to fellow supervisors, and to those in authority.

In a service business, the salespeople and others who deal with customers must often be coddled. That's why Harry Colmery and others turned down the presidency of Glore Forgan Staats, Inc. A CEO of a service company, to perhaps exagerrate, is often the servant of its stars rather than the other way around.

In a service business, the salespeople or others who deal with customers must be listened to by those who supervise them—even encouraged to speak up when they feel their company's policies and procedures are harming their company's profitability.

If information and advice had flowed upward at duPont Glore Forgan—as it usually does in a successful service business—top management would have been made aware of how important orders from institutional investors were to the firm's profitability.

Much in this chapter has heretofore been hidden: Ross's blocking the promotion of an extremely able executive because of that executive's adultery; the interview with Bob Ginsburg and his wife; Ross's asking Jim for a legal way to prevent stockbrokers from leaving; the need to refer so many decisions to Ross; duPont Glore Forgan's high ticket prices and low profit margin per ticket; and some other details of how Ross managed duPont Glore Forgan.

Ross Perot did not change his management style. Instead, a deal-maker at heart, he turned elsewhere for a solution to making duPont Glore Forgan profitable, a story to be told in a later chapter.

11

The Reality of U.S. Government Employment[1]

Jim Lynch had always been able to amicably resolve any differences he had with members of top management until Ross Perot effectively took control of F. I. duPont, Glore Forgan in late 1970. When Jim had disagreed with Russ Forgan or Harry Colmery or even with Maury Stans or Glore Forgan vice chairman Charley Hodge, Jim's objection, suggestion, or misunderstanding would be talked out, sometimes vigorously, but always with mutual respect.

Working with Edmond duPont and Wally Latour had been less easy. Matters needed to be carefully, deferentially and briefly explained to Edmond duPont—but they could be explained. And while Jim and Wally often differed, Wally would always politely and carefully consider any thoughts Jim had, and they would usually reach a conclusion through discussion.

This changed under the Perot absolute monarchy in which Mort Meyerson acted as viceroy. All too often Ross or Mort told Jim what to do, told him to do it fast, and then asked why he hadn't done what he had been ordered to do before he had time to do it. Jim found himself thinking nostalgically back to the sixties; he realized he hadn't sufficiently appreciated the aura of gentlemanly reasonableness and cooperative endeavor that Russ Forgan's and Edmond duPont's old-fashioned good manners had established.

While Jim was wondering whether he should look for another job, he got a call from Bill Casey, who offered Jim an exciting future.

President Nixon had nominated Casey to be chairman of the Securities and Exchange Commission in February 1971. Casey was one of the most knowledgeable men to hold the job. For several years before going into the OSS he had written and edited a publication on tax and securities laws. He also had had hands-on experience counseling Glore Forgan and similar clients. As SEC chairman, he felt that many changes were needed to be made in securities regulation. He especially wanted prospectuses to be more readable so that ordinary investors, not just lawyers, could understand the risks involved in any new issue of securities.

People who met Casey for the first time often under-rated him. He was never neatly dressed. Dandruff sprinkled the sleeves of the dark blue suits he usually wore. Hairs sprouted out of his ears. He often gnawed on his tie while talking. And he tended to ramble in vague generalities until he got to know his interlocutor well.

But many of those who worked with him admired and liked him. He had friends in high places all over the world. General Charles de Gaulle, for example, continued the warm relationship he had with Casey during World War II even after Casey left the OSS, even after deGaulle became President of France.

Promptly after Casey was appointed SEC chairman, he discussed his forthcoming responsibility with Jim. Among other ideas, Jim suggested an executive director be appointed to take care of the general running of the SEC. The chairman, Jim said, should not become become so involved in the nitty-gritty of administration that he did not devote enough time to considering policy, the true responsibilities of the chairman.

Casey had not only been impressed with Jim's suggestions, Casey had decided that having an executive director was a great idea, and that Jim was the ideal man for the job. But Casey had not immediately so informed Jim. He first discussed the contemplated appointment with Secretary of Commerce Maury Stans.

Maury had immediately replied: Nothing doing, he's too valuable where he is—referring to Jim's current position as general counsel and the problems F. I. duPont, Glore Forgan was having, especially the fall-out from the Penn Central bankruptcy (described in the next chapter).

Casey thereafter reorganized the SEC to include executive director but asked someone else to fill that position. A year later the position became vacant, and Casey again thought of Jim, who this time could not be deemed indispensable to F. I. duPont, Glore Forgan.

Casey telephoned Jim and offered him the executive directorship.

Jim was overjoyed. He flew to Washington and discussed the anticipated appointment with Casey.

But when he asked Casey what the position would pay, his joy turned to dismay. He couldn't live on the salary Casey offered. He had a wife and two children, and he was making monthly payments to Chemical Bank (now Chase) on the money he had borrowed to become a partner of Glore Forgan and then F. I. duPont, Glore Forgan.

"Can't the salary be increased?" Jim asked.

Casey told him that there wasn't a chance of that happening, adding that he hardly got more than what Jim would be paid.

So a disheartened Jim decided to try to adapt to the Ross Perot way of doing business.

Nowadays, just as in the seventies, the lower pay received by lawyers working at the SEC—or in any other department of the U.S. government—necessarily affects the motivations of those who work there.

Some of the lawyers, much less than half, who work at the Securities and Exchange Commission accept the SEC's lower pay primarily because the experience will significantly increase their income when they leave.[2]

The remaining big majority can be further divided into two kinds of people. A small number are those who could get jobs at much higher salaries but enjoy what they do so much that they stay where they are. Someone like Stanley Sporkin, for example, could have doubled, tripled, even quadrupled his income by becoming a partner in a law firm.

The remaining number are worth what they are paid.

All of the above is also more or less true of the SEC Commissioners. Some, like Bill Casey and Arthur Levitt, who became Chairman in 1992, take the job because they have plenty of money and want to influence the nation's affairs. Some commissioners were and are only worth what they are paid or are looking for a better paying job in the free market.

Hamer Budge, for example, fit this last category. He was a defeated politician for whom President Johnson had to find a job. Budge knew so little about the securities business that policy was decided by his fellow four commissioners.[3] He took care of the petty details and basically took orders from the other commissioners. And at the same time he overtly tried for a good-paying job in industry[4]—which he eventually got.

Consider the significance of this: The heart of the free market system, the investment business, is policed mostly by people who don't want to work in the free market or who can't make as much money in the free market. Isn't it likely, knowing human nature, that they will be antagonistic to the free market, want to socialistically control it, and sometimes damage it?

For example, in the 1990s, the SEC tried to fix the percentage that dealers could mark up stocks and bonds not listed on any Exchange that dealers bought from investors with the intention of reselling to other investors. If the SEC had succeeded, the market for the riskiest kind of stocks and bonds traded over-the-counter would have been damaged. If regulations forbade a dealer from making a big profit on a risky stock, the dealer wouldn't buy the stock in the first place. Consequently, an investor trying to sell a risky stock or bond not listed on an exchange would have had difficulty, sometimes discover it impossible, to find a buyer.

Even so, the staff of the SEC may be superior to the staffs of other federal departments. Jim Lynch, who has worked closely with the SEC for more than fifty years cannot recall any scandal involving a staff member or commissioner of the SEC. This despite the great temptations provided staff members and commissioners by virtue of their inside knowledge of the securities business.

Furthermore, the staffs of other agencies and other departments are less likely to be sympathetic to the needs of business than the staff of the SEC. This may be because few men and women who work for other federal agencies and departments—except lawyers in the Justice Department—expect to leave and benefit from the higher pay of the free-market system. Early in 2000, SEC Chairman Arthur Levitt asked Congress to raise the salaries of its employees, especially those of lawyers and accountants, so as to reduce "an alarming rate of turnover."[5]

12

How the U.S. Government Has Tried to Prevent Insider Trading—And Why It Has Failed

On December 22, 1970, the *New York Times*, the *Wall Street Journal*, and other newspapers across the country carried stories telling of insider trading by a partner of F. I. duPont Glore Forgan.[1] Some facts about that scandal not included in those and subsequent stories are worth revealing for several reasons.

This was the scandal that made it impossible for the firm's partners to raise the mere $5 million they had promised Ross Perot they would contribute to the firm's capital—and so justified Ross Perot demanding 100 percent ownership of F. I. duPont, Glore Forgan in 1971.

It involved the biggest bankruptcy of any kind of business in U.S. history till that time—that of the Penn Central Railroad.

It is an example of the arbitrary use of government power that is being used increasingly by members of the federal government.

And the telling of these facts may give some investors a valuable insight they would not otherwise gain.

The partner accused of insider trading in the newspaper stories was Charles J. Hodge, who had been the number two man at Glore Forgan Staats, Inc. and who had spurned the possibility of becoming the firm's president when Maury Stans left in 1968.

Before this scandal, Charley Hodge had never been accused of wrongdoing of any kind. In fact, he was widely liked and admired because of his character and achievements. When Jim Lynch was Glore Forgan's compliance director, he never had any problems with Charley Hodge.

Charley had already become a legendary figure on Wall Street before World War II because of his trading of railroad bonds. The prices of railroad bonds fluctuated widely during the Great Depression years, and

Charley had proved especially skillful at judging which railroad bonds to buy, which to sell, and when. Charley had been no ordinary trader. He had done his own research and was an outstanding salesman. He had made fortunes for his clients and himself.

When the Japanese bombed Pearl Harbor, Charley was a major in a socially elite National Guard cavalry unit in Essex County, New Jersey. The unit became part of General George C. Patton's Third Army, fighting its way across Europe. As a colonel, Charlie participated in the relief of Bastogne in the Battle of the Bulge. As the war ended, he was made a brigadier general.

Charley's transition into investment banking had been virtually automatic because of his skill as a trader and researcher in railroad bonds, his convivial personality, and his thoughtfulness of others. Charley had become known, liked, admired, and trusted by top executives at virtually every major railroad in the United States.

"He was the kind of a guy who could build up these warm, unbelievable friendships with people," Jim Lynch recalls. "If you needed help and he knew about it, you didn't need to ask him to do you a favor. He would anticipate your need. When my father was close to dying and I didn't know where to turn, Charley called me into his office one day and handed me a slip of paper on which was written the name of an outstanding diagnostician. He told me he had made arrangements for the specialist to see my father. How he knew that was what I needed I don't know because I had never mentioned my predicament to him."[2]

In February 1968, Charley arranged the merger of the Pennsylvania Railroad and the New York Central Railroad, thus forming the largest privately owned railroad in the United States. It appeared at the time to be the greatest achievement in his life. Glore Forgan Staats had trumpeted the glory of that merger—and the firm's genius in arranging it—in full page advertisements in the *Wall Street Journal* and the *New York Times*.[3] But the luster of the achievement vanished when the merged company went bankrupt in June 1970.

Was Charley responsible for the bankruptcy? The lead story on the first financial page of the *New York Times* on December 22, 1970, made it appear so.

"One of the saddest—and at times—one of the most sordid—pictures of the American business community that has ever been revealed in an official document," Representative Wright Patman was quoted as stating in a letter of transmittal of a report to the committee that Wright headed.

The *New York Times* story quoting the report also stated: "The Pennsylvania's disastrous non-railroad investment program was mapped to a large extent by Charles J. Hodge, a senior member of the investment firm of F. I. duPont–Glore Forgan."

This statement—that the non-railroad investment program was "disastrous"—was just plain wrong.

Federal laws and regulations at the time made it very difficult for a railroad to be profitable. Rates were set by the Interstate Commerce Commission—and the rates favored truckers in many instances.

Charley had helped the Pennsylvania Railroad make several successful acquisitions whose revenues were not set by the ICC. One was Arvida Corporation, a huge real estate company in Florida. It bought up and developed many square miles of Florida wilderness. Most of the area around Boca Raton is built on Arvida land, as is much of Disneyworld.

Charley had persuaded the directors of the railroad to start a propane gas company, Tropigas, which became the biggest supplier of propane gas in the Bahamas and West Indies. He had also helped the Pennsylvannia Railroad acquire two pipelines. All the acquisitions Charley guided into the Pennsylvania Railroad fed profits into the parent company.

There is no question, however, that Charley Hodge engaged in what would be regarded today as insider trading.[4]

Back in 1962, Charley and David C. Bevan, the top financial man at the Pennsylvania Railroad, had formed an investment club, called Penphil. Other members were their wives, other executives at Penn Central and Glore Forgan & Co., and a few friends, but Charlie and David Bevan made the decisions.[5]

The club bought shares in Great Southwest Corporation. Seventeen months later the Pennsylvania Railroad acquired the company. A few months after that Penphil sold its Great Southwest shares, realizing a net profit of $212,500—a return of 180 percent in less than 2½ years.

The members of the club actually got a much higher return from this and other investments because the club mostly bought stocks with borrowed money. Chemical Bank (in 1998 named Chase after a merger) had lent the club money at only one point above the prime rate—a very favorable rate, on it was not likely to charge other investment clubs. Penphil was charged such low interest, it was alleged, because the Pennsylvannia Railroad did so much business with Chemical.

The club bought large blocks of stock in two banks in Boca Raton, Florida, while Arvida was carrying out its intensive program of real estate development in the area. The club sold its shares three years later, nearly tripling its money.

The club invested in several other companies closely tied to the Pennsylvania Railroad and made handsome profits in each instance.[6]

Charley and David Bevan were indicted in March 1971, three months after the Congressional hearings began. The eager[7] prosecutor was Arlen Specter,[8] who later became a Senator from Pennsylvania and a Presidential aspirant.

But they were not convicted—despite the uncontested fact that they engaged in the kind of insider trading that would be considered illegal today. Why? Because there was no specific SEC regulation forbidding what they did.

Even today, buying or selling securities based on inside information is specifically forbidden only to executives in the company concerned and to owners of more than 10 percent of the stock of the company.

But what about Ivan Boesky and Michael Milken?

Neither was convicted of insider trading but both were sent to jail for fraud.[9]

There are no regulations against insider trading except by obvious insiders because the commissioners and staff of the Securities and Exchange Commission prefer not to promulgate appropriate rules or regulations.

"The main reason for not defining fraudulent insider trading is that once defined, people would get right up to the line or approach it from a different direction," an SEC spokesman stated in 1998.

In other words, what is and is not insider trading has been and is now decided not by law but by men. An individual can only judge what is likely to result in prosecution by looking at previous cases and by judging the attitude of members of the SEC and prosecutors. They have gained the power desired by despotic rulers: to prosecute whomever they please and not prosecute whomever they please for insider trading.

English history is studded with classic examples of rule by *men* increasingly[10] being replaced by rule by *law* such as the Magna Carta, the Petition of Right,[11] and the Glorious Revolution of 1688.[12]

In contrast, American history after the establishment of the present constitution in 1787 is studded with examples of individuals with political power—most conspicuouly Presidents—replacing law with what they believe to be right and/or necessary. Abraham Lincoln authorized the issuance of greenbacks—paper money not backed by gold or silver as was then required by law.[13] Franklin Delano Roosevelt forced the U.S. Supreme Court to approve measures the justices thought illegal by threatening to pack the court with additional justices who would bring in the verdicts he personally wanted.[14] Presidents Truman, Johnson, Bush, and Clinton have waged war without asking for a declaration of war by Congress, as is required by the Constitution.[15]

In every instance—or nearly so, depending upon one's politics—it can be argued that these actions were clearly in the national interest or otherwise admirable. But often law-abiding citizens suffered. Two examples: People who had saved money suffered from the inflation and resulting loss in purchasing power that Lincoln's issuance of greenbacks caused.[16] Many draftees and enlistees have been forced to risk their lives and die in wars they thought wrong or unnecessary.

Charley Hodge was a victim of that kind. In the judgement of those who knew him, he would not have engaged in the kind of insider trading he did if it had clearly been prohibited by law. The loose definition of insider trading allows the SEC and other prosecutors to ruin a man even though he has not broken any specific rule or regulation.

Charley Hodge was declared not guilty, but he was ruined both financially and personally. Ross Perot insisted that he be fired from F. I. duPont, Glore Forgan within days after the first story appeared in newspapers. Charley hired three legal firms. The litigation stretched out over several years, costing him millions. He had to sell his newly built Short Hills mansion at a loss.

What is more, the Congressional hearings revealed—and the newspapers reported—that he had behaved sexually like, unfortunately, some other men with power. Charley had helped Penn Central set up a subsidiary, Executive Jet, with an impressive board of directors. They included the actor Jimmy Stewart, who had held the rank of brigadier general in the Air Force; General Curtis LeMay, who had commanded the Strategic Air Command; and Arthur Godfrey, the entertainer, who had a great interest in aviation.

Stewardesses, as a condition of employment with Executive Jet Aviation, were expected to—and did—go out on dates with Charley and other Pennsylvania executives, even travelled overseas with them not as stewardesses but as companions.[17] Charley was married with grown children.

So deserved social disgrace was added to undeserved financial ruin.

Politicians prosecuted Charley not because he broke the law—which he hadn't—but for one or two reasons: one, perhaps to divert attention from the true cause of the Penn Central bankruptcy, inept Federal regulation; and, two, because attitudes had changed.

Whatever the motives of the politicians, the real cause of the bankruptcy of the Penn Central Railroad was hidden from the general public by politicans and a media eager to think the worst of businessmen and to lay the blame somewhere other than on government regulation.

The publicity given to the prosecution of a few blatant inside traders also has hidden until very recently the ineffectiveness of the SEC's current policy and measures.

Before World War II, nobody cared much about insider trading. Everyone knew it existed, and large numbers of investors, far from wanting to stop it, wanted to get on the inside and profit by knowing in advance when companies were going to raise their dividends, split their stock, be taken over by another company, etc.

It was then common practice for a broker who received an order to buy a big block of stock—one that would almost surely push the price of the stock up—to delay entering that order for a few seconds until he entered a small order for the same stock on his own account. He thus made a small profit when the large order pushed the price of the stock up.

Charlie Merrill made the first move to limit this "front-running" in 1940 when he established principles for the newly created Merrill Lynch, E. A. Pierce, & Cassatt. One of his ten publicized commandments designed to attract individual investors forbade the front-running of stocks by Merrill Lynch account executives. Even in the 1990s, debates would be held as to the specifics of when front-running was illegal. Several mutual fund managers would be revealed in the mid-1990s as engaging in the practice, but, while tut-tutted by the press, they would not be prosecuted by the SEC or any other governmental body.

"What was the sense on Wall Street and particularly, at The New York Stock Exchange in the 1950s of what insider information was, and was it a bad thing, or whatever?" the NYSE oral history interviewer asked Lee Arning.

"There was no sense of what it was," Arning replied. "As a matter of fact, there was a kind of belief prevailing that if you could get to know something before the other guy did, you were going to benefit and that was the way the game was played. There was nothing wrong."

This attitude changed as ownership of common stocks became more widespread. Society was only imperceptibly damaged when, in the words of Frank Zarb, the stock market "consisted of a bunch of rich people selling stocks to other rich people."[18] If an investor bought a conservative stock for dividends and long-term growth, what did it matter if he or she paid an eighth or a quarter or even a full dollar a share more for it originally? Anyway, the broker was often a relative or personal friend. And if an investor wanted to speculate, he took his chances, knowing that insider trading existed.

But when millions of individuals became modestly wealthy and thus a potential source of capital in the late fifties and sixties, blatant insider trading needed to be curbed—or appear to be curbed. Few of the millions of additional investors had rich relatives or friends on the inside who could give them valid inside information. And few were high enough up the corporate ladder to be privy to key information about their companies' future earnings and other prospects.

Consequently, to give new investors confidence they would get a fair deal by investing—and to gain votes for politicians—investors and potential investors had to be made to feel they would be treated fairly. Otherwise many would not buy stocks, thus hampering economic growth.

However, defining insider trading is not easy. Suppose a corporate treasurer of XYZ Company tells his brother that his company will soon report earnings far lower than analysts predict. If the brother sells his stock in that company promptly and the stock subsequently declines when the lower earnings are publicly reported, should the brother be declared guilty of insider trading?

Yes, according the U.S. Supreme Court.

But suppose the brother advises a friend who owns the stock that he ought to sell without giving the friend a reason—and the friend sells in time to save himself thousands of dollars. Is the friend guilty of insider trading?

Perhaps. Perhaps not.

Suppose an analyst discovers that the earnings of a highly regarded stock are fraudulent and so advises his clients before the public knows, and the price of the stock plummets. Is he guilty of abetting insider trading?

The SEC said yes in the case of Equity Funding, but the U.S. Supreme Court over-ruled, finding the analyst, Ray Dirks, not guilty.

No matter what the SEC does, it will always be true that some investors will get news affecting the price of stocks sooner than others and so be able to act more promptly and so more profitably.

When a company publicly announces some startling news that will affect the price of its stock, who does a broker call first with the news, enabling them perhaps to profit by acting more promptly than investors who get the news minutes later? Usually institutional and other large investors get called first. No regulator can stop that.

The difficulty of defining insider trading may be the reason for regulations against insider trading evolving even more slowly outside the United States. Not until 1994, for example, would the Bundestag pass a law making insider trading illegal in Germany.[19]

The prosecution of blatant inside traders under the SEC's loose definition of insider trader does reduce the amount of insider trading somewhat by making those who are tempted fear they may be caught. But mostly the efforts to curb insider trading are window-dressing to make investors feel they are getting a fair deal.

Because insider trading still goes on, the average individual investor needs to be aware that any news he or she gets about coming dividend increases, stock splits, rising or declining earnings, etc. is very probably already known—and has been acted upon—by other investors or has rightly been anticipated by skilled and knowledgeable arbitrageurs and speculators.

One example: In November 1998, shares of Mobil soared for three days prior to Exxon announcing that the two firms would merge.

Another example: On Friday, February 20, 1999, three stocks jumped in price for no publicly known reason. Sundstrand jumped 12 percent. KN Energy jumped 11 percent. And Consolidated Gas jumped 6.6 percent. Nobody seemed to know why. But they did on Monday. All three turned out to be takeover targets.

One big hedge fund manager commented, "We're back to the good old days where everything is leaked."[20]

13

The Twists and Turns toward the Reorganization of The New York Stock Exchange

The final months of 1970 and the year 1971 were even more turbulent and stress-filled than has been described in previous chapters. On November 17, 1970, President Bob Haack made a speech[1] before the Economic Club of New York that shook the very foundations of The New York Stock Exchange. The speech enraged Bunny Lasker who as you may remember had just saved giant Goodbody & Co. from bankruptcy, was strugglying to save even bigger F. I. duPont, Glore Forgan from bankruptcy, was dealing with the actual bankruptcies of several smaller firms, and was trying to get the Securities Investors Protection Corporation bill passed.

Bob Haack chose this time, when the very existence of The New York Stock Exchange was in more danger than ever before, to openly reveal his antagonism toward Bunny Lasker—or perhaps more accurately, his antagonism to Bunny's objectives and methods.

Bunny Lasker wanted not just to preserve The New York Stock Exchange; he wanted to preserve it as it always had been. His motives, in the judgment of men who knew him such as Ed O'Brien and Jim Lynch, were not just economic. His firm was profiting handsomely from the high, fixed commissions that NYSE rules mandated, but he also loved the institution for its own sake, especially the comradeship and the trust the members had in him.[2]

But he was not rigid in his defensive strategies. Like a wise commander-in-chief he avoided Pyrrhic victories. He had done little, you may remember, to prevent Dan Lufkin and his DLJ partners from changing the rules so that member firms could sell shares in their firms to the public.

Bob Haack too wanted to preserve The New York Stock Exchange. If the Exchange collapsed, he, not Bunny, would be blamed. Bunny, Felix Rohaytn, Ralph DeNunzio and the other members of the Crisis Committee were unpaid, part-time volunteers. Bob Haack was the paid, full-time professional in charge of the other professionals. What is more, Bunny was an able politician. Most of the members felt at one with him. And, of course, it couldn't be the members' own fault—could it?—if The New York Stock Exchange became just one of several stock exchanges?

In late October 1970, Bob Haack decided he was not going to put up with Bunny's ad hoc defenses any longer. Near bankruptcy! After near bankruptcy! After near *bankruptcy!* Some prevented by mergers, some by assessing members millions of dollars, some averted just by luck. The lack of planning was counter to everything taught at Harvard Business School.

And even if The New York Stock Exchange continued to exist, Bunny's reactionary attitude entailed another serious risk: That The New York Stock Exchange would lose its position as the leading stock exchange in the world.

When Bob Haack became president in 1967, only 10 percent of the orders for stocks listed on The New York Stock Exchange were executed on other exchanges or over-the-counter. By 1970—just three years later—this percentage had nearly doubled. Further, 35 percent to 45 percent of the orders for 10,000 shares or more for NYSE listed stocks were being traded elsewhere in 1970.[3]

There was every reason to believe that these debilitating trends would continue unless appropriate measures were taken, measures that Bunny showed no sign of adopting.

Bob Haack did not want to end up like Winston Churchill who, following World War II, said "I have not become the King's First Minister in order to preside over the liquidation of the British Empire"[4] but then, willy-nilly, lived to see what he feared and hated happen.

The New York Stock Exchange was losing business to other Exchanges and the over-the-counter market principally because of the way its members charged for executing orders. The commission schedule was high and fixed. Exchange rules compelled every member to charge the same rate.

In 1968 the Justice Department had challenged fixed rates so vigorously that the Exchange governors had been forced to act. But the governors had done as little as they could, voting a discount of about 40 percent on trades of 10,000 shares or more. Even with a 40 percent reduction, the commission on a large order continued to be excessive for the service performed.

Just by charging less to execute a trade, the Midwest Stock Exchange or the Pacific Coast Stock Exchange or an over-the-counter firm often got an order, especially a large order, ordinarily traded on The New York Stock Exchange.

What is more, other exchanges were allowing mutual funds and other institutional investors to become members of their exchanges. No independent brokerage firm got any commission at all!

As a consequence, The New York Stock Exchange was losing an ever-increasing number of orders to the over-the-counter market and regional exchanges.

But Bob Haack would have been wasting his time trying to persuade imperious Bunny to back a change in the fixed-rate system. As would talking to the governors; 14 out of the 33 were floor partners;[5] most, like Bunny, were eager to keep the fountain of wealth flowing from high, fixed commissions unrestrained for as long as possible.

Bunny and other floor brokers were getting very rich indeed from the many orders—especially institutional orders—that their brokerage firms were getting at non-competitive rates.

Bunny would also almost certainly vigorously oppose other radical changes in The New York Stock Exchange—changes that Bob Haack believed needed to be made if The New York Stock Exchange were to continue to exist as the world's preeminent stock exchange.

In October, Bob Haack received an invitation from the Economic Club of New York to make a speech before its members and guests on November 17, 1970. The Economic Club was and continues to be a prestigious organization consisting of top officers of big corporations and investment firms.

Bob, desperate, decided to use that speaking engagement to openly challenge Bunny and his adherents. Perhaps public opinion could force Bunny and some other governors to stop sucking blood from the weakening Exchange and instead provide it with the remedies it needed.

But before openly defying Bunny and many of the other floor partners, Bob took a step that might mollify Bunny and disgruntled NYSE members.

Bob knew how much Bunny hated Executive Vice President John Cunningham. John's personality inflamed Bunny and vice versa. Both were tough.[6]

For about two and a half years—ever since Bunny had become vice chairman and then chairman—these two combustible personalities, each accustomed to dominating, had been forced to talk regularly to each other over the telephone and in person. They often clashed at the weekly meetings of the Crisis Committee.

John Cunningham was also disliked by many members of The New York Stock Exchange for the way he had forced the Central Certificate System on them before it was perfected.

Furthermore, John had firmly backed up Bob Bishop and Lee Arning when they restricted the income-producing activities of badly managed firms. Some members were angry at these three Exchange officials because their firms had been put on restriction. Others were angry just because they had been threatened with restriction and had to find additional capital.

A third group—including the heads of firms that were well managed and well financed—were angry because they felt John, Lee, and Bob Bishop had not been strict enough with the under-financed, poorly managed firms.[7]

Lee's disarming personality deflected much of the anger of members toward the other two. John's toughness attracted the anger like a powerful magnet.[8]

In October, Bob Haack warned John, "They're after both our heads."

In November—on the Saturday before the Tuesday when Bob Haack was to make his Economic Club speech—Bob visited John's home. After a few preliminaries, Bob told John that he ought to resign.

John thought to himself, "I could fight this, but what kind of people are they?"[9]

The media, echoing the NYSE public relations officer, would later report that John's resignation was not connected to Bob's speech. Logically it wasn't—it was emotionally and tactically connected. The timing indicates that Bob Haack thought firing John Cunningham would somewhat cool the anger he anticipated his speech would inevitably arouse in Bunny Lasker and other members who wished to preserve the status quo.

"Cunningham lost his job because nobody was ready for a central certificate system," recalls Norm Swanton. "The governors had put it off, put it off, put it off for years. He forced the firms to go live." (That is, stop experimenting and actually adopt the system). "If he hadn't done it that way, we'd never have got it. Now you couldn't live without it. I credit him as having done a great service to Wall Street."[10]

John Cunningham's resignation accomplished, Bob Haack stood before an audience of business leaders at the Economic Club of New York in the Waldorf-Astoria on November 17, 1970, and said:

"I am concerned lest we bask solely in the glory of the past, and in the process become oblivious to emerging trends. . . . The New York Stock Exchange, to put it crassly, no longer has the only game in town."[11]

He also said that "our industry leaders . . . might well consider fully negotiated commissions as an ultimate objective. . . . Better would it be for the industry to make its own competitive adjustments as economic conditions warrant, rather than work on a new schedule as it has for eight years with still no end in sight."[12]

Fully negotiated commissions!

He was proposing, like a true exponent of capitalism, that the price

charged for transferring capital from one person to another be determined by market forces.

Bob went even further and struck at the very way The New York Stock
Exchange was governed: .

"In the near future I will be presenting definitive proposals to our
Board . . . which, hopefully, will lead to a major restructuring of the New
York Stock Exchange. The Exchange must, in my opinion, do all that it
can to be a most efficient, businesslike organization, responsive to the
needs of the public and membership, if it is to continue to serve as the
marketplace it has been for more than 178 years."

Bob aimed a cannon not only at the *incomes* of those who benefited
from high fixed commissions but directly at the political *power* of the
brokers!

"All kinds of hell broke loose," recalls Lee Arning."

"Wall St. Shaken By Haack Speech" shouted a *New York Times* headline.[13]

"It's a pretty sick patient to be performing major surgery on," said
Richard Jenrette, whose firm was founded on the high, fixed commissions that institutions paid.

"It's ridiculous!" said Clifford Michel, Loeb Rhoades CEO and incoming chairman of the Association of Stock Exchange Firms.

"He's way off base," said Harold A. ("Chuck")[14] Rousselot, who, as
previously noted, would later become president of F. I. duPont, Glore
Forgan. At the time, he was head of F. I. duPont, Glore Forgan's sizable
commodity division and the incoming president of the Association of
Stock Exchange Firms.

In the privacy of his office, Bunny stormed back and forth, shouting
that the president doesn't make policies.[15] To Terry Robarts of the *New
York Times* Bunny stated, "The policy of the New York Stock Exchange
is made by this board of governors, not by the president."[16]

To head off Bob Haack's revolutionary proposals, Bunny adopted a
suggestion made the day following Bob's speech by Howard Stein, CEO
of Dreyfus & Co., a mutual fund management company. Stein's suggestion seemed constructive to the unwary, but was a time-tested method
for slowing down reform: appoint a committee to study the problem.
Bunny modified Howard Stein's suggestion by reducing the committee
to one man, to be appointed by Bunny. That man could be one that
Bunny thought could be counted on to make conservative recommendations.

Bunny chose William McChesney Martin.[17] He had been president of
the Exchange from 1939 to 1941 and had recently resigned as Chairman
of the Board of Governors of the Federal Reserve System after serving
for 19 years.

Bill Martin would, as Howard Stein and Bunny probably anticipated, take many months to study the situation and deliver his recommendations.

Meanwhile the date for Bob Haack's reelection as president of the Exchange approached.

Immediately following Bob's November 17 speech, the *New York Times* had said, "In making this speech, he obviously took a calculated risk that he could literally shake his industry to its foundations and keep his job."[18]

One industry executive had gone even further: "I know Bob Haack, and he wouldn't make this speech at this time unless he was contemplating resignation."[19]

But Bob had no plans to resign. And the actions he took in the days and months leading up to July 31, 1971—the date when he would or would not be reelected president—indicate that he intended to continue as president of the Exchange.

He did much to deflect criticism by the governors.

He reneged on his promise to deliver a plan for restructuring the Exchange.[20] Perhaps Bob had thought that the proposals he made in his November 18 speech would draw widespread support, especially from the heads of the large firms. Instead they were widely booed. Retreat seemed wise.

He did not promote the obvious[21] candidate for the vacant executive vice presidency, Lee Arning, to that position. Many members resented Lee's part in restricting their activities, in making them ante up more capital, and in forcing their firms to merge with other firms. Instead Bob jumped up over Lee the man who had been running the Central Certificate System[22]—and running it well, making several improvements—to the executive vice presidency vacated by John Cunningham. At the same time, Bob took a step that might mollify Lee's supporters; in January 1971 Bob made Lee Arning a *senior* vice president.[23]

Bob also worked with Bunny to relieve members of the financial losses they risked if The New York Stock Exchange itself became bankrupt. Since its founding, The Exchange had been legally an association, making its members liable as they would be in a partnership; all its members might be assessed for the bankruptcy of any. The Exchange became a non-profit corporation on February 18, 1971.[24]

Bob worked with Bunny to tighten the capital structure of member firms. No longer would Bob Bishop have the discretion to recommend or not recommend that a firm be suspended if the ratio of its indebtness to its net capital exceeded 20 to 1. This ratio was reduced to 15 to one and made mandatory.[25]

Bob also took a step toward satisfying those members who hated Bob Bishop. In March 1971, he called Bob Bishop into his office and told an astounded Bishop that he was going to be shifted to "Special Projects" as soon as a replacement could be found.[26]

In his desire to be reelected, Bob also may have been aided by an Exchange rule regarding the chairmanship: A chairman could not serve for more than two years[27]—and Bunny had been chairman for that length of time. Bunny's successor was not a floor partner. He was an organization executive who had done much to modernize his firm: Ralph DeNunzio, executive vice president of Kidder Peabody & Co.[28]

A further fact encouraged economy-minded members to vote for Bob Haack's reelection: The Exchange would have to pay him the following year's salary even if he were not reelected. His five-year contract did not end in 1971 but on July 31, 1972.

Bob Haack was reelected on July 31, 1971.[29]

On August 5, 1971, Bill Martin delivered his report.

The report stated: "An abrupt change to fully negotiated rates would be imprudent."[30]

A victory for Bunny Lasker!

Bill Martin also recommended that mutual funds and other institutions not be allowed to become members.

Another victory for Bunny!

But a third recommendation was a clear victory for Bob Haack. Bill Martin proposed that The New York Stock Exchange be completely re-organized. Instead of the 33-member board of governors, he recommended the Exchange be governed by a "board of directors." It "would consist of 20 individuals plus a voting chairman whom the board would elect. Ten directors would be elected by vote of the member firms from the officers, partners and proprietors of the member firms and 10 directors would be initially elected from the public by vote of the member firms."

The power of the floor brokers would be virtually destroyed. Instead of 15 out of 33 governors, only three floor partners out of 20 would be members of the Exchange's board of directors. The floor partners' voting power would be reduced from 45 percent to 15 percent!

Astutely, Bill Martin had avoided making recommendations on the individual, controversial issues of negotiated commissions and institutional membership. This was not just diplomatic. He had seen that the problem was fundamental: The New York Stock Exchange could not continue to be organized and administrated the way it had been. For decades, the Exchange had existed to serve the few rich. Now it existed to serve many millions of investors of moderate means.

Furthermore, even people in the United States who didn't own stocks or weren't beneficiaries of a pension plan could be negatively affected by The New York Stock Exchange's malfunctioning. Even in the 1930s, the economy of the United States had been mostly agricultural. The industrialized economy of the 1970s required that The New York Stock Exchange be governed in a way that gave considerable weight to the public good. It could not be governed just for the benefit of members of the financial community, or even of their customers. It needed to be governed for the benefit the entire nation.

Martin also recommended that "The principal officer of the exchange would be the chairman of the board of directors who would be the chief executive officer of the exchange. The chairman would be elected by the board of directors and would be required to sever any ties with any member of the exchange or any other business. . . . The chairman would appoint the president . . . and all necessary other officers."

In other words, the Exchange should no longer be run like a club with a member serving part-time. The Exchange had become so important and its administration so time consuming that it needed a full-time professional at its head.

Would the governors approve this direct assault on their power? The heads of the biggest and most powerful firms, such as Don Regan of Merrill Lynch and Jim Davant of Paine Webber, forced the governors to do so. The firms that dealt directly with investors had the ultimate power. They, if opposed, could direct their customers' orders to other exchanges. The big firms were, in effect, the floor brokers' customers.

The coming appointment of a professional with immense powers as the chief executive officer of The New York Stock Exchange represented a clear victory for Bob Haack. A professional administrator like himself would dominate the Exchange.

But Bob soon learned he would not be that someone.

The newly elected board of directors chose James J. Needham,[31] a member of the Securities and Exchange Commission and a protege of Bill Casey. Bob Haack did not even stay on for the month between the July 31, 1972 termination of his contract and Needham's arrival on September 2. Ralph DeNunzio acted as the Exchange's CEO during the interregnum.

Yet in Bob Haack's battle against Bunny and the floor members, Bob was the victor. Like Nelson at Trafalgar, he won but was personally a casualty. His November 17 speech initiated the much-needed reorganization of The New York Stock Exchange. The de facto power of the large firms that dealt with the public became de jure, eliminating the obstructionism of the floor brokers. A single near-dictator replaced the awkward double consulship of a professional president and an unpaid chairman with a possibly self-serving agenda. And by making representatives of the public a near majority of the governing body, the Exchange became more responsive to the needs of the investing public.

Bob Haack may have been politically killed in 1972, but personally he lived very well in the following years on the handsome fees he received as a director of several corporations.

John Cunningham had a very successful career as a financial consultant and as senior vice president of Federated Department Stores.

Lee Arning also did well. Early in 1972, he welcomed a call he got from the top partner at Tucker Anthony, R. L. Day, a medium-sized brokerage firm. Arning was asked to become their CEO. He accepted, tripling his income. Several years later he became president of U.S. Life Insurance Company.

And what of Bob Bishop? An outside head-hunting firm searched for a replacement for over a year. Other efforts were made. But nobody could be found who was qualified to replace Bob as head of the member firms department. Shortly after Jim Needham became president, Jim called Bob into his office, praised him, confirmed him in his position, gave him additional responsibilities, made him a senior vice president, and raised his salary.

Not reported until now (because John Cunningham has hitherto remained silent) is the fact that Bob Haack visted John Cunningham's home and asked for John's resignation. Also hidden behind misleading press releases has been the real reason for that resignation.

Also until now, the public has been able to get only a little peek at the three principal personalities involved and how sharply they contrasted with each other. Bunny was an ad hoc solver of problems who gained power through popularity and who prized the past. Bob Haack was a diplomatic, trained executive looking to the future. John Cunningham was a leader but no diplomat. He did not fear to antagonize superiors in order to achieve what he knew was best for the organization for which he worked. And he was loyal and supportive of subordinates.

Obvious to the world has been the great significance of Bob Haack's speech. Without his initiative and daring, The New York Stock Exchange might have sunk to the status of just another regional exchange. At the very least, his speech hastened the much-needed reorganization of The New York Stock Exchange—a reorganization that has benefited investors, members of the financial community, and the economy of the United States for the next 25 years.

However, even though The New York Stock Exchange was radically reorganized, the question of fixed versus competitive commissions was not settled in the months immediately following the election of the new board of directors and the election of James Needham to the presidency in 1972.

14

How NYSE Commissions, Traditionally Fixed and High, Became Competitive and Low, Despite the Opposition of Most Members of The New York Stock Exchange

A few days after Bob Haack made his shattering speech before the Economics Club on November 17, 1970, proposing among other reforms that negotiated commission rates be considered, Chairman Bunny Lasker had hurried down to Washington to counter-attack. Bunny wanted to preserve as long as he could the tradition that all brokers charged investors the same commissions—a practice that had existed ever since The New York Stock Exchange was founded in 1792.

In dealing with the SEC commissioners, Bunny[1] copied the tactics made famous by the Roman general Fabius Maximus in successfully defending Rome: delay, delay, delay.

This was a departure from the adamant stand Gus Levy, then supported by Bob Haack, had made when the SEC suggested in 1968 that commission rates be competitive. In so doing, The New York Stock Exchange officially made several dire prognostications[2] that have proven to be wrong. The Exchange had stated making commission rates competitive would result in withdrawal of members from the Exchange, less accurate price information, less liquidity and depth, and weakened regulatory functions. At that time, Bob Haack had teamed with Gus in defense of fixed rates.

However, it had become obvious by then that if fixed rates continued, the rates would have to be revised. The huge increase in the size of institutional orders had not been envisioned when the last revisions were made in 1959. So Gus and Bob preserved the principle of fixed rates by agreeing to a very small reduction in commissions on some orders of 1,000 shares or more.[3]

Bob Haack's November 1970 speech, however, made it impossible to directly defend the principle of fixed commissions.

Before the speech, the sides were clearly drawn. The army attacking fixed commissions consisted only of some elected and appointed government officials. The defending army consisted of all the officials of The New York Stock Exchange and all of its members. In arguing that fully negotiated rates be considered, Bob Haack had defected to the attacking enemy.

Yet when Bunny spoke to the SEC commissioners in the weeks and months following Bob Haack's November 1970 speech, he did not have much trouble convincing them that imposing negotiated rates immediately would be disastrous. He could point out that hundreds of small brokerage firms would be put out of business, and that the nature of the investment business might be changed in unfathomable, undesirable ways.

Bunny was aided by the fact that the chairman, Hamer Budge, like previous SEC chairmen and commission members, was responsive to political pressures. All five members had been appointed by a president and confirmed by the Senate—and officers of Wall Street firms were heavy contributors to presidential and Senate campaigns. No commissioner wanted to antagonize the President or any Senator.

Consequently, over the next several weeks, Bunny, aided by studies costing hundreds of thousands of dollars, was able to persuade Chairman Hamer Budge and the other commissioners to allow just a token change: Commissions on orders of half a million dollars or more could be negotiated.[4]

Shortly after Bill Casey became SEC chairman in April 1971, Don Regan went down to see him.

"Anathema," was the word Don used to describe the fixed commissions to Bill. "Here we were preaching free enterprise, and the heads of a few big houses would get together and say, 'My costs are going up. How about yours?' They'd get a commission increase through the Stock Exchange board. Then they'd take it to the SEC and get it rubber stamped. It was virtually a conspiracy in restraint of trade."[5]

But Bunny was able to convince even Bill Casey not to act precipitously. Bill was anxious to get another, better job in government, and he may have thought it unwise to offend a man who regularly talked to the President. (In February 1973, Casey would become Assistant Secretary of State for Economic Affairs.)

Consequently, commissions remained fixed with only a minor revision being made. The negotiated limit was dropped from half a million dollars to $300,000 beginning April 1972.[6]

Hopes for competitive commissions were raised when The New York Stock Exchange was reorganized in 1972. The board of directors, now

FIGURE 1
COMMISSION CHARGES ON NYSE SECURITIES

STOCKS

The new interim minimum commission schedule of the New York Stock Exchange, which became effective December 5, 1968, applies a money involved formula plus a fixed amount to each single round or odd lot purchased or sold. The minimum commission charge for a 100 share round lot ranges between $6.00 and $75.00 per transaction. The amount charged need not exceed $1.50 per share or $75.00 per transaction, but it may never be less than $6.00 per transaction. In transactions for less than $100, the commission may be as mutually agreed upon. A transaction for less than the customary unit of trading, usually 100 shares, incurs an additional cost, known as the odd-lot differential.

Effective April 6, 1970, the Exchange put into force an interim service charge of not less than $15 or 50% of the minimum commission, whichever is smaller, on 1,000 shares or fewer. As of April 5, 1971, the commission on that portion of an order exceeding $500,000 may be negotiated between broker and customer.

Stocks Selling at $1.00 Per Share or Above			
Minimum Commission on First 1,000 Shares of an Order			
		Plus Stated Amount	
Money Involved	Per Cent of Money Involved	For 100 Shares[1]	For Less than 100 Shares[2]
$100 to $400	2%	$3[3]	$1[3]
$400 to $2,400	1%	7	5
$2,400 to $5,000	1/2%	19	17
Over $5,000	1/10%	39	37
Minimum Commission on Shares in Excess of 1,000 per Order			
	For 100 Shares		
Money Involved	Percent of Money Involved		Plus Stated Amount
$100 to $2,800	1/2%		$ 4
$2,800 to $3,000	Compute as $2,800		—
$3,000 to $9,000	1/2%		$ 3
Over $9,000	1/10%		$39

[1]Also, 10 to 99 shares of a 10-share unit stock.   [2]Except for 10 to 99 shares of a 10-share unit stock.
[3]Minimum $6.
Note: For transactions in excess of 100 shares, each 100-share lot or fraction thereof is considered separately. When the commission on any order computed in accordance with the foregoing schedules is in excess of $100,000, the minimum charge is $100,000.

Odd-Lot Differentials

100-Share Unit Stocks		10-Share Unit Stocks	
Effective Round-Lot Price	Differential Per Share	Effective Round-Lot Price	Differential Per Share
$55 or above	$0.25	$75⅛ or above	$0.75
Below $55	0.12½	$75	0.62½
		$74⅞	0.50
		$25⅛ through 74¾	0.37½
		$25 or below	0.25

BONDS

Bond prices are quoted as a per cent of face value. A quoted price of 90 means 90% of face value or $900 for a $1,000 bond.

Minimum Commissions

Market Value Per $1,000 Bond	Commission Per $1,000 Bond
Under $10	$0.75
$10 but under $100	1.25
$100 and above	2.50

Source: Fact Book, 1971 Data (New York: New York Stock Exchange, 1972).

headed by Chairman James H. Needham, promptly called for the abolition of fixed rates. But Jim Needham and the board soon softened their recommendation to the usual "not yet" and added a request for higher fixed rates—which they got.

Eventually an exasperated Congressman—John Moss, who had been so influential in the passing of the act establishing the Securities Investors Protection Corporation—had enough of the dilly-dallying.[7] He had been holding hearings on the Exchange's fixed commission system and similar matters since 1971. In 1973 he introduced a bill that would amend the Securities and Exchange Act of 1934 in several important ways, including making brokerage rates competitive.[8]

John Moss's bill spurred Ray Garret, Jr., whom Richard Nixon had appointed SEC chairman in 1973, into action. Ray was less ambitious politically and less beholden to politicians than his predecessors. On September 10, 1973,[9] the SEC ordered the abolition of all fixed rates on and after May 1, 1975.

In subsequent years, the abolition of fixed rates saved investors billions of dollars. But for long-term, conservative individual investors, the savings have been modest. The fixed commission schedules were complicated, but on average an investor paid a commission on the order of two percent—more on small orders, less on large orders. Two percent on his initial purchase did not matter much to an investor who held the stocks he bought for several years. It was a one-time payment. Investors in most no-load mutual funds in the 1990s pay the fund's advisors more than one-half of one percent *every year*—which mounts up. Furthermore, two percent is small when compared to the six percent to eight percent charged for transferring real estate from one owner another.

Lower rates have also made it possible for more speculators who are not members of The New York Stock Exchange to survive and prosper. High commissions doomed to insolvency most non-members who continually bought stocks one day and sold them a few days later. By the late 1990s, the combination of improved computer technology and competitive rates would make it feasible for traders who are not members of The New York Stock Exchange to switch their holdings several times during a single day.

Contrary to the blanket charges of politicians whose own actions sometimes cause wide fluctuations in stock prices, many speculators actually cushion declines and often prevent stock prices from rising excessively. These speculators buy when they think stock prices are low and sell when stock prices are high. One indicator of a market high, trusted by many experienced market watchers, is the total dollar amount of stocks sold short on margin. When stock prices fall, speculators cover, thus cushioning the fall.

The most significant benefit of the unfixing of commissions, however, was this: Unfixing commission rates strengthened the auction market for the stocks of the most important companies in the United States. The higher fixed commissions charged by the Exchange had caused many investors to divert their orders away from the Exchange to other exchanges and to the over-the-counter market where commissions were lower. When all—or very nearly all—of orders for a stock are not concentrated in one place, a buyer or seller of a stock may pay a higher or lower price than he should.

As a consequence of Bob Haack's desparate intiative in his November 1970 speech and SEC Chairman Garret's dictate in 1973, investors benefited from a centralized market place for the most important stocks in the United States for the next 25 years.

However, as the century drew to a close, the centrality of The New York Stock Exchange—and the benefits this centrality confers on investors—was again threatened. The apparent enemies now were principally electronic trading systems and the trading of stocks outside the hours when The New York Stock Exchange is open.

Again, the officers and most members did not adequately respond to the threats. And again—on September 24, 1999—a public figure made front page headlines in the *New York Times* and the *Wall Street Journal* with a speech calling upon the officers and members of The New York Stock Exchange to adapt the operations of the Exchange to new conditions.

The outspoken leader for change this time was SEC Chairman Arthur Levitt, who continued to prod officers and members of The New York Stock Exchange well into the year 2000.

15

An Unintended Consequence of the Imposition of Competitive Commission Rates: A Boom in Soft Dollars[1]

Stanley Sporkin and other members of the Securities and Exchange Commission staff got an unpleasant surprise in the months following the elimination of the fixed commission system on May 1, 1975. Here's why:

Stanley and his associates had long deplored—since the sixties—certain ways many brokerage firms attracted commission business from mutual funds. Stanley felt it was acceptable for a brokerage firm, like Donaldson, Lufkin & Jenrette, to get orders from a mutual fund by supplying the fund's advisors with information and opinions about stocks. However, Stanley did not, for example, approve of what Glore Forgan did for the advisors to Investors Overseas Service, a mutual fund that invested in other mutual funds.

In 1966, Glore Forgan Staats Inc. received more than a million dollars a month in commissions from Investors Overseas Service (a fact that was, naturally, hidden from reporters). Glore Forgan kept only about half that money. At the end of each month, Glore Forgan received a directive from IOS listing firms and people with whom they should share the commissions they received. Without question, Glore Forgan would write and send the checks.

Some checks went to firms and people who had supplied IOS with information that helped IOS invest more productively. But most of the checks went to brokers and brokerage firms that had sold IOS funds to investors. This was done so as to legally circumvent the Investment Company Act of 1940 which limited the amount of money mutual funds could pay brokerage firms and brokers who sold their funds.

Many other brokerage firms and mutual fund advisors engaged in this "giving up" of commission dollars to brokers and others who had nothing to do with the execution of the orders to buy and sell securities.

Stanley and his associates at the SEC, morally indignant, conducted a widespread investigation of give-ups in 1967 and 1968. Glore Forgan was a principal target.

Stanley wanted most of the money that Glore Forgan had disbursed to other brokers and individuals to be returned to IOS funds. His reasoning: The mutual fund, not the advisor to the fund, paid the commissions, but the advisor—not the mutual fund—was benefiting. Using the power of the commission dollars to get investment advice and information was appropriate because investors in the fund benefited. However, Stanley reasoned, using part of the commission dollars to reward brokers for selling shares in the mutual fund was not. Furthermore, he felt that diverting commissions to pay for unspecified services was reprehensible.

Jim Lynch was general counsel for Glore Forgan at that time. He spent many hours arguing with Stanley. Jim pointed out that no law or regulation forbade give-ups of any kind. Furthermore, Jim argued, give-ups were not only legal but also ethical. Businesses regularly compete with each other by providing benefits not directly related to their products or services. Savings banks, for example, were offering toasters and other gifts to attract new depositors.

Jim also countered Stanley's argument against rewarding brokers and brokerage firms for selling the fund's shares. Jim pointed out that present investors benefited because fixed costs were thus distributed over a greater number of investors, reducing their cost to present investors.

Besides, Jim pragmatically argued, returning the money was impossible. Some of the recipients had in turn passed on some of the money they received to others who had helped them help IOS.

But Stanley insisted that Glore Forgan stop passing on to others any money the firm received from IOS as, nominally, commissions on the execution of orders to buy and sell securities. Jim was forced to agree. And in 1968, the SEC issued a ruling making cash disbursements of this kind illegal for all brokerage firms.

As a consequence, many brokerage firms scrambled to provide mutual funds with an increasing number of non-execution services. E. F. Hutton would pay for, say, the printing of a mutual fund's sales booklets. Or Hayden, Stone would install a stock ticker free in a customer's office. Or McDonnell & Co. would purchase Standard & Poor's manuals and have them delivered to the client's offices. Some brokerage firms paid for messenger and telephone services, postage, and parking fees.

These payments came to be called "soft dollars."

No question but the practice resulted in all kinds of abuses. Sometimes soft dollars paid for lavish entertainment and expensive gifts. And there may have been outright bribery, as Norm Swanton suspected prior to his dismissal from Hayden, Stone:

Over the next few years, Stanley battled to reduce soft-dollar payments, but as May 1, 1975, approached, it seemed to Stanley and his associates at the SEC as well as to many other Wall Street observers that their struggles would soon be over. On that date, the fixed commission system would be abolished. The competition between brokerage firms would thus, it was thought, be reduced to which firms provided the best executions at the lowest cost.

Here's where Stanley and his associates were unpleasantly surprised. Instead of declining after May 1, 1975, the payment of soft dollars mushroomed! Brokerage firms were reluctant to lower their commission rates. Most did so modestly. Instead, many competed for mutual fund commissions by increasing the services and equipment they would pay for. Some not only supplied mutual fund advisors (and other institutional clients) with computers, free, but trained the advisors' employees in their use. Some soft dollars paid for the travel expenses of employees of the mutual fund advisors. Some soft dollars even paid advisors' rent![2]

This has gone on ever since. But market forces plus hounding by the SEC has caused the payment of soft dollars for non-research items to diminish. When the SEC examined nearly five thousand soft-dollar arrangements with advisors to mutual funds, banks, pension funds, and hedge funds in 1998, they found that only 2 percent involved non-research items.[3]

Hidden from many investors, however, because it is difficult to ferret out in mutual fund prospectuses is this: Most mutual funds—with the SEC's approval—continue to pay higher commissions than the competitive rate in order to get research information and advice. And these higher commissions affect the performance of most mutual funds when compared to the Dow Jones average and Standard & Poor's 500-stock index. These higher commissions are one reason most mutual funds most years perform less well than the Dow Jones average or the Standard & Poor's index.

16

How a Defiant Stockbroker Virtually Single-Handedly Enabled All Members of The New York Stock Exchange to Sell Annuities[1]

In 1971, Thomas C. Hofstetter, a stockbroker with Walston & Co., then one the country's largest brokerage firms, was vice chairman of The New York Stock Exchange's marketing committee. In thrashing about to find a way to increase the income of stockbrokers and their firms, his committee looked hungrily at the huge commissions that insurance agents got from selling life insurance products.

New York Stock Exchange rules, however, forbade members from engaging in any business not connected to securities.

In assessing what to do, if anything, Tom had the benefit of seeing what had happened to reformers who defied The New York Stock Exchange.

In one instance the reformers had benefited. Dan Lufkin and his partners had dared the members of The New York Stock Exchange to expel Donaldson, Lufkin & Jenrette if the firm sold shares in DLJ to the general public. Tom saw the majority give in. And he saw that Dan Lufkin and his partners had prospered accordingly.

But Tom also saw instances in which defiant reformers suffered even though they succeeded in accomplishing the reforms they proposed. John Cunningham and Lee Arning forced the Central Certificate System on Exchange members, most of whom opposed and feared virtually any automation. John had been asked to resign and Lee had been passed over for the executive vice presidency.

Tom had also seen Bob Haack force reorganization on the members of The New York Stock Exchange, a majority of whom preferred to leave the Exchange as it was. And he had seen that Bob Haack was consequently severely criticised by men with the power to prevent his being elected to the stronger presidency he had pioneered.

In contrast to the huge risks run by these defiers, Tom saw that a reformer runs little risk if he waits until the danger of not adopting the reform becomes obvious to the majority. Ralph DeNunzio had led the way toward involving the federal government in the insuring of broker- age accounts. But he had only acted when the need for the reform had become obvious, or very nearly so, to the majority.

Tom chose a middle way.

He would defy the Exchange, but he would have company.

He persuaded William C. Fleming, the president of his firm, along with Don Regan and the presidents or chairmen of all the major firms to sign a letter to Ralph DeNunzio, who had become NYSE chairman in May 1971, stating that their firms were going to sell life insurance prod- ucts whether officials of the Exchange approved their actions or not.

Shortly after Tom sent the letter, he got a call from Bob Haack who was still president of the Exchange.

Bob told Tom not to worry—that the rules would be changed.

And the rules were changed.

How was Tom rewarded?

When Tom walked into Bill Fleming's office and told him that Walston & Co. could now sell insurance, Bill followed his congratulations by say- ing he wanted Tom to become Walston's insurance sales manager.

"Hey, I don't want to do that!" a dismayed Tom blurted out. "I'm a broker. What do I know about life insurance? I don't want to get in- volved in that stuff."

Bill Fleming replied that he'd give Tom a choice. He said that Tom could become national insurance sales manager and get a big office—a very big office befitting that position—which Tom could design himself. Tom would also get other senior responsibilities and a raise.

Bill paused for a moment, but Tom said nothing. So Bill said the other alternative was that Tom would be fired.

Tom knew Bill meant precisely what he said.

"Will you give me five seconds to consider it?" Tom replied in his typical quirky manner. He then agreed to take a job he didn't want.

Year after year thereafter stockbrokers would sell annuities in increas- ing amounts. By 1998, Travelers would sell more than a billion dollars worth of annuities through its brokerage affiliate, Salomon Smith Bar- ney.[2]

Not only were the incomes of many brokers and brokerage firms thus increased, but also many investors were thus provided with an alterna- tive investment better suited to their needs and desires—an investment that they might not otherwise have considered.

The desirability of insurance companies taking over stock brokerage firms was also enhanced. When the Federal Reserve loosened the restrictions that prevented the merging of insurance companies and banks with investment firms in the 1980s, Prudential bought Bache, and Travelers, of which Sandy Weil was CEO, bought Smith Barney and Salomon Brothers.

17

The Biggest Stock Fraud in
the District Attorney's Memory[1]

Very soon after Tom Hofstetter became national insurance sales manager, he learned why Bill Fleming was extra anxious to get Walston & Co., Inc. into the insurance business. Walston & Co. needed capital, and Bill Fleming hoped that an insurance company profiting from a relationship with Walston would supply it.

The Glass-Steagall Act of 1933 had inspired the founding of Walston & Co. and spurred its early growth by forbidding commercial banks to engage in the brokerage business. Walston & Co.'s founder, Vernon C. Walston, had been the male secretary to A. P. Giannini, the CEO of the then largest bank in the United States, San Francisco-based Bank of America. Vern Walston had located Walston & Co.'s offices near those of Bank of America throughout California, and the bank had steered customers to Walston & Co.

The firm had spread northward and eastward across the country partly through mergers, partly by opening new offices, and had relocated its headquarters from San Francisco to New York City. By the sixties, Walston had more than a hundred offices from coast to coast, making it one of the largest brokerage firms in the United States.

Walston & Co.'s need for capital in 1971 and 1972 didn't, however, derive from its fast growth. Nor did it need capital because it had too many fails. Its back office operated efficiently.

Walston needed capital partly because its top officers had been overly ambitious but mostly because they made a mistake that no sensible investor would. First the story about the management being overly ambitious:

The most prestiguous firms on Wall Street were—and continue to be—

the major investment banking firms, such as Morgan Stanley and Goldman Sachs. They also are the most profitable. The pure brokerage business—that is, the buying and selling of stocks that are already issued—is only marginally profitable to the firms themselves. Individual stockbrokers are free agents. Brokerage firms compete with each other to retain them, keeping brokerage profits down. Investment banking, in contrast, can be immensely profitable. Investment bankers don't shift much from one firm to another. It's a big story in the *Wall Street Journal* when one does. The profits from an underwriting accrue to the firm. The investment bankers are closely tied to their firms by being partners or top officers in their firms. And they usually get appropriate bonuses from the deals they consummate no matter what firm they work for.

In June 1999, Paine Webber stock would sell at a lower multiple of its book value than Merrill Lynch or Morgan Stanley Dean Witter for this reason. Paine Webber is not a major underwriter. Merrill Lynch and Morgan Stanley are. Paine Webber stock was selling at 2.5 times its book value compared to 2.8 times book value for Merrill Lynch, and about four times book value for Morgan Stanley.

Observers believe that Vern Walston wanted—very much wanted—Walston & Co. to become a major investment banking firm, probably more for the prestige than the profits. He was already very wealthy. But, despite Walston & Co.'s acknowledged ability to distribute stocks to millions of investors, the majors would not include Walston in their group. Perhaps because Vern did not originate enough deals. Perhaps because Vern himself sometimes behaved the way no partner in a major banking firm would.

For example: Jim Lynch first made Vern's acquaintance in the 1950s. This was before Jim joined Glore Forgan & Co.—when Lynch was a recently graduated, young lawyer who had just joined the Association of Stock Exchange Firms. Jim got a message from his secretary that Vern Walston wanted to see him. Jim, eager to get ahead, looked forward to the meeting, hoping to make a good impression on so powerful a man.

When Jim was ushered into Vern Walston's office, he was awed by its decor. Enormous elephant tusks and heads of antelopes, leopards, and other animals Vern had killed decorated the walls. Some had been shot on safaris with Ernest Hemingway, a close friend.

Vern looked up and asked the visitor who had come at his request whether he were Jim Lynch.

"Yes, Mr. Walston," Jim replied.

That was all Vern wanted of Jim. Vern told Jim that he had just wanted to get a look at him.

Thus dismissed, Jim turned and left.

In 1964, Vern Walston followed Hemingway's example by putting the muzzle of a shotgun in his mouth and pulling the trigger.

No one knows why Vern Walston committed suicide. He was not escaping financial disaster. In 1964, most brokerage firms were prospering and, under his able management, Walston was prospering more than most. Some Wall Streeters have suggested that he couldn't stand being excluded from the major underwriting fraternity. But they may be placing too much emphasis on business pride.

Vern Walston's death left no capable number two man to succeed him. No strong number two man could have stood working for him.

Just as Alexander the Great's empire was divided among his generals after his death, so Walston's coast to coast organization was divided among three former subordinates, each governing a geographically delineated fiefdom.

Elderly Daniel J. Cullen became the legal chairman and chief executive officer but stayed in San Francisco and devoted most his time to supervising Walston's West Coast operations. Cullen had owned a big share of Walston & Co. since the firm's early days when Cullen had merged his firm into Vern Walston's. Cullen later reminsced to his son, Tipp, that the firm's name had not been changed to "Walston & Cullen" only because the two new partners wanted to save the cost of printing new stationery.

In the few marketing meetings Dan Cullen attended, he seemed to be trying to contain his anger.[2] He may have been distrustful of modern marketing methods. Or perhaps he was inwardly insecure in the top post after having been number two to a strong leader for so long.

As a consequence of Dan Cullen's attitude and location, the actual running of Walston & Co. devolved mostly upon 61-year-old Bill Fleming, located in New York City. Bill Fleming's experience and skills were administrative. He had climbed up from clerk in Walston's L.A. office to Midwest regional manager, to East Coast regional manager, and then president.[3]

The third man of the triumvirate, Glenn R. Miller, inherited Vern Walston's drive and ambition. He was executive vice president and in charge of Walston & Co.'s Midwest division. He had merged a firm he had established in Chicago into Walston & Co.

In pursuit of Vern Walston's dream of gaining major underwriting status for Walston & Co., Glenn initiated and guided the underwriting of the common stock of Four Seasons Nursing Homes of America, Inc. in 1968.

For many months after the offering, investors in Four Seasons were jubilant. The stock climbed from $11 to more than $100 a share in the late sixties.

But Allan Blair, head of Walston's municipal bond department, became skeptical. Allan had become a Walston vice president and director when he had merged the municipal bond firm he founded and headed, Allan Blair & Co., into Walston & Co. a few years previously.

When Allan's son, Doug, a neophyte market maker in Walston's over-the-counter division, mentioned that he was contemplating making a market in Four Seasons, Allan advised against it.[4]

Allan proved to be right.

In June 1970, Four Seasons declared bankruptcy.[5]

What may have happened, according to Harvey L'Hommedieu, an officer of Walston & Co., is this: Four Seasons started out as a legitimate enterprise, run honestly, when Walston & Co. first became involved. But the extraordinary profits of the early days began to taper off. The sizable earnings had come from the *construction* of nursing homes, not from their operation. When the construction slackened, so did the true earnings.

In order to keep reported earnings high and growing and so keep the price of the stock high and themselves paper multimillionaires, the top officers, according to the *New York Times*, allegedly created "sham sales of nursing homes, phony construction costs, fictitious franchises, and false financial statements."[6]

Note what Ross Perot and the Four Season founders had in common— and what they did not. Both had needed to bolster fading earnings so as to keep the price of their company's stock up, but Ross chose to expand into new territories. The Four Season founders allegedly chose illegal means.

Investors in Four Seasons lost an estimated $200 million. United States District Attorney Whitney North Seymour, Jr. called it the biggest stock fraud in his memory.[7] Legendary Ponzi took suckers for only $15 million.

Four Seasons beat by a wide margin the previous stock-fraud record perpetuated in 1963 by a customer of Ira Haupt & Co., a member of The New York Stock Exchange. An Ira Haupt customer had borrowed $150 million from the firm, putting up tanks supposedly filled with soy bean oil as collateral. The tanks had proved to be empty. To protect Ira Haupt customers from loss, the members of The New York Stock Exchange had contributed $9½ million.[8]

It was the Ira Haupt case that prompted the Exchange to set up the Special Trust Fund, colloquially called the Crisis Fund, which the governors could draw upon should they decide to assist customers in connection with the insolvency of any member firm.

The June 1970 Four Seasons bankruptcy was a blot on Walston's escutcheon, but it need not have resulted in Walston urgently needing an infusion of capital.

Only the foolish optimism of Dan Cullen, Bill Fleming, Glenn Miller and other officers made Walston desperately short of capital. They and dozens of other Walston & Co. officers had thought Four Seasons such a good investment they, through a special partnership, had put several million dollars into Four Seasons stock.

The bankruptcy of Four Seasons immediately reduced Walston & Co.'s capital. Millions of dollars of Walston & Co.'s subordinated notes were backed by Four Seasons stock. These notes became worthless.

In addition, some Walston officers needed to withdraw other subordinated capital as soon as they could so as to pay off loans they had taken personally to buy Four Seasons stock. Vice president Harvey L'Hommedieu, for example, a minor investor, immediately owed National City Bank $10,000.

Further depleting Walston's capital was a two-million-dollar loss for the fiscal year ended November 30, 1970.

Some subordinated capital was replaced by inducing customers to become subordinated lenders. The customers were attracted, despite deterring publicity, by the additional income they received without putting up any money or disturbing their investments. They got interest on the total worth of their accounts as well as the dividends and interest on the securities they owned.

In Autumn 1970, some officers of Walston pushed so hard to get customers to subordinate their accounts that the SEC alleged Walston officers violated SEC regulations.[9]

Walston's need for capital was intensified when The New York Stock Exchange announced in February 1971 that it was going to tighten its net capital rules.

Previously subordinated lenders could withdraw their capital on 90 days' notice. Under the proposed new rules, subordinated lenders would be forced to give a year's notice. Further, if withdrawal of the money would cause a firm to violate the debt-to-capital ratio, subordinated lenders could not withdraw their money at all.

And the debt-to-capital ratio rule itself was tightened.

Previously Bob Bishop had usually allowed a firm to continue to add offices and brokers so long as its ratio of indebtedness to capital was less than 15 to one. Under the new rules a firm could no longer expand if its debt-to-capital ratio exceeded 10 to one for more than 15 days. A firm would consequently soon go out of business if the greater-than-10:1 ratio persisted; account executives would leave the firm and go to a firm whose financial condition would allow them to add customers.

In an effort to get their money out before the new, tighter rules became effective, many subordinated lenders took advantage of the old rules and gave notice that they would withdraw their capital in 90 days.

Customers were soon nearly exhausted as a source of subordinated capital, so the officers of Walston & Co. looked elsewhere. The Four Seasons scandal made it impossible for them to sell stock in Walston & Co. to the general public—and also made other potential investors wary.

They needed to find an investor with many millions who had a special motive.

Ross Perot was an obvious possibility. He offered to put capital into Walston, as he had in F. I. duPont, Glore Forgan, in order to get Walston's order processing business.

No sooner did discussions with Ross become public than in April 1971 attorneys in the Justice Department made noises about Ross's investing in two competing firms being against the anti-trust laws.[10]

Luckily for Walston, record-breaking volumes on The New York Stock Exchange plus steadily rising stock prices during the first four months of 1971 improved Walston's profits and capital position.

At the end of April 1971, the talks with Ross Perot were broken off.

Almost immediately thereafter the volume of trading on The New York Stock Exchange declined.

That's why, when Hofstetter told Bill Fleming in the summer of 1971 that Walston & Co. would be able to sell life insurance, Fleming moved promptly. Fleming wanted to get an insurance company so involved in Walston's insurance-selling activities that the company would lend Walston some of its millions to bolster Walston's financial position.

Negotiations for Walston to sell products of Travelers Insurance Company were begun and went well. In November 1971 Walston became the first member firm to announce that it had reached a marketing agreement with an insurance company.

Negotiations to get Travelers to invest in Walston, however, did not go so well. The top managers of Travelers saw securities as competing for whole life insurance. They continually intoned, like a comforting mantra, that there was no better investment than whole life insurance.

Amazingly, the then top managers of Travelers were unaware of the difference between potential buyers of whole life insurance and potential buyers of securities. Whole life insurance appeals to people with little money who want to be protected against catastrophe and be forced to save. Securities appeal to people who have plenty of extra money they want to put to rewarding use. The life insurance product that appeals most to brokerage firm customers is annuities—a product which does not compete with whole life insurance.

Ironically and appropriately, an executive experienced in the investment business, Sandy Weill, took Travelers over in December 1993 and turned it into a financial conglomerate.

Even though many other investment firms made record profits in booming 1972 as stock prices climbed and the volume of trading on The New York Stock Exchange reached new records, Walston & Co.'s revenues, because of the Four Seasons publicity, declined and profits suffered.

During the three months ended August 30, 1972, Walston & Co. lost more than half a million-dollars, its first loss since 1970.[11]

Anticipating some such result, Dan Cullen and Bill Fleming, spurned by Travelers and facing tighter capital rules while officers and others withdrew subordinated capital, turned desperately in June 1972 back to Ross Perot.

18

A Cliff-Hanging Merger Meeting

In mid-1972, Ross Perot appeared to be well on his way to achieving his original objective in the investment business. Just as he had in the health insurance business, he had aimed at getting several firms in the industry to retain Electronic Data Systems, Inc. for data processing.

The third largest firm, duPont Glore Forgan, Inc., was a client.

Dominick & Dominick, Inc., a small brokerage firm, also had become a client.

And on July 7, 1972, the *Wall Street Journal* announced that Walston & Co. had become a client as well.

His relationship with Walston would be similar to that with F. I. duPont, Glore Forgan.

He obtained the Walston account by contributing capital—$15 million—to Walston, just as he had with F. I. duPont, Glore Forgan.[1] (The attorneys at the Justice Department withdrew their anti-trust threat when the firm's dire condition was revealed to them.)

And just as with F. I. duPont, Glore Forgan, the firm did not prosper thereafter. Walston's data processing costs increased—doubling according to one estimate.

At the same time, revenues declined for reasons that had nothing to do with Ross Perot. Continuing stories in the media about the Four Seasons debacle made investors wary and discouraged Walston stockbrokers. In December 1972,[2] Glenn Miller and another Walston & Co. officer were indicted. It was the first criminal fraud charge ever filed against high officers of a big investment firm. In January 1973, both Miller and the other officer pleaded guilty.[3]

Walston lost nearly a million dollars during the three months ended

February 22, 1973, and continued to lose money in succeeding months. To cut costs, more than 30 offices were closed.

Walston was by no means alone. Nor was the investment business. The entire economy of the United States began to suffer withdrawal symptoms in 1973, reacting to the loss of the stimuli Nixon and the Democrat-controlled Congress had injected into the economy in 1971 and 1972. With price controls lifted in 1973, prices rose to an intolerable level, and the Federal Reserve, in a futile effort to curb the inflation, raised interest rates,[4] enhancing the attractiveness of bonds.

In addition, investors anticipated a recession. Stock prices began to decline in January 1973 and continued to decline, month after month, as thousands of investors sold stocks.

The volume of trading on The New York Stock Exchange declined as well. From 19 million shares a day in January 1973, the volume of trading subsided to only 13 million in June 1973.[5]

Commissions declined even faster. Under the fixed commission system then in effect, the commission on an order was based on the total value of the order—the number of shares times the price. So when prices went down, so did commissions.

Reducing commissions even more, the number of institution-size orders declined for the first time since pensions funds, mutual funds, and other institutions began investing enormous sums in the sixties.

At the same time, increased costs made 100 and 200 share orders unprofitable for many investment firms. Wages of all U.S. non-agricultural workers had climbed nearly 50 percent since 1966, and wages of Wall Street workers had climbed even faster. Consequently, the firms with the biggest losses were those like Walston and duPont Glore Forgan where small orders far exceeded big orders.

By June 1973, the number of firms whose capital Bob Bishop and his crew needed to carefully watch climbed to more than 60. Nine of them might need to be liquidated, Bob thought.[6]

Walston and duPont Glore Forgan worried Bob the most. The capital of both firms was ebbing away.

duPont Glore Forgan had, like Walston, closed more than 30 offices[7] to reduce costs but was still the third largest firm. If Ross Perot allowed duPont Glore Forgan to become bankrupt, more than 300,000 customers would lose some of their money. They would not be reimbursed by the Securities Investor Protection Corporation because duPont Glore Forgan was already financially troubled prior to SIPC's recent enactment. And The New York Stock Exchange would be forced to contribute the $15 million the Exchange had promised Ross when he took over F. I. duPont, Glore Forgan in May 1971.

Though duPont Glore Forgan was in worse shape than Walston, Bob worried more about Walston. Ross Perot still had his millions, didn't he?

Furthermore, if Walston became bankrupt, hundreds of thousands of Walston's customers would lose sizable sums even though Walston was covered by SIPC. Here's why: In voting for SIPC, many members of Congress wanted to avoid appearing to appear to be saving the rich. So SIPC protected only $10,000 in cash and only $25,000 in securities. Walston had hundreds of thousands of customers with more cash and/or securities than those modest amounts.

And if duPont Glore Forgan needed the $15 million and/or Walston needed to be liquidated, Bob knew he would be the one most blamed.

Bob decided he would soon need to restrict both firms and so informed their top managements.

A possible solution seemed to be for the two firms to merge. While their orders were being processed on the same computers, the orders were processed separately, using different software. Combining the processing would reduce costs.[8]

Other savings might be even greater. Competing offices could be consolidated. Both duPont Glore Forgan and Walston had an excessive number of empty desks in their brokerage offices. Some office managers and other supervisory personnel could be dispensed with.

So at 8:00 A.M. on Sunday, July 1, 1973, the twenty directors of Walston & Co. gathered around the long table in Walston's sizable conference room at 77 Water Street to vote on Ross's offer to merge.

The outcome was very much in doubt. Some directors were known to favor the merger, others to oppose, and some had not let their opinions be known.

Chairman Dan Cullen and President Bill Fleming very much favored the merger. They had been assured that they would occupy powerful and prestigious positions in the new firm. They may also have been influenced by their close association with the Bank of America,[9] from which Walston & Co. had in effect been split off because of Glass-Steagall.

Allan Blair, the head of Walston's municipal bond department, who had suspected that something "smelled" about Four Seasons, favored the merger because he despised Walston's current management. He had often scornfully confided to his wife that his was the only department at Walston making money.

Tipp Cullen, Dan Cullen's son, who was assistant sales manager, could be expected to vote with his father.

George Thomson, Walston's chief financial officer, spoke up in favor of the merger after being assured that Mort Meyerson would not become CEO of the combined firm.[10]

Ross had been allowed to place two directors on Walston's board as a condition of his putting the $15 million into the firm. They too could be expected to vote for the merger.

Two sons of Vern Walston, Carl and Jack, were on the board. Both had favored the merger when talks had begun, but their attitudes had cooled and then heated up into opposition as they became better acquainted with Ross Perot and Mort Meyerson. It was consistent with the past that Carl Walston and Dan Cullen would be on opposite sides. Carl had continually advocated marketing methods which Dan Cullen had vetoed.

Furthermore, Carl and Jack's opposition as well as that of others on the board, had been stiffened by a report by one of Walston's top accountants, given at a meeting of some of the directors. The accountant had told the attendees that the firm was not in so bad a shape as Dan Cullen and Bill Fleming seemed to think.

Eldon Grimm, Walston's head of research, followed Carl's lead.[11]

Frederick H. Schroeder, once but no longer head of investment banking at Walston, also opposed the merger.[12] Fred had increased Walston's investment banking business considerably, despite the negative publicity resulting from the Four Seasons fiasco. Before joining Walston, Fred had made a career of searching out small, promising companies and helping them grow with sound financial advice and by raising money for them in economical ways. Half a dozen or so of those companies had loyally followed him when he joined Walston & Co.

At Walston, he had been able to arrange for Lehman Brothers to refer underwriting deals to Walston that Lehman could not handle or did not want.

As a consequence, Walston had been in more underwritings in 1972 than duPont Glore Forgan.

Fred had favored Ross putting $15 million into the firm in return for Walston's data processing business. The infusion of capital could help him move toward achieving Vern Walston's goal of making Walston & Co. a major underwriter. But Fred had clashed with Mort Meyerson over the way the merged firm would be organized. And apparently, despite Fred's value to the firm, Ross and Mort did not court Fred. They may have under-rated him because he was gray-haired, wore glasses, and was 67 years old.

Fred had told Bill Fleming how much he opposed the merger. Bill was naive in believing that Ross Perot would save the firm no matter what, Fred felt. Fred predicted that if the two firms merged, the combined firm would be bankrupt in six months.

Bill promptly fired Fred as an employee—as an executive vice president of Walston & Co.—but he could not fire Fred as a director.

Douglas E. DeTata, a West Coast sales manager, and John C. Doughty, a Midwest sales manager, also voiced their opposition to the merger.

The attitudes of the remaining directors were unknown to the other directors. Some may have been truly undecided on the day of the meeting. One, Charles W. Cox, had, however, confided his attitude to Willard H. Smith, Jr.,[13] until very recently Walston's syndicate manager. The two of them commuted together from Short Hills, N.J.

Bill Smith had been one of the capable executives who had left F. I. duPont, Glore Forgan shortly after Ross assumed control and joined Walston. As soon as Bill heard that Ross might possibly assume control of Walston, he promptly left to become syndicate manager at Ferdinand Eberstadt & Co., a highly regarded boutique underwriter.

Cox (also called "Bill" by his friends) had been a protege of Fred Schroeder. Fred had brought Cox with him from his previous firm. But Cox didn't feel the same way as his boss did about Ross Perot's merger offer. Cox said that Walston was not only short of capital but badly managed. Cox said that Dan and Tipp Cullen owed their positions to Dan having been associated with Vern Walston in the firm's early days. And that Carl and Jack Walston were officers of Walston in large part because their family owned large amounts of Walston & Co. stock.

Bill Smith, from his own observation, did not agree with Cox's description of the abilities of the two Cullens and the two Walstons. Bill and another Walston officer who was interviewed, Harvey L'Hommedieu, recall all four as intelligent, competent and capable.

From my own experience as president of Walston's advertising agency, I considered Carl Walston capable, intelligent, and forward-looking and Dan Cullen an old man over his head in his job as CEO. But I may be biased because Carl favored more advertising and Dan sometimes vetoed projects I had developed.

Cox also said that the feud between the Cullens and the Walstons weakened the firm, a view with which Bill Smith and I do not disagree.

Dan Cullen technically presided at the meeting from the head of the table, but Thomas L. Higginson, Walston's outside counsel from Sullivan & Cromwell, controlled much of what went on, introducing the various speakers. Other lawyers sat behind some of the directors who were their clients, making a total of about thirty people. The room was dark and crowded.

Dan Cullen wanted all 17 pages of the proposed merger agreement read aloud, but the directors thought that waste of time and voted to hear the several speakers slated to talk.

George Thomson described the financial condition of Walston & Co. He said it was so bad that The New York Stock Exchange would probably suspend the firm unless the merger were agreed upon. He showed that the combined firm would immediately be financially stronger.

Jack Walston promptly challenged George's advocacy of the merger. George replied just as Archie Albright had when Jim Lynch, Harry Colmery and other Glore Forgan partners had opposed the merger of Glore

Forgan with Francis I. duPont: Suggest an alternative! That quieted Jack Walston as it had the others.

Mort Meyerson made a presentation in favor of the merger. He described the unique way the two firms would function if they merged: Essentially duPont Glore Forgan would be the back office, duPont Walston the front office. He said little about the financial condition of duPont Glore Forgan, just that its debt-to-capital ratio was about ten to one.

Mort left. He was not a director of Walston and had no legal reason to be there.

The next speaker was Paul Fitzgerald,[14] a vice president of The New York Stock Exchange. Though only thirty years old, Paul was directly responsible for overseeing the financial condition of both duPont Glore Forgan and Walston & Co. Bob Bishop, now a senior vice president, and his immediate boss, nervously awaited the outcome of the meeting outside in a Walston corner office.

Paul emphasized to the directors that Walston was on the Exchange's early warning list. This meant that Walston was forbidden to add offices, account executives, or customers. Further, if losses continued to erode Walston's capital base, Paul warned that the Exchange would ultimately suspend Walston—which would mean that all accounts would be frozen and a liquidator appointed.

A director asked Paul if the Exchange favored the merger. Bob Bishop, Paul, and other officers of the Exchange had good reason to want the merger to go through. They feared the far-reaching, dangerous consequences if two big firms failed. In contrast, they thought a financially viable firm might be created if the merger went through.

But Paul told the directors that the Exchange neither endorsed nor opposed the merger—that the decision was up to the board. In being so cautious, he was following the advice of Millbank, Tweed, the Exchange's counsel.

Paul did say, however, that if the board voted for the merger, the Exchange would approve it.

When asked about duPont Glore Forgan's financial condition, Paul did not go beyond saying it "was not insolvent."

After Paul left the meeting, a lawyer from Sherman & Sterling, Walston's law firm, explained the technical terms of the proposed merger.

Tom Higginson noted that there was no antitrust problem because of the failing firm doctrine.

Carl and Jack Walston and a California lawyer they had personally retained voiced objections from time to time, but offered no thought-out alternative except for Walston & Co. to continue as before.

All the directors except Doug DeTata and John Doughty voted as anticipated. Surprisingly, they voted for the merger.

Glenn Miller voted for the merger. He had resigned as an officer but not as a director. He had pled guilty to securities fraud and had been fined $10,000 by the American Stock Exchange but had not yet been fined by the U.S. district court.[15]

Six other directors voted against the merger including George Cabell (Walston's inside counsel) and George U. Robson, an elderly, senior vice president of the firm.

The result was a ten to ten tie!

Both sides were frustrated. A long adjournment followed, during which all the directors and their lawyers went out to dinner, some in groups, some in pairs, some alone.

When they returned, they periodically talked and sat around doing nothing—thinking or waiting for others to talk. About 10:00 P.M. George Robson got up, left and never came back!

"I couldn't go on," he would explain a few days later. "I started to feel ill." Which was understandable. The meeting had started at 8:00 A.M., and he had had a heart attack six months before.

Close to midnight another vote was held. Often when a director is absent and the vote is close and important, an absent director is telephoned and his vote is counted just as valid as if he were present. Dan Cullen had this responsibility, but he did not phone and nobody on either side suggested that he do so.

The merger was approved ten to nine.

Officially the meeting was promptly adjourned, but the directors were asked to stay a little longer. Ross Perot shortly appeared along with Mort Meyerson and Walter E. Auch, who was introduced as the president of the soon-to-be-formed firm of duPont Walston, Inc.

Bill Fleming had thus been promptly and unceremoniously demoted.

Ross attempted an evangelistic pep talk, but Fred Schroeder, the Walstons, and the other opposing directors received it with skepticism.

Not till nearly 2:00 A.M. did the directors leave. The meeting had lasted almost 18 hours.

19

Déjà Vu

Ross Perot, Bob Bishop, John Fitzgerald, and others had anticipated big savings from the merger. They turned out to be right. Thirty days after the merger, duPont Walston trumpeted its financial strength in full page advertisements in the *Wall Street Journal* and the *New York Times*:[1]

"We've organized and financed ourselves to reduce risk. The New York Stock Exchange requires that a firm's indebtedness not exceed 15 times its capital. Our current indebtness is about a tenth of that requirement. The exact ratio of our service affiliate, duPont Glore Forgan Incorporated, was higher: 8.77 to 1 as of July 1, but duPont Glore Forgan is a clearing firm—is not subject to many of the risks common in the investment industry such as underwriting securities and making markets in securities."

Just as he had at F. I. duPont, Glore Forgan, as soon as he got control, Ross Perot became personally involved in managing duPont Walston. And despite what Dan Cullen, Bill Fleming, George Thomson, Walter Auch, and other executives had expected, Mort Meyerson became his all-powerful viceroy.[2]

Unfortunately, Ross Perot and Mort Meyerson had not learned that the management style that had made a success of Electronic Data Systems, Inc. could not be successfully applied to the investment business. An investment firm is no better than the people who work for it.

Carl and Jack Walston were summarily fired, which was, perhaps inevitable. But in Carl they lost an able marketing executive who was admired by many other executives in the firm.

Tom Hofstetter, another widely admired executive who increased the firm's revenues by getting The New York Stock Exchange to allow stockbrokers to sell annuities—was given a job not worthy of his capabilities and then fired.[3]

"Deke" Jackson, another widely admired executive who had been head of Glore Forgan's Northwest division, resigned even though he had been made a director of duPont Walston.

The executive in charge of trading and underwriting, who had been hired by Mort Meyerson, disagreed with Mort, went over Mort's head, and was promptly fired.

And, as previously described, two highly capable investment bankers—Fred Schroeder and Bill Smith—left Walston shortly before the merger because they opposed the way Ross Perot managed.

Paradoxically, the passage and signing of the Securities Investors Protection Corporation act hampered Ross's efforts to make duPont Walston profitable. The basic SIPC coverage usually made it actuarially feasible for insurance companies to insure brokerage accounts for higher amounts. Consequently, duPont Walston's competitors had supplemented SIPC with additional insurance of $100,000, $500,000, and more. But because of duPont Glore Forgan's prior history and the losses Walston & Co. had suffered as a consequence of the Four Seasons bankruptcy, no insurance company would insure duPont Walston's accounts. Thus the bigger and hence most profitable accounts tended to use Merrill Lynch, Paine Webber, and other firms that offered most if not all of their accounts full protection.

Benn & MacDonough, Inc. was retained as duPont Walston's advertising agency but was hampered by a directive to promote a straitjacketing concept that discouraged risk-taking by investors. It contrasted with the thinking that had made Walston & Co., Inc. so successful prior to the Four Seasons debacle. Walston's pre-Perot advertising had been successfully based on the guiding principle (but not so articulated) that stockbrokers gain clients and increase their commissions by offering investors what investors want, not by trying to reform them. And that speculators, because of their active trading, are the most profitable kind of customers. Of course, the Walston ads were always truthful and never promised more than Walston's research department and stockbrokers could deliver.

As a consequence of the shift in advertising emphasis, duPont Walston brokers got fewer leads than they had previously and fewer of the most profitable kind of leads. For this and other reasons, such as the accounts of the richest customers not being fully covered by insurance and the defection of so many admired leaders, several hundred of duPont Walston's best stockbrokers left. Most of their customers—numbering in the thousands—left with them.

In the investment business, it is easy for the best people, if irked, to get a job with a competitor.

Even favorable stock market conditions could not save duPont Walston. The volume of trading on The New York Stock Exchange climbed to more than 17 million shares a day in September, to more than 18 million in November, and to 19 million in December.[4]

Yet on January 20, 1974, Ross Perot informed a surprised[5] board of directors, through Mort Meyerson, that he wished to liquidate the firm.

The directors of duPont Walston, Inc. could only accede to Ross's wishes. The firm was declared bankrupt. Most of the firm's accounts were transferred to other, financially stronger firms. Other customers were sent stock certificates and checks.

No duPont Walston customer lost any money or securities. And the inconvenience they were caused was minimal.

Stockholders and subordinated lenders, however, lost all their money. This put many stockholders who had borrowed money in order to buy stock in the firm in debt for several years. The New York Stock Exchange was forced to contribute the $15 million promised by the governors when Ross took over F. I. duPont, Glore Forgan in 1971—but the brokerage business was now so generally profitable that this was not a serious hardship. The bankruptcy referee sued Ross Perot for $90 million and settled for an undisclosed sum and a confidentiality agreement. No payment from the Securities Investors Protection Corporation was required. And all creditors were eventually paid in full.[6]

Vern Walston cannot be blamed for the ultimate demise of the firm he founded, despite his leaving the firm to divided rule. Even though the Walston brothers and the Cullens were continually at odds, the firm prospered after Vern Walston's death. Walston, Inc. would have survived and prospered without Vern Walston—would have survived the disgrace of the Four Seasons bankruptcy and the ups and downs of the stock market—if its officers had not violated a fundamental rule of investing. They made the same mistake that officers of Long Term Capital would make in 1998. They thought they were so intelligent and knowledgable—that their judgement of what was a sound, profitable investment was so astute—that they could place a disproportionate percentage of the firm's capital in a single investment. They brushed aside the possibility that they could be wrong about the facts and the future. Like the tragic heroes of ancient Greek drama, they were destroyed by hubris.

And the same characteristic prevented Ross Perot and Mort Meyerson, when they took over Walston, from learning from the mistakes they had made in managing duPont Glore Forgan.

The good news was this: Only now, with the liquidation of duPont Walston, Inc. without any loss to the firm's customers, could Bob Bishop, Jim Lynch and other insiders rightly feel confident that The New York Stock Exchange and its preeminence in the world of investing could no longer be destroyed by the demise of a major member firm. Firms—

especially the larger firms—had been enormously strengthened financially by being able to sell shares in their firms to the public. Back offices were improving so that fails would soon no longer be a serious problem. And customers of large firms (and of many small firms as well) were insured against loss not only by SIPC but also for much higher amounts by insurance obtained from private insurance companies.

Furthermore, the extent of the dangers that had threatened to cause millions of investors to lose millions of dollars had been successfully hidden from investors, lawmakers, and the general public. Confidence in The New York Stock Exchange and in the free market system had not been shaken at a critical moment in world history.

And for this, Ross Perot must be given much credit. At that critical moment, he had resisted taking on the task of saving the third-largest investment firm from bankruptcy. But no other super-rich patriot could be found. Ross Perot saw the financial risks and assumed the responsibility because the President of the United States asked him to.

20

How and Why Discrimination Based on Class and Religion Declined on Wall Street

Ken Langone (as was mentioned in Chapter 7) was the investment banker who managed the first underwriting of stock of Ross Perot's company, Electronic Data Systems, Inc. In getting the account in June 1968 for Pressprich & Co., Ken beat out many bigger, more highly regarded firms including Merrill Lynch, Dillon Read, Goldman Sachs, Salomon Brothers, and G. H. Walker.

Shortly thereafter, Ken became Pressprich's CEO, yet only a few years previous, when Ken had tried to get a job as a stockbroker, he had been turned down time and time again. Turned down despite his obvious intelligence (he had graduated from Bucknell in 3½ years). Despite his knowledge of finance (he had gotten an M.B.A. studying nights at N.Y.U., had been a brilliant financial analyst with Equitable Life Insurance Company the previous three years, and was teaching economics nights at N.Y.U.). And despite his sales ability (he had been successfully selling since he was a teenager).

Ken explains why he wasn't hired: "You had to go to the Harvard Business School or likewise. It didn't hurt if you went to Yale or some other—. It was principally a closed society. Jews could always go to a Jewish firm—and they did: Kuhn Loeb, there was Wertheim, there was Lehman Brothers, ah, there was Salomon Brothers, Hirsch & Co., but for the most part if you looked at the other firms, Hornblower & Weeks . . . Dillon Read, Morgan Stanley, Hayden Stone, those firms were principally white Waspy firms."

Ken Langone was as courteous as the best brought up white-Anglo-Saxon-Protestant or Jew, but he wasn't either. He was big and burly, Roman Catholic and Italian-American, and his accent immediately identified him as coming from a working-class family. Neither of his parents had even attended high school. His father was a plumber. His mother had worked in the school cafeteria.[1]

The religious division between investment firms in the early sixties is indicated by the advertising agencies they patronized. Protestant-owned firms tended to patronize Doremus & Co. Its owner was a white, Anglo-Saxon–descended Protestant socialite who got many accounts through his social connections. All of its officers were fellow Wasps, except one who was Irish and Catholic. Doremus clients included Morgan Stanley, Paine Webber, Dillon Read, Halsey Stuart, and Hornblower & Weeks.

The only other sizable agency with considerable financial advertising expertise in the early sixties, Albert Frank–Guenther Law, had most of the Jewish investment firms as clients. They included Bache, Kuhn Loeb, Wertheim & Co., Hirsch & Co., and the one major Catholic firm, Mc-Donnell & Co.

But the cleavage was not clear-cut. Merrill Lynch, which was more polygenetic than most other firms dominated by Christians, patronized Albert Frank until it moved its account to Ogilvy & Mather in the sixties; and Goldman Sachs patronized Doremus.[2]

"If there was a restrictive problem, it was that the Christian firms didn't have any Jews; it was not that the Jewish firms didn't have any Christians," says John C. Whitehead. He had joined Goldman Sachs fresh out of Harvard Business School in 1947 and became Goldman's co-CEO in 1976.

"I was a non-Jew," he said, "and there were a lot of other non-Jews there. . . . Of the 250 employees, there might be fifty or something like that."

Of Goldman's seven partners at the time, four were Jews and three were not.[3]

In the sixties, the prejudice against Catholics was not so prevalent as that against Jews, but it existed. Here's an incident that illustrates the degree of anti-Catholicism then:

It was customary at annual dinner meetings of the Association of Stock Exchange firms for each governor of the Association to stand up and comment on the stock market, politics and anything else he felt would be of interest to the attendees. At the meeting held just after the Kennedy-Nixon presidential race, one governor included several anti-Catholic remarks in his speech, saying, for example, that now that Kennedy was elected, the United States would have a President who would be taking orders from the Pope.

The next speaker ignored those remarks, as did another. Then Robert A. Magowan rose. He was marketing director of Merrill Lynch, Charlie Merrill's son-in-law, and a Catholic.

Among other rebuting statements, he said he was surprised that no one else had immediately stood up to counter the anti-Catholic speaker's remarks. And that he had thought that prejudice of that kind had long since vanished. He was applauded when he sat down. *But many members did not applaud.*[4]

Those who controlled the hiring of men as incipient stockbrokers or investment bankers or traders before the sixties probably hired mostly white Protestant or Jewish men who came from upper-class families— or who sounded and looked as if they did—because of the natural inclination of people to like and want to work with people who are most like themselves. But that tendency was also encouraged by economics— that is, for a business to serve customers and potential customers in the way customers want to be served. People with money and/or power usually want to deal with someone most like themselves. And, since colonial days, nearly all the people likely to invest in stocks and bonds have been upper-class Wasps and Jews. And most of the heads of major corporations had been Wasps.[5]

In the investment business, a stockbroker or an investment banker seldom offers an obviously unique product or service. An investor can buy the same stock through hundreds of brokers. A corporation or other issuer can usually get as good a deal, so far as the issuer can determine in advance, from any of several investment bankers. Consequently, a marginal benefit can cause an investor to choose one broker rather than another, or can cause a corporate head to choose one investment banker rather than another. One marginal benefit that all competent salespeople know is this: Customers like to do business with people very much like themselves.

Despite his speech at the Association of Stock Exchange firms, Bobby Magowan knew this. In 1950, he decided Merrill Lynch would open an office in the heart of the garment district. So did he staff it with what would be considered a politically correct variety of stockbrokers? Of course not. Since virtually all the customers were going to be Jewish, he rounded up all the Jewish stockbrokers and all the qualified Jews in the firm who wanted to become stockbrokers and concentrated them in the garment district office. It was immensely successful.[6]

He was not original in tailoring an office to a specific religious or ethnic clientele. Back in the fifties, Hooker, Fay & Co. decided to open an office in the North Beach area of San Francisco. The managers of the firm staffed the office with Italian-descended stockbrokers, all of whom spoke Italian. Consequently, the office attracted some of the wealthiest wine barons of the Napa Valley and was very profitable.

How important was it for the stockbrokers to speak Italian? When Hooker, Fay was taken over by William R. Staats, Inc. (which was later merged with Glore Forgan & Co.), a new manager of the North Beach office was appointed. He got the job partly because he had an Italian name. Those who appointed him, however, failed to check if he spoke Italian. He had to go to night school to learn the preferred language of his customers.[7]

Customers may even be justified in feeling they will get a better deal from an investment firm manned by people like themselves. Here's a dramatic example:

During the 1930s, many wealthy German Jews had gotten their money out of Germany by opening accounts in the Switzerland office of Hirsch & Co. Many perished before they were able to escape Germany and claim the securities and cash they had left with the firm.

After World War II ended, people often showed up at Hirsch offices and claimed they were the rightful heirs, saying their father or other relative had died in Auschwitz or elsewhere. Many could not prove that the account holders were dead, and sometimes the claims were not legally valid for other reasons, yet Hirsch would usually give the presumptive relatives the securities and/or cash in the accounts. In so doing Hirsch took risks that other brokers and banks would not and did not. Some Swiss banks continued to hold many millions of dollars of unclaimed deposits until 1998 when they were forced to pay $1.25 billion to settle the claims of tens of thousands of Holocaust survivors. Hirsch, in contrast, risked losing millions of dollars in the late forties and early fifties by paying presumptive heirs promptly. Other people with legally valid claims might have shown up.

The news of Hirsch's humanitarian risk-taking spread throughout the Jewish European community, and many—a great many—wealthy Jews in gratitude did all their investment business with Hirsch.[8]

So how did Ken, who was neither an upper-class Jew nor an upper-class Wasp, get his foot on the first rung of an investment firm ladder? A sizable Catholic firm did exist, McDonnell & Co., but it was *Irish* Catholic.

He had one advantage: He had married into a Wasp family and his father-in-law was a stockbroker with a Wasp investment firm, Shearson, Hammill. His father-in-law was able to get him interviews with a number of firms headed by Wasps.

But getting an interview and getting a job are not the same.

In 1962, one interviewer sympathized with Ken, saying he'd like to hire Ken but that he didn't see how he could do it. (He didn't say why.)

Ken was desperate. He couldn't stand the thought of being stuck at a desk all day, studying boring reports. He craved an opportunity to use his talents, energy, and initiative. He was 27 and felt his life was slipping away.

"What do you pay secretaries?" he remembers asking.

A hundred and fifty dollars a week, he was told.

Ken had been making more than $200 a week at Equitable. He was married with one child and another on the way. He knew his former boss wanted him to come back, but his pride and his intense desire to be a stockbroker made a return impossible.

"Here's what I'll do," said Ken. "You have a good number of trainees?"

Yes, agreed the interviewer.

"If you pay me a hundred and fifty dollars a week, I'll agree to teach the training classes in addition to working here as a salesman. There's just one condition. You give me the accounts you're not doing business with."

It was an offer the interviewer, a partner at Pressprich & Co., couldn't refuse. Ken struggled for a few months, but a few years later he was making more money than any of the partners of R. W. Pressprich.

How did he do it?

His charm and abilities wouldn't have been enough if the clients and potential clients of investment firms hadn't changed.

"Thank God for the institutionalization of the market," Ken recalls. (From 1950 to 1970, the value of NYSE–listed common stocks owned by pension funds and insurance companies surged from less than $6 billion to more than $100 billion. The stocks held by mutual funds increased similarly.)

"In the old days the market was wealthy individuals," Ken recalls. "The 'carriage trade' was what they called it. There were no institutions. The people in the institutions—that were running the institutions—[had] kind of . . . my background. You didn't have the men of wealth working in the institutions . . . the burgeoning pension funds and the mutual funds, they were all pretty much staffed by people with very much my own background . . . young people. . . . If you were wealthy [or] came from a wealthy family or a family of substance, you went to work for a name firm on Wall Street or you went to work for a bank."[9]

Ken also got the EDS account because of similarities common to his client and himself. Even though a man or woman is free of class or ethnic or religious prejudice, he or she is still likely to want to do business with the person most like himself or herself in other ways.

Most of what Ken promised Ross Perot that Pressprich would and could do for EDS could have been said and promised by his competitors—and probably was. But—

"There were incredible similarities in our lives," recalls Ken about Ross Perot and himself, "including the fact that we were married the same hour, the day, the same year. It was obvious we had a lot in common. We shared a lot of values. We enjoyed each other's company."

Both had been salesmen as boys, Ross with his paper route, Ken selling Christmas cards and much else. Neither had participated in organized sports at the high schools and colleges they attended. Both came from loving families. Both were self-made men who scorned the inherited rich. Both were second children; Ken had an older brother, Ross an older sister. Ken was academically smarter than Ross who had been only a B student, but both were real-life problem solvers. Both loved deal-making. Both sometimes spoke with so much blunt self-confidence as to seem tactless to the timid. Both had attractive wives they adored and to whom they were faithful. Both were consciously patriotic, thankful to a country that had enabled them to become so successful.[10]

Ken was also helped when he began as a stockbroker by the fact that many white, Protestant Americans who fought in World War II, as well as their wives and contemporaries, were much less prejudiced in every way than the previous generation, perhaps because all Americans had to pull together to defeat two religiously and racially prejudiced nations, Germany and Japan.

Prior to World War II, for example, colleges such as Brown and Harvard, which are models of inclusivity today, had a quota for Jews—and there was no outcry from the media or elsewhere against this practice.

But the shift was gradual. Even in the 1950s, applicants for membership in the West Tennis Club in Forest Hills, where the nationals were then played, were required to indicate their religion on a form; few, if any, Jews were members.[11]

Sometime in the late fifties, Perry Hall, the ultra-Waspy CEO of ultra-Waspy Morgan Stanley called Sidney Weinberg, the CEO of Goldman Sachs. This is the dialogue as John Whitehead remembers it:

"Sidney," Perry Hall said, "I have some wonderful news to tell you." (All the CEOs of the major firms were friendly with one another. They needed to be friendly because they often got together and jointly financed big underwritings.) "Morgan Stanley," Perry Hall exulted, "has just made its first Jewish partner."

Sidney laughed and quickly replied: "Congratulations! You know, we've had them for a long time."

Another story illustrates the generational change in attitude of Christians toward Jews: In 1970, a socially prominent, white, Protestant investment banker at F. I. duPont, Glore Forgan decided to join Kuhn Loeb. He had no prejudice against Jews, but he anguished about how he was going to tell his parents.[12]

Mergers of Wall Street firms also caused the distinction between Jewish and Waspy firms to virtually disappear. Sometimes a merger made sense because a larger firm would be more efficient. Computers cost money. A Waspy firm would merge with a Jewish firm to their anticipated mutual economic advantage. Often a failing Wasp firm, such as Hornblower & Weeks–Hemphill Noyes would be saved from extinction by merging with a Jewish firm such as Loeb, Rhoades & Co.

Merrill Lynch had become polygenetic through mergers even before

World War II for a similar economic reason. In the Depression years, investment firm after investment firm verged on bankruptcy. Just as in 1970, well-managed firms took over poorly managed firms. As a consequence, well-managed E. A. Pierce & Co. became the largest NYSE member firm, and its officers and stockbrokers included a few Jews.

Just before the Depression ended, E. A. Pierce & Co., ladened with so many less-than-competent partners, itself verged on bankruptcy, and Charlie Merrill was urged by Exchange officials to take over the firm—which he did.

Charlie Merrill searched for someone to improve the back office of Merrill Lynch, E. A. Pierce & Cassatt. He found an Irish Roman Catholic who had made Safeway Stores highly efficient with modernized accounting methods. Furthermore, Merrill Lynch's back office, like the back offices of many brokerage firms, included many Irish Catholics. As institutional trading blossomed and computers became more prevalent and sophisticated, Irish Catholics, like Norm Swanton at Glore Forgan, were put into respected executive positions at many investment firms. At Merrill Lynch, some became chief executive officers.[13]

At Glore Forgan, when the idea of Hirsch joining the merger was broached in 1970, a few partners of Glore Forgan—who were all Christian—objected with anti-Semitic remarks. But when it was pointed out to them that Hirsch had plenty of capital—capital that both Glore Forgan and Francis I. duPont badly needed—their objections vanished.[14]

By 1975, anti-Semitism and anti-Catholicism had virtually disappeared on Wall Street and is indiscernible today.

But before we jump to any generalized conclusions, let's look at how blacks and women have fared on Wall Street.

21

The Different Reasons for the Decline in Racial and Gender Discrimination on Wall Street

Jewish firms had existed on Wall Street ever since—even before—the founding of The New York Stock Exchange. But no core of black firms existed in the early sixties. Not until 1970 did a black man become a member of The New York Stock Exchange.[1] He did so as an individual and became a partner in Newburger, Loeb & Co. Not until 1971 did the first firm owned by blacks become a member.[2]

So many Jews have been governors of The New York Stock Exchange since it was founded that they can't be counted. A black man became a member of the governing body of The New York Stock Exchange only in 1972[3] when the board of governors of The New York Stock Exchange was replaced by a board of directors.

No organized effort was ever made by Protestant leaders on Wall Street to push the hiring of Jews or Catholics by Protestant-dominated firms, but in the early seventies, John Whitehead and several other Wall Streeters decided to do something to increase the number of blacks holding important positions in investment firms.

John was only one of several partners at Goldman Sachs at the time, but he was chairman of the Securities Industry Association. Here's how he recalls the situation and what they did:

"The problem was that very few blacks went to graduate business school. Smart, able blacks who did well in college would go on to law school, they'd go on to medicine, but they didn't go into business because they thought there was prejudice in business, particularly on Wall Street, against blacks. . . .

"The program we started at the SIA had to do with more interviewing at black colleges, which were very good and were turning out good people. Some of them had business schools. [We put] more concentration on the very few candidates that did go to business schools. So there was competition for black students because there were only a few, and everybody wanted to hire more. So I remember we chartered a plane at Harvard and flew down to New York a fair number of black students who were at Harvard Business School and gave them a day on Wall Street. ... They visited The New York Stock Exchange, they visited Merrill Lynch, they visited Goldman Sachs, and they visited other places during this day. And listened to sales talks about the wonderful opportunities that there were for blacks in business. I think we did that two years. And all the firms stepped up their efforts to hire more blacks—with some success. Goldman Sachs hired a fair number of black students."[4]

Jews and Catholics were not helped to get jobs with Protestant investment firms by any legislation. The 1964 Civil Rights Act was passed much too late to help them. (The Act prohibits job discrimination based on race, color, religion, sex, or national origin.) But the Act certainly affected the employment of blacks by investment firms.

In 1975 the Equal Opportunity Commission charged Merrill Lynch with violating and continuing to violate the Act by discriminating against blacks, women, and other minorities. The commission pointed out that, as of May 1973, only 11 out of the more than five thousand account executives at Merrill Lynch were black.[5]

Merrill Lynch settled the suit for a modest amount and agreed to do what the commission required.[6]

In 1997 the publisher of a newsletter directed to blacks in the investment business praised Merrill as "probably the leading firm on Wall Street that is attempting to improve its diversity."[7]

Economics has helped to significantly increase the number of blacks employed on Wall Street. The number of black mayors has steadily increased, and black mayors like dealing with those municipal bond underwriters who are most like themselves. Many African countries have needed financing. And leaders of African countries also like dealing with those people most like themselves.[8]

The tight employment market of the late 1990s also helped blacks get jobs as clerks, secretaries and assistants. "There are so many black men and women on Wall Street now," remarked an interviewed white executive who had been working on Wall Street since 1966, "that one doesn't look at them as black but as people."[9]

Statistically, however, the number of blacks employed on Wall Street in 1997 was not enough to satisfy Jesse Jackson. Less than five percent of officials and managers in the securities business were black, for example.[10]

With considerable fanfare, Jesse Jackson opened an office in the Wall Street area for his Rainbow-Push Coalition saying, "We intend to struggle to end exclusion on Wall Street as we did in Selma, Alabama thirty-two years ago today."[11]

Apparently he has been able to get pension funds to use black firms as investment advisors, but he seems to have had little other effect on employment of blacks by investment firms.[12]

There can be little doubt that today the demand for black men and women with the ability to become professional investment bankers, traders and stockbrokers is greater than the supply and that discrimination against black workers qualified to fill clerical, secretarial, and similar positions is hard to find.

Wall Street's experience with women has differed from that with Jews, Catholics, or blacks.

Unlike blacks, plenty of women were employed by investment firms in the sixties. In 1966, a young executive new to the area, standing at the corner of Wall and Broad, looked around and described the inhabitants as consisting of "old men and young chicks."[13] Only a few women, however, occupied executive positions, and they were mostly in personnel or as heads of libraries. A few were in public relations and advertising. Most women by far were employed as clerks, secretaries, and assistants of one kind or another.[14]

Neither Jews, nor Catholics, nor blacks held demonstrations protesting against discrimination, but women did. In 1970, they gathered in front of The New York Stock Exchange and handed out women's rights literature, protesting against the lack of women in executive and professional positions.[15] Only two women were members of The New York Stock Exchange at the time (Muriel F. Siebert and Jane R. Larkin).[16] Merrill Lynch had one woman vice president (Mary Wrenn).[17]

The protest had little perceptible effect although a woman was elected to the board of directors of The New York Stock Exchange when the Exchange was reorganized in 1972. Twenty men were also elected.[18]

The Equal Opportunity Commission's 1975 charge against Merrill Lynch did, however, immediately change the attitude of many male Wall Street executives. A woman executive at one brokerage firm remembers immediately getting a raise and being made a vice president.[19]

John Whitehead, however, claims that the SEC accusation against Merrill Lynch "didn't send shock waves through Goldman Sachs. We liked to think that the people at our firm were better paid than at other firms."

For men of good will (as well as for those anxious not to be prosecuted by the Equal Opportunity Commission), John Whitehead recalls the problem as being similar to that with blacks:

"We recruited professionals largely out of graduate schools, and there were very, very few women who went to graduate business schools. That was a handicap for us. My class at Harvard Business School, class of 1947—a hundred people in the class— . . . there weren't any women. . . .

Then when there began to be women at the business school . . . we tried hard to hire them but we were handicapped by the fact that women who graduated from business schools tended . . . they went to work for Macy's, they went to work for consumer product companies, not Wall Street because Wall Street had a reputation of being prejudiced against women."

Over the years since then, more and more women have gone to graduate business schools; and many more women occupy influential positions in investment firms.

"There are women at Goldman Sachs," John Whitehead noted in 1998, "earning more than a million dollars a year in compensation."

No woman has yet become the CEO of a major firm, but the president of The Bond Market Association, one of the two most powerful lobbying, education, and training associations on Wall Street, has been headed by a woman since 1983.[20]

Many women still feel they have been and continue to be underpaid.

"I can't deny that there were probably some people (executives at Goldman, Sachs) who thought they could get a woman to come to us for less money than they'd have to pay a man," admitted John Whitehead.

But that's the way of the free market. Workers of equivalent ability, eager to get jobs, need to be willing to take lower pay if they are to displace other workers. Mexican immigrants, for example, have sometimes displaced black workers because the Mexicans were willing to accept lower wages.[21]

The fact is: Most workers of any sex or race or religion or class competing for work and advancement in a free market are underpaid to some degree. If they are overpaid, they are likely to be "downsized."

"If you're a woman," says John Whitehead, "you tend to think you're underpaid because you're a woman. If you're a man, you tend to think you're underpaid because they (your bosses) don't recognize your latent abilities."[22]

Some interesting, wide-ranging conclusions can be drawn from Wall Street's experience in dealing with discrimination based on class, religion, race and gender.

The experience of Jews, Catholics, men from lower-class families and, to some extent, of blacks on Wall Street supports the arguments of libertarian economists. These advocates of minimum government argue that *government* pressure aimed at preventing discrimination is not necessary because *economic* pressure will cause discrimination to disappear. That is, businesses that do not discriminate can pay lower wages and will hire on average better quality people; thus non-discriminating businesses will provide better quality products or services at lower cost; and thus non-discriminating businesses will grow and prosper while discriminating businesses will shrink and vanish.

The validity of the argument is obvious for Jews, Catholics, and men from lower-class families working or wanting to work on Wall Street. For blacks it is obvious in some instances. Black municipal bond dealers took underwriting assignments away from all-white firms when competing for the financing of cities and other local governments headed by black mayors. Black investment bankers took assignments away from all-white firms when competing for the financing of many African nations.

It may even be true—although not demonstrable—that investment firms that led the way in hiring women were and are more profitable than firms that discriminated against women. (More capable employees at lower cost.)

The investment business, however, differs in a very important way from most other businesses: It is comparatively easy for the top management of an investment firm to tell how profitable a stockbroker or an investment banker or a trader or even a securities analyst is to the firm. The investment business is intensely competitive and personal. Its assets are people and money.

Not so, for example, in a business as superficially similar as commercial banking. The entry level and promotion qualifications are not nearly so high. Among tellers, it's easy to weed out the obviously incompetent but difficult to distinguish among the rest. Some loan officers are better than others, but it's hard for top management to tell. One loan officer may make more sound loans than another just because of the location of the branch in which he is located. For the same reason, it is difficult to tell whether one branch bank manager is better than another. So there's little or no economic pressure against intolerance in hiring or promoting.

Remember Ken Langone's remark that Wasps went into the banking business?

Even in the early eighties, seven of the largest New York City banks had virtually no Jews in top executive jobs even though 50 percent of the college graduates in New York were Jews. Nationally, less than one percent of all corporate executives were Jewish then, although 10 percent of all college graduates were Jewish.[23]

Discrimination against Jews, Catholics and men with lower-class backgrounds rapidly disappeared in the investment business partly because of the post–World War II improvement in tolerance but mostly because such tolerance became *perceptibly* profitable to those who managed investment firms.

No question but that anti-Semitism declined much more rapidly in the investment business than elsewhere. Consider, for example, the behavior of Morton H. Meyerson, a vice president of EDS, when he became Ross Perot's de facto deputy at F. I. duPont, Glore Forgan in 1971.

"My first meeting with Mort," Richard McDonald recalls, "was going to have breakfast with him at the Bankers Club. I was having bacon. He said something about his being Jewish. It was interesting he brought it up. With the old guard, it might have been different, but the new guard, it didn't mean anything to us. You were either a professional and you did your job or you didn't."

Mort was probably feeling his way. He had not been an observant Jew in Texas, but working in the investment business in the seventies, he became less self-conscious and started attending synagogue regularly.[24]

In businesses where the profitability of individual employees is not so obvious, competitive economic forces may cause discrimination to disappear over the long term. But, as John Maynard Keynes said in promoting some of his political measures affecting economics, "In the long term, we're all dead."[25]

Consequently, some kind of anti-discrimination law may be desirable.

The experience with blacks on Wall Street, however, shows how bucking economic forces with the aim of achieving what are perceived to be socially desirable ends can backlash.

Some executives who pushed the hiring of blacks have quietly voiced their disappointment with the results, often citing Joseph Jett, a one-time star trader at Kidder Peabody, as an example. In 1998, "Mr. Jett was found guilty of false record keeping, ordered to repay $8.2 million of bonuses, fined $200,000 and barred from the securities business," the New York Times reported on November 22, 1999. His actions made it necessary for Kidder to sell itself to General Electric.

It may be that many well-intentioned executives were so eager to hire blacks that these executives lowered their standards or overlooked warning signs that would have stopped them from hiring a white man with similar credentials. Or possibly the blacks they hired were so conspicuous that those who failed to measure up were even more conspicuous. But it's obvious that preferential treatment of blacks has increased the antagonism some people feel toward blacks. As early as 1974, the Wall Street Journal ran a front page story headlined, "White Males Complain They Are Now Victims of Job Discrimination."[26]

For those interested in diminishing discrimination nationally or worldwide, the Wall Street experience indicates that wholesale attacks on discrimination are a mistake. Different remedies are needed for different groups. On Wall Street no legislation was needed to virtually end discrimination against Catholics, Jews and men from working class families. In stark contrast legislation was needed to diminish discrimination against hiring and promoting women to high level jobs.[27] And the experience with blacks has been still different: Legislation has not achieved the statistical goals desired by those who believe blacks continue to be discriminated against, even though the employment of blacks has been aided by both legislation and economics.

Wall Street's experience with blacks emphasizes how short-sighted the well-meaning national political efforts to help blacks have been. More blacks would be hired and occupy important positions on Wall Street if more blacks were educationally qualified. Certainly segregation was an evil that needed—still needs—to be eradicated. But consider how much better off blacks would be today if the U.S. Supreme Court, instead of directly attempting to integrate schooling in 1954,[28] had instead demanded what a Florida civil rights group sued for in 1999:[29] that blacks truly be provided with educations equal to those of whites. Segregation would today have been substantially reduced by economics.

22

Significance

This book is partly about a kind of class warfare, but one continually waged within the free market system. On one side are forward-looking, competent executives who learn by experience and identify their own futures with that of the organizations to which they belong, whether they own a company, head a business association, or are just officers or employees. Their enemies are many: Executives who pursue personal goals, usually wealth, at the expense of the organizations to which they belong. Incompetent executives who have gained power by inheritance or by personal qualities that have no relation to executive ability. Executives who impede the adaptation of their organizations to new challenges. Executives who hire, promote, or favor less competent subordinates over more competent subordinates because of class, religion, race or sex. And otherwise competent executives who are blinded by their own arrogance as to what should be done.

But this book is not written to show that the victories of its heroes were and will be inevitable.

Nor is it written to show that individuals by their actions determine the outcomes that in restrospect we call history. It is written from the conviction that it is hard to tell what would have happened if the individual had not done what he did. One can only estimate degrees of likelihood.

Consider, for example, the actions of Dan Lufkin and his partners. They forced members of The New York Stock Exchange to allow their firm and other member-firms to sell shares in their firms to the general public. It's likely, given the economic need and desirability, that this would have happened anyway—that Dan Lufkin and his partners just made it happen sooner. But we can't be 100 percent sure.

At the other extreme, the actions of Ross Perot and Richard Nixon in saving F. I. duPont, Glore Forgan from bankruptcy very likely changed history to a significant degree, given the disastrous effect the collapse of The New York Stock Exchange would have had on millions of investors, especially at a time when the country was at war and sentiment in the United States and worldwide favoring socialism was widespread and growing.

History is useful in showing how we got where we are by the interaction of economic and other major forces with the deeds of individuals. History can also show how the free market works. For example:

When a major economic change occurs, a few businesses promptly adapt and profit. Most, however, adapt slowly. Some not at all. This was the pattern followed when the development of pension funds and mutual funds caused orders for stocks to increase enormously from hundreds of shares per order to many thousands of shares per order. Donaldson, Lufkin & Jenrette; Cogan, Berlind, Weill & Levitt; and a few other firms promptly profited by furnishing detailed information about potential investments to institutions. Merrill Lynch and some other firms soon followed their lead. But the majority of brokerage firms only reluctantly and slowly adapted. Some never did.

When machines threaten to displace men, the men resist. This was the reaction of most members of The New York Stock exchange to the introduction of the Central Certificate System. If John Cunningham and Lee Arning had not forced the Central Certificate System on the members of The New York Stock Exchange, other Exchanges would probably have supplanted The New York Stock Exchange.

The "creative destruction"[1] of businesses caused by patterns such as these make free-market economies increasingly efficient. In contrast, the slow, if ever, adaptation by socialist economies to changing needs of customers, changing size and character of the workforce, changing methods of production, transportation or communication—to virtually any change that comes along—hampers their growth.

As efficient as the free market system is, however, and despite the high standard of living it delivers to consumers, past patterns show that businesses need regulating by governments. Left alone, business people will not keep free markets free but usually try to fix prices at a high level so as to maximize profits. Members of The New York Stock Exchange were able to keep commissions high and fixed for nearly two hundred years until the U.S. government forced them to compete on the basis of price as well as service.

Unless curbed by government actions, businesses will also, through mutual agreement, use other ways to profit at the expense of consumers. Many brokerage firms got big orders from many institutions for many years through the excessive use of soft dollars.

What a majority of citizens consider sufficiently immoral to warrant legislation (such as birth control and abortion) shifts. Few people worried about the immorality of "front-running" and other uses of inside information in the 1930s. Nor did most Wasp businessmen then believe they were being immoral in discriminating against men from working-class families, Jews, blacks and women.

While businesses need to be regulated, well-intended regulation can also make businesses less efficient to the detriment of consumers. Tariffs impede the free market system and so make goods more costly to consumers. The Central Certificate System would have been adopted much earlier if the laws in many states had not made the issuance of stock certificates mandatory. The biggest bankruptcy in U.S. history up to 1970—that of the Penn Central Railroad—occurred primarily because the U.S. government set impractically low shipping rates on railroads.

Sometimes businesses and governments need to work together to protect consumers, such as in the establishment of the Federal Deposit Insurance Corporation for bank depositors and the creation of the Securities Investors Protection Association for investors.

It is sometimes in the national interest for a government to prevent an individual business from failing. This is obvious when the failure of a company, like Lockheed in 1971, would weaken national defense. (The U.S. government guaranteed private loans of $250 million.)

Government help is also necessary when the demise of a badly managed, giant company, such as Chrysler in 1980 and F. I. duPont, Glore Forgan in 1970 and 1971, would cause many other companies that are well managed to fail as well. (The U.S. government guaranteed $1.5 billion of private loans to Chrysler. In saving F. I. duPont, Glore Forgan, the U.S. government did not risk losing any money. Only a couple of pleading or arm-twisting phone calls were needed.)

These rescues, however, were extreme. Businesses are usually best helped by other businesses, overseen by government. Not only are tax dollars saved, but business people usually know better than government officials what is needed and how to do it, and can act more promptly. Prior to 1971, the members of The New York Stock Exchange taxed themselves many millions of dollars to prevent investment firm after investment firm from failing. In 1998, the president of the Federal Reserve Bank of New York (which is owned by member banks) got Long Term Capital's creditors together to save that hedge fund from bankruptcy, again at no cost to the government.

This subject—how and to what extent businesses should be controlled and helped—has been of increasing political importance in the Western world ever since the Industrial Revolution began. It will become even more critically important worldwide in the twenty-first century. Especially important will be the search for ways to control and help large financial entities, especially countries, whose mismanagement can have dire international results.

One can safely assume that many patterns of the future will be much like those of the past. Look, for example, at the pattern of activity that established SIPC:

1. Several investment firms were so badly managed that they were unable to pay their debts.

2. Their failure to pay their debts would damage other, well-managed firms.

3. The saving of each firm was haphazard, without well-defined, guiding principles or rules. Many failing companies were saved ad hoc by a capital infusion by The New York Stock Exchange or in one instance by loans from Ross Perot.

4. The politicians diddled but eventually minimized the damaging effect of the failure of any firm by establishing a super-organization with well-defined rules and obligations.

Compare this activity with the international financial pattern in the 1990s and beyond. Except for tenses, only the italicized words make the following description different from that above:

1. Several *countries* were and are so badly managed that they were and are unable to pay their debts.

2. Their failure to pay their debts would damage other, well-managed *countries*.

3. The saving of each *country* has been haphazard, without well-defined, firm guiding principles or rules. Many failing *countries* have been saved by an ad hoc infusion of capital from the *International Monetary Fund* or loans from *the United States*.

4. The politicians are diddling but they are likely to eventually minimize the damage caused by any *country's* financial mismanagement by establishing a super-organization with well-defined rules.

Other patterns likely to be repeated:

Chief executive officers who have seemingly achieved miracles at their companies will be lured away to assume command of other companies near failure. Some will succeed in turning around the failing companies. But some of these extravagantly praised CEO's, like Ross Perot with F. I. duPont, Glore Forgan in the seventies and Albert J. Dunlap with Sunbeam in the late 1990s, will fail ignominiously. The methods that resulted in their fame will not be applicable to the problems of the failing companies.

The hubris of the top management of a giant company will cause it to fail. If its failure would cause great damage to other, well-managed companies, the hubristic company will be saved by its government.

Many U.S. government employees, such as those at the SEC and the Department of Justice, will continue to be grossly underpaid for the immense responsibilities they bear. Consequently, some will work for the U.S. government only because they are emotionally anti-business—and some because they hope to get much higher-paying jobs with the industry they regulate.

Unintended consequences will result from the passage of some well-intended government regulations and laws. In 1975, SEC officials were astonished to find that eliminating fixed commissions resulted in some investment firms in effect bribing mutual funds with soft dollars in order to get their business. In 1982, Congress greatly lightened restrictions on the kinds of loans that savings and loan associations could make while continuing to insure deposits. The change in the law was intended to stimulate the economy, but instead it resulted in widespread fraud and was a contributing cause of the serious recession of the early 1990s.

Governments seem likely to continue to try to diminish discrimination worldwide by law, just as the U.S. government tried on Wall Street for blacks and women, without giving sufficient consideration to other measures, such as improved education, that may be necessary as well.

The continual repetition of some of these patterns may dismay those who feel human progress is inevitable. But consider: All over the world there are and will continue to be men (and women) like Bob Bishop and Lee Arning who inconspicuously struggle to save their organizations from destruction.

And all over the world there are and will continually be men (and women) like Norm Swanton, the name partners of Donaldson, Lufkin and Jenrette, John Cunningham, Bob Haack, and Tom Hofstetter who follow this pattern: They first fulfill their designated responsibilities to their organizations, then find that the attitudes of those above them limit further improvement, and so, because of their characters, challenge those in power to make much-needed changes. Sometimes these idealists succeed, sometimes not. Seldom are they appropriately rewarded for what they accomplish for their organizations—they may even be punished—but most prosper anyway because of their abilities.

23

Aftermath: The Perils of Partnerships[1]

In the sixties and seventies, few wives of investment executives worked for a living. And though most were college-educated, few would be able to earn much money if they needed to. Consequently, wives feared any loss or decline in family income as intensely—or even more—than did their husbands.

For some wives whose husbands had been partners in Francis I. duPont or F. I. duPont, Glore Forgan, those fears were renewed and lasted for years after those firms and duPont Walston, Inc. no longer existed.

Bill Smith's wife, Barbara, was one.

Her terror began with an unexpected ring of the doorbell one sunny Summer day shortly after duPont Walston was liquidated. She went to the door, holding her one-year-old, diapered son in her arms. Her three-year-old daughter trailed behind.

When she opened the door, a man uniformed like a policeman apologetically handed her a bulky envelope and left. Over his shoulder, she saw a car emblazoned with the word, "Sheriff."

Barbara opened the envelope and read that her husband, along with several other men, was being sued for $3½ million—a sum equivalent to many times that amount today. She envisioned losing her home, her car, and more—of being forced to live miserably while she and Bill tried to repay the money.

Meanwhile, the sheriff was driving to another Short Hills home. There he handed a similar notice to Richard McDonald's wife, Pat.

Bill Smith and Richard McDonald, along with Jim Lynch and several other former partners of F. I. duPont, Glore Forgan, were being sued as a consequence of a secret action by that firm's senior partner.

Back in 1970, when Ross Perot was connected to F. I. duPont, Glore Forgan only by his ownership of Wall Street Leasing, Edmond duPont, in his search for capital to bolster the firm's financial condition, borrowed $3½ million on behalf of the partnership without informing the partners of what he had done.

Even so, Edmond duPont's partners were equally responsible by law for repayment of the loan.

Negotiations regarding payment of the loan dragged on for several years. And during those years, Barbara continually worried about the possibility of poverty, even though Jim Lynch had assured her and Bill that the suit would be settled for less than $3½ million.

When the suit was eventually settled, Barbara was relieved. The multi-million dollar threat made the settlement seem modest. Still, Bill Smith, Richard McDonald, and similarly ranked partners were forced to pay $50,000 each. Higher ranked partners, such as Harry Colmery and Jim Lynch, were stuck for $150,000 each. Norm Swanton escaped because he was never a partner of F. I. duPont, Glore Forgan. Those partners who didn't have a sufficient cash reserve—which included Bill Smith, Richard McDonald, and Jim Lynch—were allowed to pay in installments over several years.

The law regarding the liability of partners for the actions of any other partner, such as secretly borrowing money on behalf of the partnership, is the same today as it was then.

Appendix

Table 1
Stock Prices, Volumes, and Fails, 1968

Month	Stock Prices* High	Low	Volume (Millions of Shares)	Fails (Millions of Dollars)
April**	912	861	11.9	2,670
May	920	892	9.2	3,466
June	918	989	14.8	3,769
July	924	883	13.3	3,675
August	896	970	14.3	3,095
September	938	900	13.4	3,082
October	967	942	15.1	3,358
November	985	946	14.8	3,274
December	985	944	14.9	4,127

* Dow Jones Industrial Average.
** Fails data not available prior to April 1968.
Sources: Fact Book, 1968 Data (New York: New York Stock Exchange, 1969), p. 6; *Fact Book 1974* (New York: New York Stock Exchange, 1975), p. 20; *The Dow Jones Averages 1885–1990* (Homewood, IL: Business One Irwin, 1991) (pages not numbered).

Table 2
Stock Prices, Volumes, and Fails, 1969

Month	Stock Prices* High	Low	Volume (Millions of Shares)	Fails (Millions of Dollars)
January	952	921	12.1	3,300
February	953	900	11.7	2,969
March	935	904	10.0	2,319
April	950	918	11.3	2,319
May	969	937	12.2	2,551
June	933	870	11.2	2,183
July	886	802	10.9	1,668
August	837	809	9.6	1,399
September	838	812	10.4	1,468
October	862	802	13.5	1,869
November	863	807	11.3	1,691
December	805	770	12.4	1,837

* Dow Jones Industrial Average.
Sources: Fact Book, 1969 Data (New York: New York Stock Exchange, 1970), p. 6; Fact Book 1974 (New York: New York Stock Exchange, 1975), p. 20; The Dow Jones Averages 1885–1990 (Homewood, IL: Business One Irwin, 1991) (pages not numbered).

Table 3
Stock Prices, Volumes, and Fails, 1970

Month	Stock Prices* High	Low	Volume (Millions of Shares)	Fails (Millions of Dollars)
January	811	744	10.5	1,457
February	778	746	11.5	1,316
March	791	763	10.1	1,060
April	793	724	10.2	968
May	774	631	12.3	830
June	720	683	10.3	790
July	736	669	10.4	780
August	766	707	10.4	782
September	773	747	10.4	898
October	784	754	11.9	825
November	794	754	11.5	1,087
December	842	794	15.2	1,392

* Dow Jones Industrial Average.
Sources: Fact Book, 1970 Data (New York: New York Stock Exchange, 1971), p. 6; Fact Book 1974 (New York: New York Stock Exchange, 1975), p. 20; The Dow Jones Averages 1885–1990 (Homewood, IL: Business One Irwin, 1991) (pages not numbered).

Table 4
Stock Prices, Volumes, and Fails, 1971

Month	Stock Prices* High	Low	Volume (Millions of Shares)	Fails (Millions of Dollars)
January	869	830	17.4	1,559
February	890	869	19.5	1,801
March	917	882	17.0	1,738
April	951	903	19.1	1,801
May	940	908	15.2	1,523
June	923	873	13.8	1,460
July	903	858	12.6	1,106
August	908	840	14.6	1,247
September	921	883	12.0	1,138
October	902	836	13.3	1,202
November	834	798	13.2	941
December	894	846	17.2	1,363

* Dow Jones Industrial Average.

Sources: Fact Book, 1971 Data (New York: New York Stock Exchange, 1972), p. 6; *Fact Book 1974* (New York: New York Stock Exchange, 1975), p. 20; *The Dow Jones Averages 1885–1990* (Homewood, IL: Business One Irwin, 1991) (pages not numbered).

Table 5
Stock Prices, Volumes, and Fails, 1972

Month	Stock Prices*		Volume (Millions of Shares)	Fails (Millions of Dollars)
	High	Low		
January	917	889	18.1	1,346
February	928	902	18.8	1,484
March	950	929	18.4	1,392
April	968	941	18.4	1,415
May	971	925	15.2	1,280
June	961	926	14.3	1,064
July	942	910	14.5	1,028
August	974	930	15.5	1,130
September	970	936	12.3	773
October	956	922	14.4	960
November	1,025	968	20.3	1,396
December	1,036	1,000	18.1	1,753

* Dow Jones Industrial Average.
Sources: Fact Book, 1972 Data (New York: New York Stock Exchange, 1973), p. 6; *Fact Book 1974* (New York: New York Stock Exchange, 1975), p. 20; *The Dow Jones Averages 1885–1990* (Homewood, IL: Business One Irwin, 1991) (pages not numbered).

Table 6
Stock Prices, Volumes, and Fails, 1973

Month	Stock Prices* High	Stock Prices* Low	Volume (Millions of Shares)	Fails (Millions of Dollars)
January	1,052	993	18.8	1,511
February	997	948	16.8	1,298
March	980	923	15.6	803
April	967	921	13.9	866
May	957	887	15.3	816
June	927	869	12.8	775
July	937	870	14.7	1,035
August	913	852	11.8	1,030
September	953	881	17.3	1,465
October	987	949	18.4	1,225
November	949	818	19.0	1,125
December	851	788	19.2	1,137

* Dow Jones Industrial Average.
Sources: Fact Book, 1973 Data (New York: New York Stock Exchange, 1974), p. 6; *Fact Book 1974* (New York: New York Stock Exchange, 1975), p. 20; *The Dow Jones Averages 1885–1990* (Homewood, IL: Business One Irwin, 1991) (pages not numbered).

Table 7
Some Statistics Affecting Stock Prices and Volumes, 1965–1975

Year	Unemployment	Federal Budget ($billions)	GNP Change*	Consumer Prices Up**	Interest Rates#	Corporate Profits ($billions)	Stock Prices***	NYSE Volume##
1965	4.5%	−1.6	6.0%	1.9%	4.9%	80.0	911	6.2
1966	3.8	−3.8	6.0	3.4	5.7	85.1	874	7.5
1967	3.8	−8.7	2.7	3.0	6.2	82.4	879	10.1
1968	3.6	−25.2	4.6	4.7	6.9	89.1	906	13.0
1969	3.5	+3.2	2.8	6.1	7.8	85.1	877	11.4
1970	4.9	−2.8	−0.2	5.5	9.1	71.4	753	11.6
1971	5.9	−23.0	3.4	3.4	8.6	83.2	885	15.4
1972	5.6	−24.4	5.7	3.4	8.2	96.6	951	16.5
1973	4.9	−14.9	5.8	8.8	8.2	108.3	924	16.1
1974	5.6	−4.7	−0.6	12.2	9.5	94.9	759	13.9
1975	8.5	−45.1	−1.1	7.0	10.6	110.5	802	18.6

* Adjusted for inflation.
** December to December.
# Baa bonds.
*** Dow Jones Industrial Average, average of daily closing prices.
Average daily volume in millions of shares.

Sources:
Economic Report of the President Transmitted to the Congress, January 1981 (Washington, DC: U.S. Government Printing Office, 1981). Unemployment: Table B-31, p. 269; Federal Budget Surplus or Deficit: Table B-71, p. 316; Gross National Product Change: Table B-2, p. 235; Consumer Prices: Table B-53, p. 293; Interest Rates: Table B-65, p. 308; Corporate Profits: Table B-80, p. 325; Stock Prices: Dow Jones Industrial Average, Average of Daily Closing Prices, Table B-90, p. 335.

Fact Book, 1992 Data (New York: New York Stock Exchange, 1993), Daily Average Volume in Millions of Shares, p. 83.

Notes

CHAPTER 1: HOW MEMBERS OF THE NEW YORK STOCK EXCHANGE GAINED THE RIGHT TO SELL SHARES IN THEIR FIRMS TO THE GENERAL PUBLIC DESPITE THE OPPOSITION OF A MAJORITY OF THE MEMBERS

1. Personal observation, concurred in by Jim Lynch.
2. Taped interview with Jim Lynch in the early 1990s.
3. Ibid.
4. Taped interviews with Norman F. Swanton and Jim Lynch, both in the early 1990s, plus personal observation.
5. Taped interview with Norman F. Swanton, early 1990s.
6. All from note 5 to note 6 is ibid.
7. Personal observation and experience. In the forties, nearly, if not all, investment research consisted of statistics and turgid commentaries by security analysts who seemed to delight in writing long, involved sentences with long, Latin-rooted words. I was hired in 1948 at the suggestion of Winthrop Smith, the CEO of what was then named Merrill Lynch, Pierce, Fenner & Beane, to write industry analyses that could be easily understood by men and women with little knowledge of finance.
8. Personal observation concurred in by Jim Lynch. Common knowledge at the time.
9. Taped interview with Dan Lufkin in the early 1990s. Also in Lee Arning's oral history taken by The New York Stock Exchange from May 21 to June 1, 1984.
10. Lufkin, op cit.
11. Not Dan Lufkin's words in the taped interview but their import.
12. Lufkin, op cit.
13. Taped interview with Edward O'Brien in the mid-1990s.

14. Lufkin, op cit.
15. Ibid.
16. Ibid.
17. Ibid.
18. O'Brien, op cit.
19. Ibid.
20. *Fact Book, 1969 Data* (New York: New York Stock Exchange, 1970), p. 3.
21. Clipping obtained from the library of Donaldson, Lufkin & Jenrette of an article that appeared in the *Times-Union* (Albany, NY) on December 26, 1969.

CHAPTER 2: HOW THE CENTRAL CERTIFICATE SYSTEM WAS INTRODUCED AND OTHER EARLY BUMBLING WITH COMPUTERS

1. Arning, op cit.
2. Ibid.
3. *Fact Book, 1992 Data* (New York: New York Stock Exchange, 1993), p. 83.
4. *Fact Book, 1970 Data* (New York: New York Stock Exchange, 1971), p. 46.
5. *Historical Statistics of the United States, Colonial Times to 1970* (Washington, DC: U.S. Department of Commerce, Bureau of the Census, 1975), p. 343.
6. *Fact Book, 1970 Data*, p. 50.
7. *New York Times*, April 24, 1967, p. 3. The two were Donald C. Cook, president of American Electric Power, and Edwin D. Etherington, former vice president of The New York Stock Exchange and former president of the American Stock Exchange.
8. Taped interview of Lee Arning taken in the early 1990s.
9. Personal observation. Endorsed by Lee Arning and Jim Lynch.
10. Telephone conversation with John Cunningham in the mid-1990s. Cunningham's character traits are concurred in by Jim Lynch and Lee Arning.
11. *Fact Book, 1970 Data*, p. 19.
12. Arning, op cit.
13. *Wall Street Journal*, Eastern edition, March 7, 1969, p. 5.
14. See tables of stock prices, volumes, and fails in Appendix.
15. Swanton, op cit. Endorsed by Jim Lynch.
16. Lynch, op cit., and personal knowledge from my years with Merrill Lynch.
17. Swanton, op cit.; Lynch, op cit.
18. My observation and conclusion, concurred in by Jim Lynch.
19. Swanton, op cit.; Lynch, op cit.
20. Ibid.
21. Swanton, op cit.
22. Lynch, op cit.
23. Swanton, op cit.
24. Ibid.
25. Ibid.
26. See tables and sources in Appendix.
27. *Memorandum on NYSE Special Closings* in the files of the Research Department of The New York Stock Exchange, p. 11.

28. My conclusion based on many years of being an executive working under other executives and two years as a Naval officer in charge of a top secret project about which my superiors knew little—as well as observation of other executives in hierarchies.

29. Swanton, op cit.

30. Lynch, op cit.

31. Ibid.

32. Personal knowledge from my years at Merrill Lynch.

33. Lynch, op cit.

34. Personal knowledge from my years at Merrill Lynch.

35. Arning, op cit.

CHAPTER 3: THE HAIR-RAISING WAY BROKERAGE ACCOUNTS CAME TO BE INSURED

1. Off-the-record comments by interviewees. Concurred in by Jim Lynch. Also obvious from what happens later.

2. See tables in Appendix.

3. *Economic Report of the President Transmitted to the Congress, February 1990* (Washington, DC: U.S. Government Printing Office, 1990), Table C-76, p. 383.

4. Ibid., Table C-71, p. 376.

5. Bob Bishop's oral history taken from November 21, 1984 to December 4, 1984.

6. Arning, op cit.

7. Ibid.

8. Ibid.

9. Bishop, op cit.

10. Ibid.

11. *Fact Book, 1969 Data*, p. 2.

12. Report of the Committee on Banking and Currency, Subcommittee on Securities on S. 2348 (Federal Broker-Dealer Insurance Corporation), U.S. Senate, April 16, 1970, p. 8.

13. Private papers of Jim Lynch.

14. Bishop, op cit.

15. Personal observation based on confidential statements by brokerage firm partners.

16. Bishop, op cit.; Arning, op cit. .

17. Vincent P. Carosso, *The Morgans: Private International Bankers* (Cambridge, MA: Harvard University Press, 1987), p. 181; Frank G. Zarb and Gabriel T. Kerekes, *The Stock Market Handbook* (Homewood, IL: Dow Jones–Irwin, 1970), p. 75.

18. *Wall Street Journal*, January 31, 1969, p. 1.

19. Bishop, op cit. and Arning, op cit., but not the way they phrased it.

20. Bishop, op cit.

21. Arning, op cit.

22. *1970 Annual Report* (New York: New York Stock Exchange, 1971), p. 6. Also Report of the Committee on Banking and Currency, op cit., p. 143.

23. Carosso, op cit., p. 73.

24. Bishop, op cit.; Arning, op cit.

25. Ibid.

26. Arning, op cit.

27. Ibid.

28. *1970 Annual Report*, p. 8.

29. Arning, op cit.

30. Personal knowledge. Walston was a client of Benn & MacDonough.

31. Willard H. Smith, Jr., syndicate manager in turn at Glore Forgan Staats, Inc.; F. I. duPont, Glore Forgan; Walston & Co.; and Ferdinand Eberstadt, Inc.; as well as my personal knowledge.

32. Swanton, op cit.

33. Arning, op cit.

34. Interview with Theodore H. Focht, in 1970 Special Counsel, House Interstate and Foreign Commerce Committee in 1998 (the House committee that introduced the bill in the House).

35. Ibid.

36. Statement of Donald T. Regan, President, Merrill Lynch, Pierce, Fenner & Smith re S. 2348 (Federal Broker-Dealer Insurance Corporation) before the Subcommittee on Securities, Committee on Banking and Currency, U.S. Senate, April 16, 1970, p. 29.

37. Arning, op cit. Also the *New York Times* reported on June 5, 1970, p. 33: "Most leaders of the securities industry have indicated they would prefer to establish their own system of insurance."

38. *Wall Street Journal*, July 17, 1970, p. 17, and confirmed by subsequent developments.

39. Testimony of Hamer Budge before the Subcommittee on Securities, Committee on Banking and Currency re S. 2348 (Federal Broker-Dealer Insurance Corporation), U.S. Senate, April 16, 1970, p. 2 and following.

40. Statement of Ralph D. DeNunzio before the Subcommittee on Securities, Committee on Banking and Currency re S. 2348 (Federal Broker-Dealer Insurance Corporation), U.S. Senate, June 18, 1970, p. 225.

41. Arning, op cit.; Bishop, op cit.

42. Bishop, op cit. and Bishop's private papers.

43. Ibid.

44. Bishop's private papers.

45. Confidential source.

46. Bishop, op cit.; Arning, op cit.

47. *New York Times*, July 28, 1970, p. 3 and July 25, 1970, p. 20.

48. Interview taken in the mid-1990s with George B. Munroe, a governor of The New York Stock Exchange in 1970.

49. Confidential source.

50. Arning, op cit.

51. Ibid.

52. *New York Times*, September 28, 1970, p. 63.

53. Arning, op cit.

54. *Wall Street Journal*, October 1, 1970, p. 1.

55. New York Stock Exchange news release, dated October 1, 1970.
56. Ibid.
57. Arning, op cit.
58. Ibid.
59. Ibid.
60. Ibid.
61. Ibid.
62. *New York Times*, October 30, 1970, p. 1 and December 10, 1970, p. 73.
63. Focht, op cit.
64. *Wall Street Journal*, November 17, 1970, p. 2.
65. *Wall Street Journal*, November 13, 1970, p. 4.
66. *Wall Street Journal*, December 21, 1970, p. 5 and December 23, 1970, p. 2.

CHAPTER 4: THE DESIRABILITY OF PERMANENT CAPITAL

1. Except where otherwise indicated or obvious, the facts in this chapter are as told to me by Jim Lynch or are from my personal observation. I was president of Glore Forgan's advertising and public relations agency during this period. Also, any speculations of mine are concurred in by Jim Lynch based on our detailed knowledge of the situation and the people involved.
2. Confidential source.
3. See tables in Appendix.
4. Robert J. Gersky. He is the source for the story in an interview taken in the early 1990s.

CHAPTER 5: NEGOTIATING A MERGER

1. Except where otherwise indicated or obvious, the facts in this chapter are as told to me by Jim Lynch or are from my personal observation. I was president of Glore Forgan's advertising and public relations agency, Benn & MacDonough, Inc., up to the merger. After the merger, Benn & MacDonough, Inc. became F. I. duPont, Glore Forgan's advertising agency. I personally wrote the ad announcing the merger. Also, I knew Wally Latour personally. Years before the events in this chapter, he was president of the Westchester County Tennis League at the same time I was treasurer. Also we were at Merrill Lynch at the same time.
2. Statement of Wallace C. Latour, Senior Managing Partner, Francis. I. duPont & Co. before the Subcommittee on Securities, Committee on Banking and Currency, U.S. Senate, April 16, 1970, p. 39. Repeated on p. 45.
3. Willard Smith, concurred in by Jim Lynch; Arning, op cit.
4. Arning, op. cit.
5. Ibid.
6. See Appendix.
7. Memorandum on NYSE Special Closings in the files of the Research Department of The New York Stock Exchange, p. 11.
8. *Fact Book, 1992 Data*, p. 68.

CHAPTER 6: OBSTACLES TO THE MERGER

1. The description of the meeting and comments are based on interviews of Harry Colmery and Jim Lynch.

2. Based mostly on interviews of Norm Swanton. Jim Lynch, who was at the meeting, concurs but doesn't remember Swanton and Latour coming quite as close to blows as Swanton describes, but Jim couldn't read Swanton's mind.

3. Swanton, op cit.

4. Ibid.

5. Interview with Jim Lynch in the 1990s. Concurred in by Mrs. Russell J. Forgan and Aline Countess Romanones, who was an American spy during World War II, in personal conversations with me. Russ Forgan drew up the original plans for the CIA.

6. As remembered by Jim Lynch and confidentially concurred in by the utterer.

7. Maurice Meyer, Jr. He was interviewed in early 1990s.

8. Interview with Gilbert Bach taken in the early 1990s.

9. Ibid.

10. Ibid.

11. Roger Fraiman. He declined to be interviewed, but he confirmed this fact. Also stated by Gil Bach.

12. Interview of Jim Lynch in the 1990s.

13. Ibid.

14. Interview of Richard MacDonald, taken in the mid-1990s.

15. Ibid.

16. MacDonald, op cit.; Lynch, op cit.

CHAPTER 7: HOW AND WHY ROSS PEROT SAVED THE NEW YORK STOCK EXCHANGE FROM POSSIBLE COLLAPSE

1. Bishop, op cit.; Arning, op cit.

2. 1968 and 1969 Annual Reports of Electronic Data Services, Inc.

3. Todd Mason, *Perot: An Unauthorized Biography* (New York: Business One Irwin, 1990), p. 71.

4. 1969 Annual Report of Electronic Data Service, Inc.

5. See Appendix.

6. Arning, op cit.

7. Lynch, op cit.

8. Ibid.

9. Willard F. Smith, Jr. in an interview taken in the 1990s.

10. Lynch, op cit.

11. *New York Times*, July 6, 1970, p. 46; *Wall Street Journal*, July 6, 1970, p. 9.

CHAPTER 8: HOW THE NEW YORK STOCK EXCHANGE CAME CLOSER—MUCH, MUCH CLOSER—TO COLLAPSE THE SECOND TIME

1. McDonald, op cit.
2. Colmery, op cit.; Lynch, op cit.; Swanton, op cit.; and private papers.
3. Colmery, op cit.
4. My conclusion, concurred in by Jim Lynch.
5. Swanton, op cit.; Lynch, op cit.
6. Lynch, op cit.
7. My analysis. In my career in advertising, I have written for others and made myself many successful sales presentations of the kind Frank Lautenberg made.
8. Lynch, op cit.
9. The facts that follow about how Ross Perot got accounts prior to 1970 are from Mason, op cit., pp. 36–42.
10. Lynch, private papers.
11. Arning, op cit.; Lynch, op cit.
12. Lynch, op cit.; Lynch, private papers.
13. See tables in Appendix.
14. Ibid.
15. Lynch, op cit.
16. *New York Times*, December 11, 1970, p. 73.
17. Bishop, op cit.; Arning, op cit.
18. Bishop's private papers and interview.
19. McDonald, op cit.
20. Langone, op cit.; Arning, op cit.
21. Arning, op cit.
22. Ibid.; Bishop, op cit.
23. Ibid.
24. Ibid.
25. *Wall Street Journal*, October 9, 1970, p. 3. The figures are for profit or loss before federal income taxes, the best measure of how well the firms were managed. The Francis I. duPont loss was reduced to $19 million after tax rebates. The DLJ profit was reduced to $18 million after taxes.
26. Swanton, op cit. Concurred in by others.
27. Arning, op cit.
28. My opinion. Two additional reasons for this conclusion: (1) Previous threats occurred when the economy of the United States was mostly agricultural; consequently, the demise of The New York Stock Exchange would previously not have been devastating. (2) Never before had the adoption of socialistic measures that would hamper economic growth been so possible. For more on this subject see Robert Sobel, *Panic on Wall Street: A History of America's Financial Disasters* (New York: The Macmillan Company, 1968).
29. Logical conclusion from previous paragraphs. Concured in by Jim Lynch.

30. Langone, op cit.

31. Richard Nixon, *The Memoirs of Richard Nixon* (New York: Grosset & Dunlap, 1978), pp. 494–495.

32. H. R. Haldeman, *The Haldeman Diaries* (New York: Putnam's Sons, 1994), p. 211.

33. Nixon, op cit., p. 489.

34. Ibid., p. 493.

35. Arning, op cit.

36. My speculation, concurred in by Jim Lynch and a financial advisor who prefers not to be named.

37. My speculation, concurred in by Jim Lynch.

38. Broadus Mitchell, *Depression Decade, Volume IX: The Economic History of the United States* (New York and Toronto: Rinehart & Co., 1947), pp. 83, 84.

39. Arning, op cit.

40. Lynch, op cit.

41. Ibid.

42. My speculation.

43. Lynch, op cit.

44. Ibid.

45. Ibid.

46. Ibid.

47. Arning, op cit.

48. *Business Week*, December 5, 1970, p. 78.

49. I was especially alert at the time to any such information. Benn & MacDonough, Inc., instead of Francis I. duPont's advertising agency, had been chosen to be the advertising agency for F. I. duPont, Glore Forgan.

50. *New York Times*, November 26, 1970, p. 65.

51. Sam Freedman revealed the call and the story that follows to a group of intimates many years later. The source is confidential. If Lee Arning or Bob Bishop had known about this call, they would have reported it in their oral histories. Lee Arning reviewed a previous draft of this book and did not contradict this statement.

52. Ibid.

53. 1969 EDS Annual Report.

CHAPTER 9: HOW A GIANT INVESTMENT FIRM VERY NEARLY WENT BANKRUPT IN 1971, POTENTIALLY CAUSING INVESTORS TO LOSE MILLIONS OF DOLLARS DESPITE THE EXISTENCE OF THE SECURITIES INVESTORS PROTECTION CORPORATION

1. *Wall Street Journal*, December 14, 1970, p. 5.

2. *Fortune*, July 1971, p. 91.

3. I didn't know until I was told it by a confidential source in the 1990s, and if I, who was close to many of the people in F. I. duPont, Glore Forgan and attentive to any information about my biggest client, didn't know, other outsiders didn't know.

4. Again, if I didn't know, outsiders didn't know.

5. Lynch, op cit.

6. Ibid.

7. Ibid.

8. Ibid.

9. Bishop, private papers.

10. Lynch, op cit.

11. Ibid.

12. Even I, president of F. I. duPont, Glore Forgan's advertising agency, was at the time ignorant of how precarious the firm's finances were.

13. Forcht, op cit.

14. Ibid. The terms of SIPC were that if the industry had not yet contributed sufficient funds to SIPC to cover a disaster that the U.S. Treasury could be called upon to contribute the money promptly but temporarily.

15. Lynch, op cit.

16. Ibid.

17. Ibid.

18. Lynch, private papers.

19. *Fact Book, 1970 Data*, p. 3.

20. Ibid.

21. Lynch, private papers.

22. Ibid.

23. Arning, op cit.

CHAPTER 10: THE IMPORTANCE OF MANAGEMENT STYLE

1. Thomas J. Peters, *In Search of Excellence* (New York: Harper & Row, 1982), p. 15.

2. McDonald, op cit.

3. Colmery op cit.; Lynch, op cit.

4. Lynch, op cit. and a confidential source.

5. My conclusion based on experience in doing cold-calling, writing cold-calling scripts, and knowing many stockbrokers.

6. Lynch, op cit.

7. Ibid. Ginsburg related the incident to Lynch.

8. Last page of an unpaged reprint of an article in *Fortune*, July 1971, entitled "Ross Perot Moves in on Wall Street." It was reprinted "solely for the information of the staff of duPont Glore Forgan Inc."

9. Confidential source.

10. More than one confidential source.

11. McDonald, op cit.

12. Colmery, op cit.

13. Lynch, op cit.

14. Ibid.

15. Personal knowledge.

16. Mason, op cit., p. 85.

17. See Table in Appendix.

18. *New York Times*, August 16, 1971, p. 1.

19. *New York Times*, June 26, 1971, p. 37 (first financial page).

20. Herbert Stein, *Presidential Economics* (New York: Simon and Schuster, 1984), p. 167.

21. Ibid., p. 164.

22. See Tables in Appendix.

23. See Tables in Appendix.

24. *Fact Book, 1972 Data*, p. 3.

CHAPTER 11: THE REALITY OF U.S. GOVERNMENT EMPLOYMENT

1. The facts in this chapter are almost entirely based on interviews of Jim Lynch. The conclusions are mine, concurred in by Jim Lynch.

2. This is widely accepted by people conversant with Wall Street and the SEC. Example: in 1999, the director of the SEC's division of market regulation asked Chairman Arthur Levitt to help him get a higher-paying job on Wall Street. The Chairman recommended him to Bear Stearns even though Bear Stearns was being investigated by the SEC at the time. The director got the job. Source: *Wall Street Journal*, May 19, 1999 (first financial page).

3. Lynch, op cit.

4. Joel Seligman, *The Transformation of Wall Street* (Boston: Houghton Mifflin, 1982), p. 443.

5. "SEC Chairman Levitt Calls for Pay Raises to Retain Employees," *Wall Street Journal*, February 28, 2000, p. B14.

CHAPTER 12: HOW THE U.S. GOVERNMENT HAS TRIED TO PREVENT INSIDER TRADING—AND WHY IT HAS FAILED

1. *New York Times*, December 21, 1970, p. 59 (first financial page); *Wall Street Journal*, December 21, 1970, p. 6.

2. Lynch, op cit. Much of this chapter is from interviews of Jim Lynch.

3. *New York Times*, February 1, 1968, p. 38; *Wall Street Journal*, February 1, 1968, p. 7.

4. There were other reasons Penn Central failed, including paying high dividends. See *Finance*, December 1970, p. 58. But my analysis made at the time, based largely upon knowledge of railroad finance gained by writing an analysis of railroads for Merrill Lynch in 1950, was that federal regulation favoring the trucking industry over railroads was the principal cause.

5. *The Penn Central Failure and the Role of Financial Institutions. Part II, Case Study of a Penn Central Subsidiary Executive: Jet Aviation, and Part III Penphil: The Misuse of Corporate Power, Staff Report of the Committee on Banking and Currency, House of Representatives, 92nd Congress, First Session, February 15, 1971* (Washington, DC: Superintendent of Documents, U.S. Government Printing Office, 1971).

6. Ibid.; Lynch, op cit.

7. The "eager" is based on confidential information from a former intimate of Senator Specter. Also, Specter did not need to prosecute.

8. *New York Times*, January 5, 1972, p. 1.

9. Taped telephone conversation with John Heine, Deputy Director of Public Affairs, Securities and Exchange Commission.

10. "The leaders of the barons in 1215 groped in the dim light towards a fundamental principle. Government must henceforward mean something more than the arbitrary rule of any man, and custom and the law must stand even before the King." Winston S. Churchill, *The Birth of Britain* (New York: Dodd, Mead & Company, 1956), p. 253.

11. 1628. "The Petition complained against forced loans, imprisonment without trial, billeting, and martial law." Ibid., p. 186.

12. The Glorious Revolution of 1688 resulted in the Bill of Rights being enacted in 1689. An extract is included in Edward P. Cheyney, *Readings in English History Drawn from Original Sources* (Boston, New York, Chicago, and London: Ginn and Company, 1922), pp. 546–547.

13. "In Lincoln's case, the solution was much more direct: the national government simply printed new money, nearly $500 million in a new currency called "greenbacks," and spent it. The immediate result in every instance was dramatic growth and an explosive burst of inflation afterward." From William Greider, *Secrets of the Temple* (New York: Simon and Schuster, 1987), pp. 100–101.

14. Ted Morgan, *FDR, A Biography* (New York: Simon and Schuster, 1985), pp. 467–473.

15. Fast strikes, as in the war against Grenada (1983) initiated by Reagan and the war against Panama (1989) by Bush, may possibly be justified because of the military desirability for surprise. Moreover, they were quickly over. Truman acted promptly and wisely in 1950 by acting immediately to repel the invasion of South Korea by North Korea, but he had plenty of time thereafter to ask Congress to declare war. Similarly, the Vietnam War (begun gradually in the early 1960s), lasted long enough for Johnson to ask Congress to declare war. And it is difficult to find any constitutional justification for Bush not asking for Congress to declare war against Iraq (1991) or for Clinton not asking for a declaration of war against Serbia (1999). These two wars resulted from the countries the United States invaded ignoring threats by the United States; there was plenty of time to ask Congress for declarations of war, both before and after the wars had begun. The military pretext of the desirability of surprise did not apply. Moreover, asking Congress to declare war would have strengthened the power of the threats.

16. See note 13.

17. *The Penn Central Failure and the Role of Financial Institutions.*

18. Speech before The Bond Market Association at Boca Raton, Florida, on March 7, 1998.

19. *New York Times*, July 11, 1994, p. D5.

20. *Wall Street Journal*, February 23, 1999, pp. C1 and C2.

CHAPTER 13: THE TWISTS AND TURNS TOWARD THE REORGANIZATION OF THE NEW YORK STOCK EXCHANGE

1. *Competition and the Future of The New York Stock Exchange, Remarks of Robert W. Haack, President of the New York Stock Exchange at the Economic Club of New*

York, Waldorf Astoria, New York, November 17, 1970—as distributed by The New York Stock Exchange and obtained from the private files of Jim Lynch; *New York Times*, November 18, 1970, p. 1.

2. O'Brien, op cit.; Lynch, op cit.; Cunningham, op cit.

3. *Competition and the Future of The New York Stock Exchange*, p. 4.

4. Speech at the Lord Mayor's Day Luncheon, London, November 10, 1942 as stated by John Bartlett, *Familiar Quotations, Thirteenth and Centennial Edition* (Boston and Toronto: Little, Brown and Company, 1955), p. 871.

5. *Wall Street Journal*, November 19, 1970, p. 4.

6. My opinion based on multiple sources such as interviews with John Cunningham, Jim Lynch, Norm Swanton, Bob Bishop, and interviewees who were in the investment business who prefer to remain anonymous.

7. Ibid.

8. Ibid.

9. Cunningham, op cit.

10. Swanton, op cit.

11. *Competition and the Future of the New York Stock Exchange*, pp. 4–5.

12. Ibid., pp. 6–7.

13. *New York Times*, November 19, 1970, p. 67.

14. Jenrette, Michel, and Rouselot quotes are from the *Wall Street Journal*, November 18, 1970, p. 3.

15. Arning, op cit.

16. *New York Times*, November 18, 1970, p. 76. Also, " 'The President's job is to administer the affairs of the New York Stock Exchange' . . . was the icily expressed comment of Bernard J. Lasker" in the *Wall Street Journal*, November 18, 1970, p. 3.

17. *Wall Street Journal*, January 12, 1971, p. 32 and January 21, 1971, p. 3.

18. *New York Times*, November 24, 1970, p. 55.

19. *Wall Street Journal*, November 18, 1970, p. 3.

20. *Wall Street Journal*, January 12, 1971, p. 32.

21. *Wall Street Journal*, November 23, 1970, p. 2.

22. *New York Times*, January 22, 1971, p. 27.

23. *New York Times*, February 19, 1971, p. 57.

24. *New York Times*, February 25, 1971, p. 53.

25. *Wall Street Journal*, March 29, 1971, p. 1; Bishop, op cit.

26. *New York Times*, December 3, 1970, p. 73 (first financial page).

27. *New York Stock Exchange Constitution and Rules*, June 15, 1971, p. 1054.

28. *New York Times*, May 11, 1971, p. 51.

29. *New York Times*, August 6, 1971, p. 1.

30. All quotes and facts from the Martin report are from the *New York Times*, August 6, 1971, p. 47 headlined "Excerpts from Report on Securities Markets Submitted by Martin to Big Board."

31. *New York Times*, July 14, 1972, p. 1.

CHAPTER 14: HOW NYSE COMMISSIONS, TRADITIONALLY FIXED AND HIGH, BECAME COMPETITIVE AND LOW, DESPITE THE OPPOSITION OF MOST MEMBERS OF THE NEW YORK STOCK EXCHANGE

1. My analysis based on interviews with Jim Lynch, Ed O'Brien, and others, and on Lee Arning's oral history. Concurred in by Jim Lynch and Ed O'Brien. Also substantiated by what follows.

2. *1968 Annual Report*, The New York Stock Exchange, p. 7.

3. Ibid., p. 4.

4. *1971 Annual Report*, The New York Stock Exchange, p. 7.

5. Joseph E. Persico, *Casey from the OSS to the CIA* (New York: Viking, 1990), p. 147.

6. *1972 Annual Report*, The New York Stock Exchange, p. 11.

7. My opinion of John Moss's attitude based on my reading of news stories and talking to Ted Forcht.

8. *New York Times*, March 2, 1973, p. 47.

9. *1973 Annual Report*, The New York Stock Exchange, p. 5.

CHAPTER 15: AN UNINTENDED CONSEQUENCE OF THE IMPOSITION OF COMPETITIVE COMMISSION RATES: A BOOM IN SOFT DOLLARS

1. Except where noted or obvious, the information in this chapter comes from Lynch, op cit.

2. Arning, op cit.; Lynch, op cit.

3. *Inspection Report on the Soft Dollar Practices of Broker-Dealers, Investment Advisers and Mutual Funds September 22, 1998*, The Office of Compliance Inspections and Examinations, U.S. Securities & Exchange Commission, Appendix D, p. 2.

CHAPTER 16: HOW A DEFIANT STOCKBROKER VIRTUALLY SINGLE-HANDEDLY ENABLED ALL MEMBERS OF THE NEW YORK STOCK EXCHANGE TO SELL ANNUITIES

1. Based almost entirely on an interview with Tom Hofstetter in the mid-1990s.

2. Keith Anderson, Travelers Life Insurance Company.

CHAPTER 17: THE BIGGEST STOCK FRAUD IN THE DISTRICT ATTORNEY'S MEMORY

1. The title of this chapter is taken from a front page article in the *New York Times*, December 21, 1972. This chapter is mostly derived from interviews of Jim Lynch, Bill Smith, Harvey L'Hommedieu, Tom Hofstetter, Mrs. Allan Blair, Doug

Blair, Tipp Cullen, and others at Walston & Co. who prefer to remain anonymous, plus the oral histories of Lee Arning and Bob Bishop, plus my own personal experience. Walston & Co. had been a Benn & MacDonough client since 1967. Often what each said duplicated or overlapped what others said and what I had experienced or knew.

2. Personal observation from the meetings I attended.

3. Obituary, *New York Times*, December 21, 1994, p. B16.

4. Douglas Blair telephone interview in 1995.

5. *Wall Street Journal*, June 29, 1971, p. 5.

6. *New York Times*, December 21, 1972, p. 62.

7. Ibid., p. 1.

8. Arning, op cit.

9. *New York Times*, October 8, 1971, p. 61.

10. *New York Times*, April 28, 1971, p. 63.

11. *New York Times*, October 6, 1972, p. 59.

CHAPTER 18: A CLIFF-HANGING MERGER MEETING

1. *New York Times*, July 7, 1972, p. 48.

2. *New York Times*, December 21, 1972, p. 62.

3. *Wall Street Journal*, January 9, 1973.

4. Three month bills went from 4 percent in 1972 to 7 percent in 1973. Baa bonds, however, went up only from 8.16 percent to 8.24 percent. Source: *Economic Report of the President, Transmitted to the Congress February 1990* (Washington, DC: U.S. Government Printing Office, 1990), Table C-71, p. 376. The Federal Reserve through its buying and selling of short-term securities directly and immediately influences short-term rates. It has seldom taken actions that influence long-term rates directly.

5. See tables in Appendix.

6. Bishop, op cit.

7. Lynch, private papers.

8. Lynch, op cit.

9. Confidential source.

10. Telephone conversation with George Thomson in mid-1990s. He was one of the sources for what went on in the meeting.

11. Some of the information regarding the meeting and the attitude of the directors is from a confidential source.

12. Frederick H. Schroeder, Jr. attended the meeting as his father's lawyer. He was a valuable source for the atmosphere of the meeting and what went on.

13. Smith, op cit.

14. Paul Fitzgerald was interviewed in mid-1995 and was a valuable source for what went on while he was present as well as other background information.

15. *Wall Street Journal*, February 28, 1974, p. 12.

CHAPTER 19: DÉJÀ VU

1. *Wall Street Journal*, August 27, 1973, p. 13.

2. Interview of Walter Auch in mid-1990s; Thomson, op cit.; Lynch, op cit.

3. The sources for the dismissals and resignation are several overlapping interviews including those of Jim Lynch, Tom Hofstetter, Harvey L'Hommedieu, and a confidential source, besides my being told at the time.

4. See table in Appendix.

5. The board had met to consider a number of other problems including a lawsuit against the firm by Nella Walston, Vern Walston's widow. Source: Agenda for the Board of Directors meeting supplied by Harvey L'Hommedieu. In interviews, three directors, Jim Lynch, Harvey L'Hommedieu, and Walter Auch, confirmed that they and the rest of the board were surprised.

6. L'Hommedieu, op cit.; Lynch, op cit.; Fitzgerald, op cit.; Auch, op cit.; Bishop, op cit.; a confidential written source; and personal knowledge. Benn & MacDonough, Inc. was one of the creditors who were eventually paid in full.

CHAPTER 20: HOW AND WHY DISCRIMINATION BASED ON CLASS AND RELIGION DECLINED ON WALL STREET

1. Taped interview of Ken Langone.

2. My own experience. I was a copywriter and then copy director and a vice president of Doremus & Co. in the fifties and sixties.

3. Interview of John Whitehead.

4. Interview of Jim Lynch. He was there.

5. Charles A. Beard and Mary R. Beard, *The Rise of American Civilization*, Vol. II (New York: The MacMillan Company, 1940), p. 173. Also Sobel, *Panic on Wall Street*.

6. Personal knowledge. I was a public relations writer at Merrill Lynch at the time.

7. Lynch, op cit.

8. Interviews of Jim Lynch and Gil Bach.

9. Langone, op cit.

10. Compiled from several often overlapping sources: the taped interviews of Ken Langone and Jim Lynch plus Mason, op cit., and personal observation.

11. Mostly confidential sources. Also personal observation. When I went to Brown University in the thirties, there were several Christian fraternities and one Jewish fraternity. I became a member of Phi Kappa Psi, and we members all felt proud that we were so tolerant as to allow one Jew to join. I belonged to the West Side Tennis Club in Forest Hills in the fifties and sixties. When I had applied for membership, my proposer had asked me what religion I was. I told him "none." He persisted, saying he had to put down something on the form. I told him I had been christened as an infant in the Church of England, which delighted him, and he put "Episcopal" on the form.

12. Confidential source.

13. Personal knowledge gained largely from talking to long-time partners and employees of Merrill Lynch and predecessor firms while I was at Merrill Lynch.

14. Lynch, op cit.

CHAPTER 21: THE DIFFERENT REASONS FOR THE DECLINE IN RACIAL AND GENDER DISCRIMINATION ON WALL STREET

1. He was Joseph L. Seales. *New York Times*, February 13, 1970, p. 55.

2. Daniels & Bell, Inc. *New York Times*, June 25, 1971, p. 55.

3. Jerome H. Holland. *1973 Annual Report*, The New York Stock Exchange, p. 3.

4. Whitehead, op cit.

5. *New York Times*, September 9, 1975, p. 53 (first financial page).

6. Telephone conversations with Selena Morris of Merrill Lynch Public Relations in 1999.

7. *New York Times*, March 22, 1997, p. 39.

8. My conversations with black and white investment bankers.

9. Caroline M. Benn, op cit.

10. Clipping from the *Manchester Guardian*, January 27, 1997, obtained from a confidential source.

11. *Moneyline*, CNN, March 11, 1997, 7:00–7:30 P.M. EST. Transcript obtained through a confidencial source. In referring to Selma, Alabama, Jesse Jackson apparently was not aware of an exhaustive study of conditions in Selma, Alabama, that the *New York Times* made in 1994 and reported on August 2, 1994, p. 1. It stated, "The schools are still segregated, with the old white schools virtually all black and the whites—working class and as well as wealthy—in private academies . . . the tax code still protects the interests of the white landowners." The article, which began on the front page with a sizable picture and continued for a full page inside with additional sizable pictures of conditions in Selma, also quoted a resident white man as saying, "children are now more racist than their parents had ever been."

12. *Wall Street Journal*, July 21, 1997, p. B2.

13. Caroline M. Benn.

14. Personal knowledge as well as interview of John Whitehead.

15. The demonstration ocurred in August 1970. Source: a round-up story in the *New York Times*, October 11, 1970, section III, p. 3.

16. *New York Times*, December 29, 1967, p. 35 and May 21, 1970, p. 55 (first financial page). Jane R. Larkin was a partner in Hirsch & Co.

17. *New York Times*, October 11, 1970, section III, p. 3. Mary Wrenn was the only woman security analyst at Merrill Lynch in 1948–1950 when I was at Merrill Lynch.

18. *1973 Annual Report*, The New York Stock Exchange, p. 3. She was Juanita Kreps.

19. Caroline M. Benn.

20. She is Heather Ruth. Personal knowledge and that of Caroline M. Benn.

21. *Democrat and Chronicle* (Rochester, NY), March 8, 1992, p. 1F. Also the article headlined "The Jobs Immigrants Take" in the *New York Times*, March 11, 1996, Op-Ed page. Also *Immigration in the National Interest Act of 1995, Report of the Committee on the Judiciary, House of Representatives on H.R. 2202*, March 4, 1996 (Washington, DC: U.S. Government Printing Office, 1996). Also *Skill Differences*

and the Effect of Immigrants on the Wages of Natives, Working Paper 273, December 1995, Bureau of Labor Statistics, U.S. Department of Labor, obtained from the Federation for American Immigration Reform, 1666 Connecticut Avenue, N.W. 400, Washington, DC 20009.

22. All the quotations of John Whitehead are from a taped interview with him.

23. According to the U.S. Commission on Civil Rights as reported in the *Washington Times*, October 12, 1983, in an article headlined "Religious Bias Seen Still Strong."

24. McDonald, op cit.; Lynch, op. cit.

25. Robert Leckachman, *The Age of Keynes* (New York: Random House, 1966), p. 64: "In the long run we are all dead. Economists set themselves too easy, too useless a task if in temptuous seasons they can only tell us that when the storm is long past the ocean is flat again."

26. *Wall Street Journal*, February 8, 1974, front page.

27. The need and effectiveness of legislation in reducing discrimination against hiring and promoting women to high level jobs with little or no backlash may be a special case. Donald L. Horwitz analyzed discrimination in many societies in Africa and Asia and concluded: "Especially with respect to education and employment, there is reason to expect most preferential policies to *accentuate* ethnic conflict over the short term. In the medium term, there is additional reason to expect preferential policies to *increase ethnic conflict*. . . . Ultimately perhaps there will be less ethnic conflict if all groups are proportionately represented in all sectors of the economy. One reason the truth of this proposition remains elusive is that few, if any societies have ever approximated this description" (emphasis added). See Donald L. Horowitz, *Ethnic Groups in Conflict* (Berkley, Los Angeles, and London: University of California Press, 1985), pp. 676–677.

28. *Brown v. Board of Education.*

29. *New York Times*, January 9, 1999, p. A8.

CHAPTER 22: SIGNIFICANCE

1. Joseph A. Schumpeter, *Capitalism, Socialism and Democracy* (New York: Harper & Row, 1962). Chapter on creative destruction begins on page 81. The following quote is on page 83: ". . . process of industrial mutation . . . incessantly revolutionizes the economic structure from within, incessantly destroying the old one, incessantly creating a new one. This process of Creative Destruction is the essential fact of capitalism." Also see *Forbes*, July 13, 1987, p. 49.

CHAPTER 23: AFTERMATH: THE PERILS OF PARTNERSHIPS

1. Almost entirely based on interviews of Bill and Barbara Smith. Some information from Richard MacDonald and Jim Lynch, who concur on the financial information.

Selected Bibliography

Beard, Charles A. and Mary R. Beard. *The Rise of American Civilization*, Vol. II. New York: The Macmillan Company, 1940.

Blume, Marshall, Jeremy Siegel, and Dan Rottenberg. *Revolution on Wall Street*. New York: W. W. Norton & Company, 1993.

Brooks, John. *The Go-Go Years*. New York: Weybright and Talley, 1973.

Carosso, Vincent P. *The Morgans: Private International Bankers*. Cambridge, MA: Harvard University Press, 1987.

Endlich, Lisa. *Goldman Sachs*. New York: Alfred A. Knopf, 1999.

Galbraith, John Kenneth. *The Great Crash of 1929*. New York: Penguin Books, 1990.

Greider, William. *Secrets of the Temple*. New York: Simon and Schuster, 1987.

Leckman, Robert. *The Age of Keynes*. New York: Random House, 1966.

Mason, Todd. *Perot: An Unauthorized Biography*. New York: Business One Irwin, 1990.

Mayer, Martin. *New Breed on Wall Street*. Toronto: The Macmillan Company, 1969.

Mitchell, Broadus. *Depression Decade, Volume IX: The Economic History of the United States*. New York and Toronto: Rinehart & Co., 1947.

Nixon, Richard. *The Memoirs of Richard Nixon*. New York: Grosset & Dunlap, 1978.

Persico, Joseph E. *Casey: From the OSS to the CIA*. New York: Viking, 1990.

Peters, Thomas J. *In Search of Excellence*. New York: Harper & Row, 1982.

Schumpeter, Joseph A. *Capitalism, Socialism and Democracy*. New York: Harper & Row, 1962.

Seligman, Joel. *The Transformation of Wall Street*. Boston: Houghton Mifflin, 1982.

Sloane, Leonard. *The Anatomy of the Floor*. Garden City, NY: Doubleday & Company, 1980.

Sobel, Robert. *Panic on Wall Street: A History of America's Financial Disasters*. New York: The Macmillan Company, 1968.

Stans, Maurice. *The Terrors of Justice*. Washington, DC: Regnery Books, 1985.

Stein, Herbert. *Presidential Economics*. New York: Simon and Schuster, 1984.

Wells, Chris. *The Last Days of the Club*. New York: Dutton, 1975.

Zarb, Frank G. and Kerekes, Gabriel T. *The Stock Market Handbook*. Homewood, IL: Dow Jones–Irwin, 1970.

Index

About the Author

ALEC BENN, now retired, was president of Benn & MacDonough, Inc., an advertising and public relations agency in New York City serving the financial and investment communities. Previously a vice president at Doremus & Co., one of the largest financial services advertising agencies in the United States, and before that a writer of industry studies at Merrill Lynch, Benn holds an engineering degree from Brown University and has studied writing and economics at New York University and Columbia University. He is author of *Advertising Financial Products and Services* (Quorum, 1986); *The 27 Most Common Mistakes in Advertising* (1978), and *The 23 Most Common Mistakes in Public Relations* (1982). Mr. Benn has also written articles and columns for publications in his fields and a television drama, and is an award-winning playwright.